Anarchic Solidarity

Anarchic Solidarity
Autonomy, Equality, and Fellowship in Southeast Asia

THOMAS GIBSON
KENNETH SILLANDER

Editors

Monograph 60/Yale Southeast Asia Studies

Library of Congress Catalog Card Number: *2011925069*
International Standard Book Number: *paper* *978-0-938692-94-2*
          cloth   *978-0-938692-95-9*

Distributor:
Yale University Southeast Asia Studies
P.O. Box 208206
New Haven, Connecticut 06520-8206
U.S.A.

Printed in U.S.A.

Contents

Illustrations

Tables

Contributors

GEOFFREY BENJAMIN, Anthropology, Centre for Liberal Arts and Social Sciences, Nanyang Technological University

ROBERT DENTAN, Anthropology, University at Buffalo, State University of New York

JAMES F. EDER, Anthropology, Arizona State University

KIRK ENDICOTT, Anthropology, Dartmouth College

THOMAS GIBSON, Anthropology, University of Rochester

SIGNE HOWELL, Anthropology, University of Oslo

LARS KASKIJA, Anthropology, University of Gothenburg

CHARLES MACDONALD, Anthropology, Centre National de la Recherche Scientifique (CNRS), Université de la Méditerranée

CLIFFORD SATHER, Anthropology, Borneo Research Council

KENNETH SILLANDER, Anthropology, University of Helsinki

Introduction

THIS VOLUME ANALYZES a group of Southeast Asian societies whose members have achieved a remarkably rigorous balance among the moral values of autonomy, equality, and fellowship. It also suggests some moral and political lessons that readers who share these values might apply to their own societies, in line with recent suggestions concerning the relevance of the anthropology of egalitarian societies to the theory and practice of anarchism (e.g., Clastres [1974] 1977; Graeber 2007).

The volume brings together a number of societies that are normally placed in distinct analytical frameworks according to their traditional modes of subsistence: nomadic hunter-gatherers, shifting cultivators, sea nomads, and peasants embedded in a market economy. The authors came together to produce it because they have concluded that these societies have something more fundamental in common: a mode of sociality that maximizes personal autonomy, political egalitarianism, and inclusive forms of social solidarity. Personal autonomy is maintained through the principle of "open aggregation," in which all groups beyond the domestic family are loosely defined, ephemeral, and weakly corporate, and in which membership is fluid, elective, and overlapping. Political autonomy is maintained by occupying areas that are difficult for states to administer, such as mountains, swamps, and the open sea. Economic equality is maintained through the use of subsistence techniques that require little in the way of accumulated physical capital. Social solidarity, or fellowship, is achieved through the investment of considerable effort and material resources into voluntary social relations in the absence of coercion and structural constraints. In short, the members of these societies are characterized by a strong commitment to solidarity while simultaneously defending an extensive degree of personal autonomy. They have practiced for generations forms of political anarchy

1

and social solidarity that appear in many other kinds of societies only in evanescent millenarian movements or as utopian ideals.

The volume is based on a project that was conceived by Charles Macdonald and Kenneth Sillander in February 2008 during a discussion of a presentation by Macdonald at the University of Helsinki (Macdonald 2008). Most of the essays were first presented in a session entitled "Sources of Solidarity in Open-Aggregated Communities," which was organized and chaired by Thomas Gibson at the annual meetings of the Association for Asian Studies, held in Chicago in March 2009. The concept of open aggregation, referring to the ease whereby social relations and groups in societies with anarchic solidarity characteristically are formed and dissolved, served as a key concept enabling the development of anarchic solidarity as a common analytical focus among the contributors to the volume.

In this introduction, we will provide a summary of the contribution that each of the chapters makes to our general argument and then situate our volume in relation to other theoretical traditions that draw on the concepts of anarchy and anarchism to analyze certain forms of social organization.

~

The theoretical overview provided in chapter 1 by Charles Macdonald outlines the internal logic of our argument. He presents the principal sources of solidarity identified by the contributors in the different societies studied and the principal mechanisms whereby they perpetuate themselves through time. He identifies three clusters of factors accounting for this, which are centered on the concept of sharing; on kinship and child care; and on a category of values relating to ethics, ideology, and ontology. He argues that these societies lack so many of the institutions once thought to be essential to the functioning of any society—corporate groups, debt and reciprocity, authority and ranking—that it might be better not to describe them as "societies" operating according to "social" principles at all.

The next two chapters, by Signe Howell and Kirk Endicott, provide detailed ethnographic analyses of two groups of hunter-gatherers living on the Malay Peninsula who provide classic exemplars of the sort of anarchic solidarity found among "immediate-return" hunter-gatherers elsewhere in Asia and Africa. The authors stress the ways in which principles of inter-

Map 1 *Location of peoples discussed in this volume*

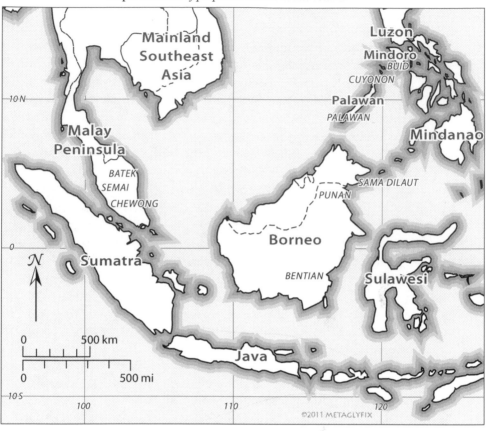

personal conduct and the cosmological beliefs and practices of the Chewong and Batek of the Malay Peninsula inculcate compassion for fellow humans and respect for the animal and spirit worlds as central social values.

In chapter 2, Signe Howell explores how Chewong personal and social interaction is predicated on their metaphysical and ontological understanding. With no formal political system and an egalitarian ethos that values autonomy, they also display a profound sense of communality—the outer boundary of which coincides with their animated forest environment in which humans and "spirits" stand in a continuous exchange relationship. Sources of solidarity may be traced to this shared perception of the universe and a number of rules that govern behavior. These have moral connotations, and the sharing of all forest produce is the paramount rule. The chapter concludes with a consideration of threats to the previous grammar of social life. As the Chewong begin to move out of the forest and become involved in a monetary economy, the ontology of the forest is losing its relevance.

In chapter 3, Kirk Endicott examines the ethical principles that influence the behavior of the Batek, a nomadic foraging people living in the rainforest of Peninsular Malaysia These principles support individual autonomy while also encouraging cooperation and group solidarity. They include obligations to respect others, help others, and be self-reliant, nonviolent, and non-competitive. Endicott also examines the main types of Batek social groups and the bases of their solidarity. Through his analysis of Batek ethical principles and group organization, he illuminates how Batek balance personal autonomy and obligations to others according to a pattern that he calls "cooperative autonomy."

The next four essays provide ethnographic analyses of societies practicing shifting cultivation that employ a number of mechanisms to achieve a form of anarchic solidarity very similar to that of the hunter-gatherers. In chapter 4, Robert Dentan addresses the question of whether the analytical construct "society" is necessary to understand the lives of peaceable Southeast Asian egalitarian peoples like the "east Semai" of central Peninsular Malaysia. The main body of the chapter discusses the centrality of children in human evolution and east Semai social life in general, and in the local band in particular. He concludes that child care provides sufficient "social glue" to account for Semai social solidarity without any need to introduce the concept of "society."

In chapter 5, Charles Macdonald examines the role of kinship and cooperative activities in generating solidarity among the Palawan, a group of swidden agriculturalists inhabiting the southern part of Palawan Island in the Philippines. Palawan kinship does not generate corporate groups but instead provides a framework within which fluid residential groups are built around a core of married female siblings. Kinship is also used as a formal grid that indicates appropriate forms of deference and closeness for any pair of interlocutors. The most frequent occasions for large-scale cooperation occur for judicial, ritual, and aesthetic reasons, not utilitarian ones. He suggests that the concept of "fellowship" best captures a mode of association based on a wealth of weak ties complemented by strong ethical norms of solidarity that prevails in this community.

In chapter 6, Kenneth Sillander analyzes kinship as a source of solidarity among the Bentian of Indonesian Borneo. He explores how forms of aggregation and social ties in Bentian communities are influenced by kinship, and by other principles or practices in combination with kinship. He examines how inclusive and flexible notions of relatedness enable the creation and multiplication of social ties, and how kinship ideology and lived experience of practical association motivate compliance with kinship obligations in interpersonal relationships. He also provides a general understanding of how Bentian solidarity is generated through egocentric social action and regularly enacted cultural practices integrating people through "shared activity." These processes account for the simultaneous salience of individual autonomy and social solidarity in Bentian society, a condition reflecting its open-aggregated character.

In chapter 7, Geoffrey Benjamin compares and contrasts the endogenous populations of what he calls the Malay World. They have long shared the same cultural pool and are therefore interconnected as a regional array of varying social formations, both egalitarian and ranked, rather than as an assemblage of distinct "societies." These formations have derived in large measure from different reshapings of certain shared kinship features—relative age, unifiliative bias, preferential marriage patterns, and so on—which have served to maintain the mutually distinctive societal traditions he examines: the Semang (tribal, egalitarian), the Senoi (tribal, egalitarian), and the Malayic (ranked tribal populations and centralized Malay states). These traditions emerged through a series of deliberate mutual adjustments, both assimilatory and dissimilatory, between populations that were each seeking complementary advantages vis-à-vis each other. The autonomy, equality and fellowship that have characterized several of these populations therefore cannot be fully understood except in relation to their long-term contact with populations that have exhibited various forms of ranking.

The next two essays carry the analysis one step further by analyzing what happens when societies in which the dominant mode of sociality is anarchic solidarity interact with neighboring societies organized in a fundamentally different way. In chapter 8, Lars Kaskija discusses four subdivisions of the formerly nomadic Punan of the Malinau area of Indonesian Borneo that have been encapsulated by a number of smaller groups of agriculturalists. Each of these subdivisions show marked variation in their social values and practices depending on the kind of agricultural society with which they are most closely associated. He suggests that local variation between individuals and bands reflects the specifics of this encapsulation, which is remarkably diverse and variable. Kaskija also describes the most salient form of Punan self-identity, developed in relation to the world around them, which is a sense of shared deprivation. This sense of deprivation is exemplified by *pelulup urip*, a ritualized form of communal commiseration that becomes an emotional expression of group solidarity and a distinct way of life.

In chapter 9, Clifford Sather explores the role played by mobility, the performative use of speech, and food sharing in maintaining conditions of "gregarious sociality" among a community of once-nomadic maritime fishing people. He is concerned in particular with the ways in which the Sama Dilaut of northeastern Borneo use speech to both express and manage conflict and with how, until recently, they maintained solidarity among community, kin, and neighbors through a flow of reciprocal gifts while, at the same time, they engaged in formalized, boundary-defining commodity trade with outsiders. The Sama Dilaut represent an example of a group that has long maintained its cultural and social autonomy and an open-aggregated pattern of sociality despite intensive engagement with the encompassing maritime economy of the region.

The final two essays apply the lessons of the previous essays to societies in which the dominant form of sociality is based on ascribed rank, the assertion of exclusive rights to productive resources, and formal political offices. In chapter 10, James F. Eder examines traditional modes of sociality among the Cuyonon of the central Philippines through the lens of their nicknaming practices, until recent decades a vibrant part of Cuyonon culture. Both nicknames themselves and the playful manner in which they were deployed in social interaction exemplified the teasing, self-effacement, and intimacy characteristic of everyday Cuyonon social life and thereby promoted the values of egalitarianism and personal autonomy on which this social life rested. With development and modernity, Eder shows, came the demise of nicknaming, but the continued presence of related, solidarity-generating cultural practices among a people who are today thoroughly integrated into the Philippine state provides a useful comparative perspective on the persistence of older modes of egalitarian, open-aggregated sociality in contemporary complex societies.

In chapter 11, Thomas Gibson argues that the egalitarianism, sharing, and individual autonomy characteristic of many societies in the highlands of Southeast Asia represent a set of mutually reinforcing ethical values that developed in opposition to the debt bondage, tribute extraction, and social hierarchy found in the lowlands of the region. The development and maintenance of these values depended on access to modes of subsistence such as hunting, fishing, gathering, and shifting cultivation that freed people from the need to defend productive resources that had absorbed large amounts of previous labor, and to accept subordination to political authorities. The egalitarianism found in these societies is thus a secondary reaction to the predatory ranking of their neighbors and may be contrasted with the primary egalitarianism found in foraging societies, the spiritual egalitarianism found in world religions, and the civic egalitarianism associated with the modern nation-state.

The persistence of societies based on these principles throughout Southeast Asia into the twenty-first century presents something of a paradox since this region was dominated for centuries by societies based on debt bondage, tribute extraction, and social hierarchy. It thus has special relevance to a long tradition of theorizing on the relationship between agrarian states and their "tribal" neighbors and on how tribal political systems must be understood as a negation of these state systems. This tradition goes back at least to Ibn Khaldun, who wrote on the relationship between Arabs and Berbers in North Africa ([1377] 1967). In the twentieth century, it included Owen Lattimore on Central Asia (1940), Edmund Leach on Highland Burma (1954), and Ernest Gellner on North Africa (1969). The tribal societies these authors had in mind may have defined themselves in opposition to the agrarian states that were their neighbors, but, unlike the societies organized according to the principle of anarchic solidarity discussed in this volume, they were internally stratified according to wealth, power, and prestige; they operated according to an ethic of competition that often resulted in systematic violence; and they were organized into corporate kinship groups.

The precise mechanisms by which societies can function without formal political offices, corporate kinship groups, or the assertion of long-term rights to productive resources were first described by ethnographers working among nomadic hunter-gatherers in Africa and South Asia during the 1950s and 1960s such as Lorna Marshall (1961), Colin Turnbull (1965), Peter Gardner (1966), Richard Lee and Irven DeVore (1968), James Woodburn

(1982), and a few others. The values of these societies were so different from those of the classic exemplars of this mode of subsistence in Australia, the Andaman Islands, and the Northwest Coast of North America that the ethnographies were at first rejected as deficient or the peoples being described were dismissed as enclaved remnants of more conventional societies and so irrelevant to general social theory. It was only as the pioneering work of the first generation of ethnographers was corroborated by a second generation working in other parts of the world such as South America and Southeast Asia that a new school of thought began to emerge in which this way of life appeared not only as an entirely coherent way of organizing social relations but perhaps even as one of the oldest and most stable ways of doing so (Clastres [1974] 1977; Benjamin 1985; Gibson 1990). According to this view, it is the appearance of political office, corporate kinship groups, and social hierarchy that requires special explanation, while the advantages displayed by the anarchic solidarity of nomadic hunter-gatherers are almost self-evident (Macdonald 2009).

Outside of anthropology, there has been a broad revival of interest in the theory and practice of anarchy over the past twenty years among both political scientists and political activists. A discussion of two recent works by political scientists will clarify how our usage of the term *anarchic* relates to their use of *anarchism*. This discussion is directly relevant to the current movement to recognize the rights of indigenous peoples around the world. The recent revival of interest in anarchy and indigeneity recalls a time in the late nineteenth century when Marxism was a parochial movement that addressed itself only to the industrial workers of Northern Europe and anarchism developed into a cosmopolitan movement that addressed itself to the peasants, agricultural workers, and bohemian intellectuals of both the metropoles and the colonies (Anderson 2005:2). The globalization of resistance movements at that time was facilitated by the advent of cheap transportation by steamship, enabling intellectuals from colonized territories to travel and meet radicals of all persuasions and to imagine new destinies for their homelands.

Anarchism receded during the first half of the twentieth century when Marxist leaders from predominantly agrarian nations like Russia and China forged new movements based on an alliance of workers and peasants and so managed to globalize the communist movement. The anarchist tradition was correspondingly marginalized until it was rediscovered by the student-based "new left" movements of the 1960s, culminating in the events of May 1968 in France. The introduction of cheap travel on jet airplanes in the 1970s had an effect similar to that of cheap travel on steamships in the 1870s, enabling nonelite workers and intellectuals to travel around the globe at a rate previously unimaginable.

With the collapse of the Soviet Union in 1991 and the acceleration of market reforms in the People's Republic of China in 1992, disillusionment with Marxist ideas and the revival of anarchist ideas began to develop on a global scale. Resistance to the restructuring of the global economy on "neoliberal" lines during the 1990s was often expressed in anarchist terms, most dramatically during the street protests organized during the meetings of a variety of international organizations such as the International Monetary Fund and World Bank in Berlin (1988), Madrid (1994), and Washington (2000); the World Trade Organization in Seattle (1999); the G8 in Genoa (2001); and the G7 in Washington (2002).

During the same period, Marxist conceptions of rural agricultural producers as belonging to a global class of "peasants" were increasingly rejected in favor of a new conception of many of the same individuals as belonging to a diverse assortment of "indigenous peoples." The reclassification of peasants as indigenous peoples began in Latin America. It was brought to global attention by the Zapatista uprising in southern Mexico, which was launched in January 1994 to protest the implementation of the North American Free Trade Agreement. Zapatista ideology draws heavily on anarchism and libertarian socialism (Jung 2008). The indigenous rights movement spread rapidly throughout the Americas and beyond. By 2007, the concept was enshrined by the United Nations in the Declaration of the Rights of Indigenous Peoples.

The relevance of the concept of indigeneity in the context of Southeast Asia is problematic since the minority peoples of the highlands are no more indigenous than the majority peoples of the lowlands (Winzeler 1997; Erni 2008a; Benjamin, this volume). The distinctions between them have less to do with language, race, and culture than with political values and ways of life. As a number of authors in this volume note, it has always been possible for individuals to move back and forth across the boundaries between the egalitarian social systems of the highlands and the hierarchical social systems of the lowlands. The groups we are discussing in this volume are defined not by their distinctive cultural traditions but by their distinctive ways of life. But it is precisely these ways of life and not particular forms of language and culture that have long attracted those interested in the possibility of organizing social relationships in the absence of organized violence and the state. What this volume provides is a detailed description of several forms of "actually existing anarchy," as opposed to the utopian models of anarchism formulated by European intellectuals.

In a recent book on the influence of anarchist thought on the anticolonial Filipinos in the late nineteenth century, Benedict Anderson has drawn attention to the fact that as early as 1885, an Ilocano intellectual called Isabelo de los Reyes identified himself "as a brother of the forest dwellers: the Aetas, Igorots and Tinguians" (de los Reyes 1994:21). He did this in a Spanish scientific journal on the new discipline of folklore.

> Folklore—comparative folklore—enabled him to bridge the deepest chasm in colonial society, which lay not between colonized and colonizers—they all lived in the lowlands, they were all Catholics, and they dealt with one another all the time. It was the abyss between all of these people and those whom we would today call "tribal minorities": hill-people, nomadic swidden farmers, "head-hunters," men, women and children facing a future of—possibly violent—assimilation, even extermination.
>
> (Anderson 2005:17)

De los Reyes was later caught up in the Philippine revolution of 1896 and exiled to Barcelona, where he shared a cell with a Catalan anarchist called Ramon Sempau. He returned to the Philippines in 1901 and immediately put into practice "what the anarchists had taught him in organizing the first serious and militant trade union central in the Philippines" (Anderson 2005:7). The Democratic Union of Workers disbanded in 1903, "but out of its ashes came many other labor organizations, and eventually a Socialist and Communist party which merged in 1938, led the Hukbalahap guerilla movement against the Japanese military invaders, and ultimately carried on a revolutionary war against the American-arranged Second Republic, inaugurated on—when else?—July 4, 1946" (229).

The anarcho-syndicalist ideas developed in southern Europe thus found a fertile soil in the lowland Philippines. As James F. Eder argues in his contribution to this volume, and as Charles Macdonald has argued elsewhere, ordinary lowland Filipinos share many of the values that the highlanders discussed in the present volume do, among them a commitment to what is called in Tagalog *pakikisama* or flexible, egalitarian solidarity with one's

companions (Macdonald, forthcoming). Alongside this value, lowland Filipinos also recognize the value of *utang na loob*, a generalized and enduring
debt of gratitude toward one's more powerful benefactors. In this one may
recognize a legacy of Spanish colonial theology, where one's debt toward
God is transferred to the Church, and from the Church to the friars who
ruled the islands for over 300 years. And yet, as Reynaldo Ileto showed in
his study of popular movements between 1840 and 1910, such deference to
superiors is liable to be thrown off at any time and replaced by a horizontal
sense of solidarity with one's equals based on *damay*, "compassion," and
awa, "pity."

> *Damay*, which today usually means sympathy and/or condolence for
> another's misfortune, has a much older meaning of "participating in another's
> work." The whole point of the singing of the pasyon is the evocation of
> damay with Christ; the text itself is filled with examples that suggest this
> mode of behavior: expressions of sorrow and compassion, tearful weeping,
> individuals helping Christ carry his Cross, changing their state of loob to
> lead a pure life and follow Christ's example.
>
> (Ileto 1979:65–66)

As de los Reyes recognized 125 years ago, there is no hard and fast
opposition between the values according to which the anarchic peoples of
the forest live and the values according to which many of the oppressed
peoples of the lowlands would like to live.

James Scott tells a different story about anarchism in his recent book,
*The Art of Not Being Governed: An Anarchist History of Upland Southeast
Asia*. He sees it as a form of resistance to domination by states based on the
extraction of tribute from the cultivators of irrigated rice fields, a process
that began two thousand years ago. He develops the model first proposed
by Edmund Leach in *Political Systems of Highland Burma* according to
which the peoples of the highlands developed egalitarian political cultures
in opposition to the hierarchical political cultures of the lowland padi
states. Scott generalizes this model by synthesizing an enormous array of
ethnographic and ethnohistorical material on the highland populations of
seven Asian countries. He identifies certain features of their environment,
technology, social organization, and ethnic identity that minimized the
ability of neighboring states to control them. These included residential
mobility, dispersion, and the occupation of landscapes inaccessible to lowland armies; diversified subsistence strategies and the cultivation of root

crops that are more difficult to appropriate than grain crops; acephalous, segmentary and fluid social structures; and transient and overlapping ethnic identities. In developing his model, he ranges far beyond Southeast Asia, noting similar antistate adaptations in many other parts of the world where the natural environment was inhospitable to the sedentary agriculture that formed the basis for most premodern states.

In many ways, Scott's volume, whose focus is on the anarchic peoples living in the highlands of mainland Southeast Asia, is complementary to the present volume, which focuses on the anarchic peoples living in island Southeast Asia and the Malay Peninsula. First, Scott's book is essentially a work in comparative political science that stresses the role of "objective" factors, such as the occupation of mountainous terrain and the cultivation of root crops, which enable people to escape predatory states. In contrast, ours is essentially a work in comparative anthropology that stresses the role of "subjective" factors, such as the positive evaluation of personal autonomy, egalitarianism, and collective ritual, which generate a form of sociality that is attractive in its own right.

Second, Scott is concerned with the entire range of social formations that organized themselves without centralized state institutions, including those that are organized into large-scale corporate descent groups that may be ranked in relation to one another. We are concerned only with social formations at the most anarchic, egalitarian end of the spectrum, formations whose members reject the subordination of individuals to any group larger than the household and who make their living by techniques than require the minimal accumulation of property, such as fishing, hunting, gathering, and shifting cultivation. The fundamental differences between the political values of hierarchical state systems and those organized according to the principles of anarchic solidarity are even more evident in these cases than in those discussed by Scott.

Third, Scott relies primarily on the written documents left by agents of lowland states, for whom the operative principles of anarchic societies were bound to be obscure. He is thus led at times to follow Malcolm Yapp in characterizing highland societies as lacking all internal structure like "jelly-fish" (Scott 2009:210, quoting Yapp 1980). We have relied primarily on long-term participant observation in existing societies of this sort and have been able to describe the precise and often subtle mechanisms through which they organize their lives. These are indeed more elusive than the corporate kinship groups, royal dynasties, and bounded nation-states that define the social structure of lowland societies in the area, but they are no less real for that.

Fourth, while Scott tends to explain every aspect of the highland way of life in terms of its utility in escaping control by lowland states, we stress the way that practices like shifting cultivation possess an intrinsic value quite apart from this function. As Scott notes, it is now well established that where population densities are low enough, shifting cultivation produces greater returns on labor, a more sustainable relationship with the natural environment, a more balanced and varied diet, and lower risks from epidemic disease than fixed field agriculture. The seminomadic way of life enabled by shifting cultivation provides individuals greater freedom in choosing whom they will live with than does permanent-field agriculture. Many peoples have chosen to live this way even when they were not under direct threat by states and when they were well aware of alternative methods of subsistence.

Perhaps the biggest difference between this book and that of Scott is that he wrote his book as an elegy for a way of life that he sees as having effectively come to an end fifty years ago. Toward the end of the book, he makes a somewhat oblique reference to "indigenism" as only the latest in a series of utopian ideologies like millenarian Buddhism, Christianity, socialism, and nationalism. "Most have failed, and some have ended at least as badly as millenarian uprisings" (Scott 2009:323). In his conclusion, he goes on to characterize the current era as one "in which virtually the entire globe is 'administered space' and the periphery is not much more than a folkloric remnant" (324).

This conclusion seems unduly pessimistic to us. There is nothing utopian about the anarchic social systems discussed in this book, which have persisted throughout Southeast Asia for generations. The authors of the chapters in this book have all done their fieldwork during the last fifty years, and the way of life described in them was still very much alive at the time fieldwork was first conducted, although it has come under growing pressure everywhere since then. Furthermore, as we saw in the discussion of Anderson's book on anarchist ideas in Southeast Asia and as we will see in many of the essays in this volume, there are many grounds for solidarity between the egalitarian peoples of the highlands and the peoples at the bottom of the hierarchies of the lowlands. The peoples described in this book have in many cases begun to develop alliances with lowland opponents of political elites in their own countries and with international nongovernmental organizations (NGOS) that have taken up the cause of indigenous rights (Erni 2008b; Padilla 2008). While our primary purpose is the description and analysis of the specific systems of anarchic solidarity discussed in this book, it is also our hope that these peoples may serve as an inspiration to all who value autonomy and equality and who feel the same solidarity with the forest dwellers that Isabelo de los Reyes expressed in 1885.

References

Anderson, Benedict. 2005. *Under Three Flags: Anarchism and the Anti-colonial Imagination*. London: Verso.

Benjamin, Geoffrey. 1985. "In the long term: Three themes in Malayan cultural ecology." In K. L. Hutterer, A. T. Rambo, and G. Lovelace, eds., *Cultural Values and Human Ecology in Southeast Asia*, 219–78. Ann Arbor: Center for South and Southeast Asian Studies, University of Michigan.

Clastres, Pierre. [1974] 1977. *Society against the State: The Leader as Servant and the Humane Uses of Power among the Indians of the Americas*. Translated by Robert Hurley, in collaboration with Abe Stein. New York: Urizen Books.

de los Reyes, Isabelo. 1994. *El Folk-Lore Filipino*. Quezon City: University of the Philippines Press.

Erni, Christian, ed. 2008a. *The Concept of Indigenous Peoples in Asia: A Resource Book*. Documents, no. 123. Copenhagen and Chiang Mai: International Work Group for Indigenous Affairs.

Erni, Christian. 2008b. "Non-violence in a frontier: The strategy of avoidance and the struggle for indigenous control over land and resources on Mindoro Island." In Danilo Geiger, ed., *Frontier Encounters: Indigenous Communities and Settlers in Asia and Latin America*, 287–345. Documents, no. 120. Copenhagen and Chiang Mai: International Work Group for Indigenous Affairs.

Gardner, Peter. 1966. "Symmetric respect and memorate knowledge: The structure and ecology of individualistic culture." *Southwestern Journal of Anthropology* 22 (4):389–415.

Gellner, Ernest. 1969. *Saints of the Atlas*. Chicago: University of Chicago Press.

Gibson, Thomas. 1990. "Raiding, trading, and tribal autonomy in insular Southeast Asia." In J. Haas, ed., *The Anthropology of War*, 125–145. New York: Cambridge University Press.

Graeber, David. 2007. *Possibilities: Essays on Hierarchy, Rebellion, and Desire.* Oakland, CA; Edinburgh: AK Press.

Ibn Khaldun. [1377] 1967. *The Muqaddimah: An Introduction to History.* Princeton: Princeton University Press.

Ileto, Reynaldo. 1979. *Pasyon and Revolution: Popular Movements in the Philippines, 1840–1910.* Manila: Ateneo de Manila University Press.

Jung, Courtney. 2008. *The Moral Force of Indigenous Politics: Critical Liberalism and the Zapatistas.* Cambridge: Cambridge University Press.

Lattimore, Owen. 1940. *Inner Asian Frontiers of China.* New York: American Geographical Society.

Leach, Edmund. 1954. *Political Systems of Highland Burma: A Study of Kachin Social Structure.* London: Athlone Press.

Lee, Richard, and Irven Devore, eds. 1968. *Man the Hunter.* Chicago: Aldine.

Macdonald, Charles. 2008. "Order against harmony: Are humans always social?" *Suomen Antropologi: Journal of the Finnish Anthropological Society* 33 (2):5–21.

———. 2009. *The Anthropology of Anarchy.* Occasional Papers from the School of Social Science, no. 35. Princeton, New Jersey: Institute for Advanced Study.

———. Forthcoming. "Uncrystallized society: The Filipino as anarchist." To appear in a volume in honor of Professor Y. Kikuchi edited by M. Nishimura. Tokyo: Waseda University Press.

Marshall, Lorna. 1961. "Sharing, talking, and giving: Relief of social tensions among the !Kung Bushmen." *Africa: Journal of the International African Institute* 31 (3):231–49.

Padilla, Sabino G. 2008. "Indigenous peoples, settlers, and the Philippine Ancestral Domain land titling program." In Danilo Geiger, ed., *Frontier Encounters: Indigenous Communities and Settlers in Asia and Latin America,* 449–481. Documents, no. 120. Copenhagen and Chiang Mai: International Work Group for Indigenous Affairs.

Scott, James C. 2009. *The Art of Not Being Governed: An Anarchist History of Upland Southeast Asia.* New Haven: Yale University Press.

Turnbull, Colin. 1965. *Wayward Servants: The Two Worlds of the African Pygmies.* Garden City: Natural History Press.

Winzeler, Robert L., ed. 1997. *Indigenous Peoples and the State: Politics, Land, and Ethnicity in the Malayan Peninsula and Borneo.* Monographs. no. 46. New Haven: Council on Southeast Asia Studies, Yale University.

Woodburn, James. 1982. "Egalitarian societies." *Man*, N.S., 17 (3):431–51.

Yapp, Malcolm. 1980. *Tribes and States in the Khyber, 1838–1842*. Oxford: Clarendon.

1

A Theoretical Overview of Anarchic Solidarity

CHARLES MACDONALD

Strange Societies

IN THIS VOLUME anthropologists with long field experience tackle an issue of general relevance to human organizations but of particular concern for insular Southeast Asia: sources of solidarity in communities that seem to reject any form of coercion and ranking. The area this book explores is comprised of the Malay Peninsula, Borneo, and the Philippines. It contains numerous small indigenous populations whose way of life and collective organization are clearly marked by similar traits: bilateral kinship, flexible rules of aggregation, egalitarian spirit with no or very little difference in status, no central government, mostly peaceful and nonviolent norms of conduct, a consensual strategy in collective affairs, and a high degree of individual autonomy. They lack the political and stratified class structure, and even the descent groups, territorial divisions, status competition, and ranking that characterize other societies in Southeast Asia and elsewhere. In a number of cases we have extreme instances of egalitarianism and peacefulness. There are to be sure a number of societies in the region that do not fit this pattern, but in Sabah, Sarawak, Kalimantan, Peninsular Malaysia, Luzon, Palawan, Mindoro, and Mindanao, indigenous communities that can be described in similar terms are common: East Semai, Temiar, Batek, Chewong (Cheq Wong), Dusun, Bidayuh, Bentian, Punan, Sama Dilaut, Palawan (Pala'wan), Batak (from Palawan Island), Ilongot, Subanun, Tiruray

(Teduray), Buid, Hanunoo—to name a few. In spite of cultural, technological, historical, and linguistic differences, there is more than a superficial *air de famille* between these groups.

Indigenous and local communities that are the major focus of study in this volume can thus be compared using the simple grid of five basic traits found in table 1.1.

Table 1.1 *Comparison of Nine Groups along Five Dimensions*

	1 Open aggregation	2 Egalitarianism	3 Sharing	4 Autonomy	5 Peaceable ethos
Chewong	+	+	+	+	++
Batek	+	+	+	+	++
Temiar	+	+	+	+	++
East Semai	+	+	+	+	++
Palawan	+	+	+	+	++
Sama Dilaut	+	+	+	+	++
Buid	+	+	+	+	++
Bentian	+	+	+	+	+–
Punan	+	+	+	+	–

Explanation of signs: + present; ++ strongly marked; – absent; +– weakly marked

Ethnographies reveal conformity of habits and manners along four dimensions.[1]

1. A general absence of corporate groups outside the domestic family, together with free association, frequent shifts in group membership, and an inclusive policy, is a situation indicated in this volume with the phrase "open aggregation." Groups are weakly delineated, and overlapping; individuals or domestic families can join or leave them at will.

2. Strictly ascribed egalitarianism and no ranking.

3. Sharing (as opposed to debt/reciprocity) as an important but not sole mode of transaction.

4. A great deal of personal autonomy and the acknowledged right for individuals to decide for themselves, irrespective of what other people tell them to do, but with an obligation to respect other people's rights.

5. The fifth column in the table ("Peaceable ethos") shows a more nuanced response and a departure to the norm of nonviolence, which is asserted with extreme force in at least seven cases. An unquestionable peaceability (rather than dogmatic pacifism) and strictly nonviolent manners coupled with a taste for tranquility characterize the Semai, the Buid, the Chewong, and four others almost to the same degree. The Punan, or at least some sections of the Punan population, are a noted exception.

Since the populations examined in this volume have no corporate groups outside the domestic family, since they adhere to an ideal of sharing rather than a debt-inspired sense of reciprocity, and since they strictly refuse hierarchy as a way to relate to each other (they are die-hard anarchists in this sense), they indeed look like they are contravening some of the basic social rules found in a majority of societies throughout the world. Their organizational principles are so elusive that one starts wondering if they should be called "societies" at all. Hence one of the questions this volume addresses: to what extent can one apply to them the notion of society?

In spite of their apparent lack of structure they do show an unquestionable concern for togetherness. We look at communities that are nurturing and friendly, creating, in Endicott's words (this volume), "a moral community." Each author in this volume will vouch indeed for the extreme degree to which these people will go in order to share with, care for, help, trust, and rely on each other. In almost all cases a vernacular term glossed as "compassion" is one of the foremost notions used by respondents to explain ethics of interpersonal conduct. In other words people described in this volume show both unity and altruistic behavior, that is, solidarity. And yet individuals are not apparently bound by a system of social control, there are no mechanisms for coercion, and individuals do pretty much as they please. Hence the major question this volume addresses: how can one make sense of a state of internal solidarity in view of an anarchic, open-aggregated type of organization? How do such individualistic and anarchic people manage to cooperate and maintain order, solve conflicts, and eventually stay together? All the authors provide answers, many of them compatible and complementary if different.

There are two other questions, not unrelated to the first but entailing a different sort of argument. One is the degree of connection between all traits mentioned in table 1.1: do the open-aggregated character of the community plus the norms of equality, sharing, individual autonomy, and nonviolence entail each other as part of a cohesive and logical pattern? This particular problem finds answers in several of the following contributions.

The final question concerns the ultimate cause or origin of this specific cluster of traits, what makes these communities become and stay the way they are and stubbornly adhere to values that are after all rather paradoxical. Here again there are different answers. One is more historical, focusing on the presence and interaction of various polities in the region, in a process of complementary schismogenesis. Another is based on material and economic factors using a modified form of Woodburn's now classic model of an immediate-return economy. Another yet is more broadly evolutionary and encased in a definition of human nature. None of these answers can be excluded to the detriment of the others. It is quite plausible that, capitalizing on a basic human trait (like a need for a felicitous kind of interaction), a specific way of life evolved under environmental and historically determined conditions that shaped its present form. Among the factors permitting this form of sociality is a sufficient supply of resources and a low demographic density—thereby limiting competition—combined with outside pressure from neighboring predatory groups.

Loose Ends

One of the distinctive aspects of the contributions presented in this volume is that they retrace their steps to a now forgotten debate in anthropology. In the 1960s and 1970s and up to the early 1980s, there was a "conversation"— to use Bird-David's phrase (1994)—on what social groups were all about, and how to define them. It had been spurred by previous descent theories and functionalist views operating on the basis of a deterministic epistemology. It was mostly a conversation on descent groups and their fate when exported from their African anthropological birthplace to other regions of the world, particularly the New Guinea Highlands, where they did not seem to fare so well (Barnes 1962; Watson 1970; Wagner 1974; Brown 1978; Feil 1984).

This out-of-Africa story was related to another one concerning the kindred and what to do with a very widespread and somewhat annoying human habit of counting one's relatives on every side, something that the French aptly call *indifférencié* (undifferentiated), thus pointing—more clearly than its English gloss "bilateral"—to the perplexing properties of this kinship type. What was at stake was, to some extent, the very notion of group, one that is as necessary to a notion of society as water is to the existence of life as we understand it. Anthropologists had gone quite far in questioning this supposed evidence that groups are always there or that the notion of group is simple or self-explanatory (Boissevain 1968; Wagner 1974). The Southeast Asianists among them were trying to sort out or redefine groups, and particularly kin groups, in cognatic kinship systems (Appell 1983; Kemp 1991). This "conversation" seems to have died out in the mid-1980s, and anthropologists busied themselves with other matters.[2] Since anthropology, social or cultural, is so dominated by fashion, the crowd has gathered elsewhere, getting excited about other matters, forgetting about its prior concerns. It is an unfinished conversation, and the present contributions suggest we take it up again.

In this general indifference toward any theoretical attempt at making real sense of the bizarre and incomplete mess of kindreds, quasi groups, nongroups, and general looseness of everything, there were a few flickers of interest in the vicinity of our area of concern. One is the discussion around the concept of society (Strathern 1989), another the stubborn hunter-and-gathererists' commitment to explain to the unbelieving public what they had seen and witnessed as something truly true and truly other—such as sharing (Woodburn 1998), equality (Boehm 1993), and another sort of sociality (Ingold, Riches, and Woodburn 1988; Ingold 1999; Bird-David 1994). Peace studies (Howell and Willis 1989; Dentan 1994, 2008a, 2008b; Fry 2006) and the belated epiphany of deep human peacefulness have also been of the essence in these marginal attempts at bringing to the fore an anthropological understanding of organizational oddities, quite unlike those we generally live with or live by. A recent interest in anarchy and anarchic aspects of human life (Barclay 1997; Graeber 2004, 2007; Dentan 2008b; Macdonald 2008a, 2009b) has added some spice to these uncoordinated efforts.

The question of group formation was then tied up with kinship studies, another central concern that latter-day anthropologists chose, in the 1970s, to discard or at least put on the back burner. The likes of Rodney Needham (1971) and David Schneider (1984) had pronounced kinship a nonobject, and students were tired of drawing kinship diagrams anyway. However, in a 1995 review of kinship studies, Michael Peletz writes in a concluding remark that they are "still vital to the discipline" (1995:367). I deem this to be

true today in 2011. Moreover kinship is "a force of fundamental social significance," to use a phrase Kenneth Sillander applies to the Bentian (Sillander
2004:109), but that is equally valid for the Palawan, the Semang, and Senoi
groups examined by Benjamin (this volume) and for a number of other
indigenous communities in many different places. Whether kinship is the
foundation of society is another question, but it has an unquestionable pervasiveness, at least as an idiom for social and interpersonal relation on the
one hand, and as a moral ideology on the other. Kinship is multitasking: it
tells one where one stands relative to others and more or less something
about the content of the relationship, whether close or distant, affectionate
or indifferent, respectful or informal, playful or serious, and what obligations
go with it in the form of services or support or in the form of norms of
conduct (avoidance, joking, use of personal names, etc.). In the Palawan
language all terms for permanent offices that are nonkinship statuses (like
"chief," *panglima*, or "judge," *ukum*) are borrowed terms. Social statuses are
kinship statuses (Macdonald 1977, 2007).

Among the tasks cognatic kinship is not performing, however, is to
automatically generate groups. Because early anthropologists saw society
as essentially subdivided into groups, the most felicitous gift to a theory of
primitive society was the discovery that certain kinds of kinship systems—
unilineal descent systems—could divide the social body into distinct groups.
Moreover these groups were endowed with a jural essence; they had property, they had a chief, and they existed in perpetuity (corporations never
die we should be reminded). In a word, they had this most precious of all
transcendent properties: a corporate essence. The descent group theory
with its sequels, one being the Leiden School and Lévi-Straussian corollary
of group connectivity through marriage, had a stunning force that immobi-
lized the anthropological imagination for close to a century. Since kinship
is inherently something that has to do (or rather appears as having to do)
with blood ties, and therefore instincts, and since it was also found as
leading to the creation of entities endowed with a corporate essence—in
tune with the legalistic thinking dear to British anthropology of Radcliffe-
Brown's time—a whole theory of primitive society was premised on its
ground, one that tied together the two poles of the social evolutionary
process as defined by Maine: blood to contract, instinct to law, savagery to
barbarism (see Orenstein 1968). Transcendental sociality originating in a
quasi-instinctual perception of the next of kin has indeed been the sub-

merged and all-powerful paradigm of the anthropology of kinship, one that has prevented a clear realization that in many instances kinship either creates groups with little or no corporate reality or just does not create any groups at all. The long discussion about the kindred initiated by Murdock (1960) and Freeman (1961) is just that, running in circles around the same conundrum of an elusive and in many cases fictitious group-generating principle in kinship.

Gregarious Anarchists

Humans are born equipped with abilities to develop specific communicative and relational skills. Far from being blank slates on which a transcendent and supernatural entity called "society" writes whatever text or program it devises, individuals process and develop, together with the input their immediate nurturing environment offers, innate abilities to interact with their conspecifics. Humans are most probably born with the psychological and biological need to interact with other human beings (see Howell, this volume). We know that individuals entirely deprived of human contact either do not develop fully (the case of savage children raised by other animal species; see Ashley Montagu 1943) or disintegrate (prisoners of war or inmates forced into long-term solitary confinement; see Grassian 1993; Frintner 2005; Cohen 2008; Gawande 2009). Humans are therefore essentially gregarious. They, however, are not necessarily "social" with the meaning we will give this term below. Gregariousness is therefore not a trait acquired through circumstances or training, any more than the ability to learn a natural language is created by the linguistic community into which the speaker is born. Competence to learn a language is hardwired into the brain of the child as are the preconditions, and the need, to communicate and interact. There are, however, as many ways to interact as there are ways to turn an ability to speak into a specific competence for a natural language.

Social science specialists have thought long and hard about what is at the bottom of society and what makes people cohere into collective bodies that are rationally organized entities, possessed of self-awareness, endowed with relative stability through time but also with a capacity for change. Anthropologists who since the second part of the nineteenth century have been engaged in the study of a great variety of societies in many ways different from their own have come up with three fundamental principles that together give rise to what is called in this essay "society."

The most obvious of these is what can be called the "corporation principle." A collective entity is a society if and only if it can be divided into durable and clearly identifiable groups. What is referred to as social organization is oftentimes nothing but a relation between such groups, be they domestic units, clans, villages, classes, castes, strata, professional corporations, or other. These elements must be corporate, that is, minimally defined as bounded and having continuity. "Society is to be viewed as a system of corporations in Maine's sense," as Leach wrote (1968:485). This entails another fundamental aspect of society: transcendence. Corporate entities live at an abstract level and "never die," just like gods.

The second principle is that of reciprocity as seminally theorized by Mauss and since adopted under various modifications by a great majority of anthropologists. This principle includes at its core an asymmetrical and binding relationship: debt.

The third principle is that of hierarchy or ranking, in a continuum from the pecking order of chickens to hierarchy in primate behavior and dominance among humans. Together with the principle of corporation and sometimes associated with a certain kind of kinship arrangement (the segmentary lineage), hierarchy generates systems on which a relation of partial order is predicated, systems that have great explanatory value in a number of cases and for a number of reasons, but not always. Society is therefore this sort of collective clockwork organization premised on corporation, reciprocity, and ranking. Individuals are likewise placed in a nest of groups and subgroups, are subjected to rules of reciprocity and ranking, and are thought of as socialized human beings as a result of this process.

My position is that while the above principles work out as a (at least preliminary) theory of society in a large number of cases, including our complex, urban, industrial, large-scale, modern societies, it does not seem to work very well for the kind of indigenous small-scale communities studied in this volume. As long as the principles defined above (corporation, debt reciprocity, and ranking) do not operate as the fundamental principles of organization, I feel entitled to declare these communities "nonsocial." Not all the authors in this volume, however, are willing to go to such an extremity, and some, like Benjamin, Endicott, and Howell, prefer to keep the terms *social* and *society*. A good reason for that is that my definition of *society*, solely based on these three principles, can easily be viewed as too restrictive. But when calling such communities "nonsocial" I do not mean that they are "subsocial"; I mean that their "sociality" or, better, "gregarious nature" is not subservient to the principles I have just indicated. Likewise I do not suggest that "nonsocial" organizations are devoid of organization. I mean that their organizing principles are fundamentally different.

What, then, are the principles that make their continuous operation possible, since of course we are speaking of relatively stable collective entities, obeying rational rules, or rules that can be rationally grasped? The purpose of this volume is to look for answers to this question. Authors offer a number of very plausible answers explaining solidarity (unity and altruism) and interdependence. It is probably useful to place these answers into three overlapping circles. One is centered on the concept of sharing, the second on kinship and child care, and the third on ethics, ideology, and a specific ontology.

Sharing

Sharing has several meanings. Because of its polysemy the word must be used cautiously. *Sharing* is firstly applied to material resources and commodities being circulated or apportioned. The word here has two opposite denotations: either sharing of something one owns—giving away altruistically as in "please come and share our meal"—or dividing a common good (a prey, land) between several people equally and without any mandatory reciprocity. This is the true sense of sharing defined in contradistinction to debt reciprocity (Woodburn 1998). In any case the basic idea is that of equal access by all concerned to a common collective good

In the sense of "taking part" and "being part of," it refers to activities, space, or substance. It means to be "part of" a totality, being "at one with," as one shares in a common state (e.g., sentiments) or a common good (e.g., a country). It is in this sense that *sharing* has the meaning of belonging to a group, like a Semai band, a Palawan neighborhood, a Sama Dilaut moorage, or a Batek hunting party. Membership, in the examples given in this volume (see the essays by Sillander and Benjamin among others), does not depend on a common substance, as Gibson has argued (1985), nor is it conditional on any external authority, but on the engagement of individual actors on a voluntary basis—something I call subjective membership because it is created by the voluntary action of the participants, not by mandatory rules of exclusive membership, nor by any chiefly authority. Access is free and based on active participation (like taking up residence with a band or participating in rotating agricultural activities). Sharing is seen as agency, but it can be perceived at the receiving end of a flow of activities, when actors are in the position of passive beneficiaries of things produced or harvested by others.

Sharing then concerns primarily three different objects: goods or commodities—food being the most important—then words and information (words can also be said to be exchanged, circulated or in flux; see Sather, this volume; and Eder, this volume, on names), then activities and also, in a metaphorical way, space (as a metaphor for dwelling or tagging along or exploiting the same geographical sector). Sharing can even be extended to what sociologists call *habitus*, a Latin word meaning "habit" or "durable disposition," and this can include a series of attitudes and shared values, like most typically in the cases studied here, peaceability, a distaste for competition, what I call reciprocal humility and a desire for interpersonal harmony.

What makes sharing a good explanation for solidarity? The first reason that comes to mind is that sharing is by definition an act of unity and mutual concern. There is, then, some circularity in the argument. Why share if one is not feeling solidary and mutually obligated? How can one be solidary if one does not share? Sharing, however, when applied to the distribution of commodities, may have a certain practical value as an insurance policy (Endicott, this volume), an argument that has been debated before (see Woodburn 1998).

Sharing, then, might not be the explanation for solidarity, just a better word for it, but the different modalities of sharing are probably the best descriptions of solidarity and the most direct and convincing way to show how it works. The reader will find in this book illuminating instances of sharing of activities, goods, sentiments, work, and persons, especially children. What eventually makes sharing so special, inasmuch as it is not confused with reciprocity, is its sociocentric rather than egocentric focus. Sharing binds individuals to a collective third party. They are concretely aggregated as persons and totalities, while not being captive abstractions in aggregations thus formed.

Kinship and Child Care

This volume is not centrally concerned about kinship, but several contributors devote some special attention to discussing it and evaluating the force of kin ties as well as their discriminatory properties when it comes to understanding solidarity and gregariousness. Kinship is a concept related to genetic as well as cognitive, semantic, and ultimately social ties. It is partly concerned with the conjugal or nuclear family, the core domestic unit minimally comprised of parents and children. This object, the true crucible of human sociality, was one of the casualties in the general downfall of kinship studies. It is now revived with good reason together with a renewed interest in kinship studies (Barnes 2006:351; Dziebel 2007:124). Every single society or group studied in this volume puts the domestic family at the center of its operation or, in the case of peasantized societies, holds it as one of its dearest institutions.

Kinship ties people together, but at the same time it divides them into distinct categories. It goes both ways as creating solidarity and fostering difference. How child care creates unity is forcefully analyzed by Dentan in this volume. It is children who generate society, and kinship aggregates are best understood as centered on descendants rather than ancestors. Not only is child care in itself a binding tie, but it is extended outside the mother-child pair. One of its most important human aspects is indeed multiple caring by individuals other than the mother, including males. Alloparents play a decisive role in what Dentan and others call K-strategy, and the mutual concern for nurturance and alloparenthood derived or extended from the mother-child tie is both a constitutive element of sociality (gregariousness) and a blueprint for it. This is in a way an "extentionist" view of kinship, reminiscent of functionalist theories positing an extension of a primary link (especially the sibling tie) to the entire sphere of kinship (Radcliffe-Brown 1952).[3] It only looks like that because in truth it is not just the mother-child link that is extended but the entire K-strategy that is applied to the sphere of human relations. "Babies as social glue" is a felicitous phrase that points not only to the centrality of child care as an archetypal mechanism of aggregation but to the principle of "descendent-centered" rather than "ancestor-centered" bilateral kinship systems.

On the other hand all kinship systems create distinct categories of kin. Those discussed in this volume typically separate younger and older by age and generation, close and distant by collaterality, and consanguines and affines by marriage. This introduces another dimension interpreted by several authors in this volume (Sillander, Sather, Macdonald) as generating strategically vital asymmetrical ties. In behavioral terms these ties are characterized by avoidance, deference, or restraint and contrast with symmetrical ties characterized by familiarity, informality, and joking. The interplay between asymmetrical and symmetrical ties or between age, generation, and/or affinity on the one hand and collaterality on the other enables the system to give any dyadic relation a value on a gradient, from most respectful to relatively subservient. It does not create an overall ranking system because the system is ego centered and relations are not transitive. The existence of asymmetric ties is theorized by Macdonald as making relationships more "manageable," because a difference in status facilitates conflict management, no matter how gregarious and egalitarian the norm is. But difference between kin categories and their behavioral correlates also have a structural effect. Rules of cross-sex avoidance, for instance, promote a situation of segmentation making conjugal family groups detachable units, a situation favorable to nomadism (Benjamin, this volume). By being either inclusive (everybody is a relative) or exclusive (some are relatives, others are strangers) kinship plays the role of a social envelope, with the capacity of uniting here and dividing there.

Moreover, as an idiom of interpersonal relations and status ascription, kinship entails a moral dimension of togetherness and common belonging. It defines "relatedness in a broad sense" as Sillander writes in this volume. Kinship usually connotes closeness or solidarity, and speakers tend to remind listeners that they are "not just strangers," as the Palawan say, but brothers and sisters, parents and children. Solidarity is at the heart of kinship even when it creates distinct and ordered classes of relatives. The various aspects and functional properties of cognatic kinship systems studied in this volume highlight the apparent contradictions of these "strange societies" by allowing maximum individual autonomy ("even the closest kin ties can be repudiated," as Sather informs us in his essay) and intense mutual obligation, and by promoting equality while using asymmetric ties.

Another source of solidarity lies in moral values and a conception of the world grounded in a special ontology and conception of personhood that sees all animated beings as belonging to a "single moral universe" (Howell, this volume) thus erasing conceptual barriers between humans and nonhumans (Descola 2005:176). Morality and cosmology are closely linked to the point of forming just one continuous domain wherein behavior is sanctioned by forces coming from within the sphere of human relations and from without. Disrespect toward animals and other members of the group, particularly affines, meets equally with physical sanctions in the form of thunderclaps, storms, swelling of the belly, and other psychosomatic diseases. Likewise conflict and enmity are a source of misfortune. Human affairs involve the natural and spiritual world, which in turn has immediate effects on humans. It is easy to see in this a self-reinforcing loop placing members of the community into a binding web of interdependent ties.

All the factors and dimensions that have been reviewed (and these do not exhaust the store of meaningful traits singled out in this volume) are, as I said, overlapping interpretive circles where factors implicate each other in a general feedback circuit. One shares because one is kin, but one is kin because one shares. Friendship creates kinship, but kinship is recognized among friends, and it ends up defining them, both kinship by friendship and friendship in terms of kinship. Aggregates are made of interdependent moral units, but interdependence is ultimately validated by an ideology of human unity that encompasses natural forces and extends the human realm to all living creatures.

Free in the Forest

I have insisted so far on the problem of solidarity in view of the absence of coercive structure and the presence of high levels of personal autonomy.[4] However, our burden as anthropologists is to account not only for factors of cohesion and unity leading to aggregation but also for divisive and centrifugal factors spelling potential disaggregation. In a classic Durkheimian view of society, freedom is dangerous and logically entails the possibility of disorder or anomy, while order (stasis) depends on orders (in the sense of commandments).

Equality is clearly a valued state of things for the indigenous communities we are discussing. Among the Cuyonon, the Malay, and other lowland societies that are otherwise ranked or stratified, the value of equality is also asserted at least in some marginal sectors of activities: the playful, the ludic, the ritual. People are committed to maintaining equality and go to some length to enforce it by shunning displays of arrogance or boastfulness, by showing reciprocal humility and biting humor, by avoiding competition even when playing games (by not scoring points, by not declaring winners or losers). As mentioned here and there in the following pages, gender symmetry is the rule, and if asymmetry or inequality in status is to be found it is in age rather than sex. Persons of some substance, usually respected elders, keep lecturing the young on good behavior and proper manners. Specialists in customary law deliver long lectures and "teachings," *usyat* as the Palawan say, when a verdict of guilt is pronounced. But orders are not given. If they are, people listen but do not necessarily obey. If you want to live with the Semai, the Batek, or the Palawan you have got to take no for an answer, even when it comes from the mouth of a child.

Autonomy and equality are the two sides of the same coin. If there is authority, it is in the form of Weberian rational authority, based on acknowledged competence or experience, not in the form of ontological dominance. Strict egalitarianism found in these communities is actually compatible with a measure of control. As this volume does not make this topic a central issue, I will not dwell on it. Let it be said that there are several ways whereby norms of equality and respect for others are enforced among the populations studied in this volume. Apart from those sanctions I mentioned before (disease and catastrophic events inflicted by nonhuman agents) there is informal public opinion (gossip), formal public opinion using a traditional system of customary law (*adat*), avoidance and ostracism, and finally there is murder (very rare indeed but a last resort against incestuous couples and dangerous individuals who are a hazard to others, like psychotic killers, madmen, violent bullies, and possibly witches). Punishment, however, is meted out parsimoniously in the best of cases. Considerable freedom is left to individuals concerning some of the most important choices they can make, one being the choice of residence and association with others.

If, as Gibson writes in this volume, egalitarianism and autonomy, as well as sharing, are "mutually reinforcing ethical values" and if there is a logical consistency in holding to this set of interconnected principles, it is done at a price: vulnerability to hostile, better organized, and militarily powerful others. Pacifism has to come into the picture sooner or later. For some authors it appears as the crux of the matter (see Dentan, this volume, and 2008a and 2008b). But whatever its origin or nature, the peaceful and nonviolent ethos of all the people studied in this volume (with the exception of some Punan groups used as mercenaries by their stratified neighbors—see Kaskija, this volume) is one of the most striking and important traits of their way of life. For my part I do not see egalitarianism as entailing pacifism (Iban and Ilongot testify to the existence of aggressive and violence-prone egalitarians), but the fact remains that, as far as the quasi totality of indigenous communities discussed in this volume is concerned, a commitment to nonviolence is a major aspect of their ideology. Even Cuyonon are to be considered as at least moderately nonviolent (Eder, this volume, and personal communication). Several studies have been written about peace in recent years (Howell and Willis 1989; Silverberg and Gray 1992; Kemp and Fry 2004; Fry 2006), and several contributors to this volume, particularly Howell and Dentan, have shown peaceability to be a trait that is innate among humans.

If sharing and a desire to be equal, together with a tendency toward peace and nonviolence, are innate and universal, why are some peoples, a majority of them actually, violent and unequal? This is where a general explanation is required, whether the explicandum is the kind of egalitarian, sharing, and nonviolent ethos that we are discussing here or whether, as Dentan would have it, it is inegalitarian, market-oriented, and aggressive relations that require an explanation. As several of the contributors remind us, we owe to anthropologists who specialize in hunter-gatherers and foragers the full realization that true egalitarianism and sharing as a distinct mode of togetherness are a fact sui generis among humans, found among some (though not all) hunter-gatherers in a pure or almost pure form (Boehm 1993; Woodburn 1982). To account for this, anthropologists used a Marxist-inspired model of determinism based on a mode of production. Woodburn's brilliant idea of immediate-return economy seemed to be the best way of making sense of egalitarianism by using economic factors. But what happens when delayed-return economies allow for the kind of strict egalitarianism and radical sharing ethos that !Kung Bushmen, Hadza, or Mbuti pygmies are practicing? It is the merit of Gibson, an editor of this volume, to have identified an almost perfect Hadza-like sociality among the Buid horticulturalists in the Philippines (1986). But in doing so he undermined the model, or at least weakened the explanatory virtue of the immediate-return factor.

It is probably the presence of an exceptionally high commitment to both egalitarianism and nonviolence (at least in the organized form of warfare, and with some exceptions like the Ilongot [see R. Rosaldo 1980; and M. Rosaldo 1980]) among horticulturalists that has thrown an anthropological bridge between hunters and gatherers on the one hand and sedentary or semisedentary people on the other, thus creating a new and critical perspective on the old typology of bands, tribes, chiefdoms, and states. At least it blurred some of the divisions between categories based on techno-economic criteria alone, and it puts an assortment of sea nomads, peasants, foragers, and shifting agriculturists more or less in the same class.

It is now clearly realized (see the essays by Endicott and Dentan in this volume) that horticulturalists and others, like the sea nomads described by Sather, also adhere to the egalitarians' club, and there is every reason to consider them as full members. The explicans is not, in other words, to be found exclusively in economic and technical constraints. Even if economic and demographic constraints severely limit the existence and operation of open-aggregated formations with an ethos of pure sharing, one has to throw in other good reasons for such a stubborn addiction to egalitarianism, mutualism, and, in most cases, pacifism (or peaceable habitus).

Several authors, mainly Dentan, Kaskija, and Gibson, see enclavement as an answer. The discussion we have around this theme is probably one of the most significant contributions this volume has to offer. Enclavement here is taken as meaning geographical containment as well as entailing a particular form of social interaction between enclaved and enclaving groups. All the indigenous communities discussed here are surrounded by dominant state-oriented lowland or coastal cultures or by stratified agriculturists. It is the reactions to these dominant polities that—according to said authors— account for their outlook on life. For Dentan it is a situation best explained by psychology, a reaction of defeated individuals or populations who learn helplessness through repeated defeat, accept their powerlessness, and live with it, eventually turning their surrender into positive thinking (this volume and 1994, 2004). For Gibson it is a refusal and an inversion of a model offered by their lowland neighbors—defined by hierarchy and aggression— what he calls a "secondary reaction to predatory ranking." For Kaskija it is a more subtle strategy of either pretending to be like one's neighbors or maybe adopting temporarily some of their traits. Benjamin also sees the nomads' consciousness as actively maintaining a distance from and rejecting the social model offered by neighboring farmers. But in the end each of these groups is retreating and, as best as it can, hiding or fleeing. They take refuge in difficult terrain, high valleys, deep forests, and high seas and basi-cally put as much distance as they can between themselves and their pursuers. The degree of isolation can vary however, nomadic Semang being less isolated than other peninsular groups. Slave raiding is in any case one of the most important elements in the history of the region. To account for the way it influenced and even shaped the consciousness of the native populations, one has to keep present in mind its looming terror and the fact that all of the people we are discussing (again with the exception of lowland populations like the Cuyonon) were systematically treated as chattel, enslaved, and at times massacred like animals (Gibson this volume; Dentan 2008b). Forever hiding or running away from their aggressors, they rejected what the slavers and neighboring bullies stood for. They were freeing themselves from the predators but also from the constraints of organized belligerence. That and living with the consequences of this choice realistically describe the situation experienced by the Buid, Palawan, Semai, and others. Social ranking and corporation had to be left behind as just other tools of enslavement or compromises were reached whereby super-ficial and borrowed forms of stratification were adopted. A commitment to everything that is not like states or stratified agricultural societies has become the determining factor, thus vindicating Clastres's antistate hypothesis (1989).

From my own point of view, the "reactionist" explanation, cogently argued by the authors I have mentioned, needs another element. The popu-lations discussed here are clearly dwelling in secluded places, "refuges," "islands in a predatory sea," as Gibson aptly terms it. But can we explain refugees by the refuge? Why in the first place are they running away and offering no armed resistance to their enemies? It may be that they stay where they stay—not in open space, at the bottoms of valleys, or on the beaches and estuaries of inland seas—because they have been actively pur-sued and hunted, destroyed, and eradicated for what they stood for in the first place. If these people are where they are it is probably because they prefer something rather than just refusing something, something supremely precious in their way of life rather than something they dislike in others.

Actually we may never know what came first, but if I were allowed to guess, I would vouch for a preference rather than a refusal. Their gregarious way of life was what made them prey, so to speak, even before being preyed upon. They did not become open aggregated only because they had to dodge their enemies; they developed an independent predisposition toward this egalitarian, free, and community-based way of life. It made them vulnerable. They were surrendered before surrendering, happily lost before being found, as it was their amazing disgrace to be. When predators came, they ran for sure, and they took refuge in the margins of the habited world.

Anarchic Solidarity

> I can't get no satisfaction.
> —Rolling Stones

And it might be nothing else but an innate gregarious cline that makes humans need satisfactory interaction, without being straightjacketed by ranking and other stifling norms, and thus prefer to stick with a way of life that satisfies this need. There are two opposite ways for humans to live together, and most certainly many intermediate solutions. One is to get seriously organized in groups, invest in property, develop hierarchy, put everyone in a nest of constraining boxes, and value discipline and order, so that everyone is told what to do. Another one is to live and let live. We are familiar with the first solution, having adopted it since the Neolithic and maybe even before, but not at all with the second. Sociology and anthropology have theorized society and extracted from it its basic principles: reciprocity and exchange, ranking and hierarchy, corporation and transcendence of the collective over the individual. I am suggesting here that we have barely started to understand the other way of life, one that is totally *not* based on these principles. This volume, however, is one that explores this kind of sociality. Whatever the ultimate explanation in evolutionary or genetic terms, or any other terms, there is a need to find a vocabulary to describe it and make sense of it in rational terms.

I have tried, in other publications (Macdonald 2008, 2009), to find appropriate words that have the capacity to name some of the dimensions, mechanisms, relations, and organizing principles at work under such different conditions. Some of these words have found their way into this volume. One is the concept of the *weak tie*, borrowed and modified from Granovetter (1973, 1983), seen as the main functional tie binding persons to each other in open aggregates (see also Endicott, this volume). Another concept is that of *fellowship*, almost identical with Gibson's *companionship*, a most apt substitute for the concept of group and one that accounts for the twin characteristics of openness and aggregation in communities with an- archic solidarity. A third is what I name elsewhere (Macdonald 2008:15) *conditions of felicity.* By this I mean certain requisites for successful and continued interaction. It is a way to give meaning to what people seek in gregarious relatedness. Other ingredients needed for community building are caught in the concepts of *complexity, immediacy, multistranded relations, immanence,* and *subjective membership.* Limitations of time and space prevent me from developing these notions further.

No matter in what exact terms the authors in this volume couch their arguments, they testify for something special in the characters they describe from long acquaintance and intimate knowledge. One is that they are, certainly, different and puzzling to an extent, but also that they are intensely moral people, and even in their own fashion exemplary. People discussed in this volume give reality and presence to a pure and almost utopian kind of selfless ethos, in spite of whatever unhappiness, stress, and strife that may otherwise characterize their lives. Were it not for the postedenic and Hobbesian spell that weighs on social sciences (Sahlins 2008), or the ten- dency to take an anti-Rousseauian stance as hard-nosed intellectualism, this could be said without apology.

Notes

1 In table 1.1, the Cuyonon are not included. As a peasant society and a Christian lowland group the Cuyonon are embedded (not enclaved or just surrounded) in a wider state society structured around principles (social differentiation, cor- poration, and inequality) different from those adopted by indigenous groups like the Batek, Chewong, Palawan, Buid, and so on. It makes their inclusion in this particular comparative grid problematic. The description of their social behavior by Eder in chapter 9 is essential, however, to understanding the nature and pervasiveness of the open-aggregated and peaceful ethos that lies at the core of the Cuyonon's and possibly other lowlanders' sociality.

2 In spite of my attempts to find discussions in the anthropological literature con- cerning the definition of *groups* and *kin groups* after the 1980s—using search engines and databases like the JSTOR—I could not find many. Like Shryer's (2001), most discussions are done by sociologists interested in ethnicity and modern societies. There is a huge literature on "reference groups" and network theory, but these concerns depart from those anthropologists had about kinship and social structure in premodern societies.

3 Dentan proposed an extentionist interpretation of Semai kin terms based on the analysis of their semantic and cognitive components (1970).

4 The phrase "free in the forest" is borrowed from G. Hickey's book with the same title (1982)

References

Appell, George N. 1983. "Methodological problems with the concepts of corporation, corporate social groupings, and cognatic descent group." *American Ethnologist* 10 (2):302–11.

Ashley Montagu, M.F. 1943. "Review of wolf-children and feral man, by J.A. Singh and R.M. Zingg." *American Anthropologist* 45 (3):468–472.

Barclay, Harold. 1997. *Culture and Anarchism*. London: Freedom Press.

Barnes, J.A. 1962. "African models in the New Guinea Highlands." *Man* 62 (1–2):5–9.

Barnes, Robert H. 2006. "Maurice Godelier and the Metamorphosis of Kinship: A review essay." *Journal of the Society for the Comparative Study of Society and History* 48(2):326–58.

Bird-David, Nurit. 1994. "Solidarity and immediacy, or past and present conversations on bands." *Man* 29 (3):583–603.

Boehm, C. 1993. "Egalitarian behavior and reverse dominance hierarchy." *Current Anthropology* 34 (3):227–54.

Boissevain, Jeremy. 1968. "The place of non-groups in the social sciences." *Man*, N.S., 3 (4):542–56.

Brown, Paula. 1978. "New Guinea: Ecology, society, and culture." *Annual Review of Anthropology* 7:263–91.

Clastres, Pierre. 1989. *Society against the State: Essays in Political Anthropology*. Trans. R. Hurley. New York: Zone Books.

Cohen, Fred. 2008. "Penal isolation: Beyond the seriously mental ill." *Criminal Justice and Behavior* 35 (8):1017–45.

Dentan, Robert K. 1970. "Hocus pocus and extensionism in Central Malaya: Notes on Semai kinship terminology." *American Anthropologist* 70 (2):358–62.

———. 1994. "Surrendered men: Peaceable enclaves in the post-Enlightenment West." In L. Sponsel and T. Gregor, eds., *The Anthropology of Peace and Nonviolence*, 69–108. Boulder and London: Lynne Riener.

————. 2004. "Cautious, alert, polite, and elusive: The Semai of Central Peninsular Malaysia." In D. Kemp and D. Fry, eds., *Keeping the Peace. Conflict Resolution and Peaceful Societies around the World*. New York and London: Routledge.

————. 2008a. "Recent studies on violence: What's in and what's out?" *Reviews in Anthropology* 37 (1):1–27.

————. 2008b. *Overwhelming Terror: Love, Fear, Peace and Violence among the Semai of Malaysia*. Lanham, MD, and Boulder: Rowman and Littlefield.

Descola, Philippe. 2005. *Par-delà Nature et Culture*. Paris: Gallimard.

Dziebel, German V. 2007. *The Genius of Kinship*. Youngstown and New York: Cambria Press.

Feil, D.K. 1984. "Beyond patriliny in the New Guinea Highlands." *Man* 19 (1):50–76.

Freeman, J. Derek. 1961. "On the concept of the kindred." *Journal of the Royal Anthropological Institute* 91:192–220.

Frintner, Carly. 2005. "Lonely madness: The effects of solitary confinement and social isolation on mental and emotional health." Serendip Third Web Papers. http://serendip.brynmawr.edu/exchange/node/1898. Accessed November 8, 2010.

Fry, Douglas P. 2006. *The Human Potential for Peace: An Anthropological Challenge to Assumptions about War and Violence*. New York and Oxford: Oxford University Press.

Gawande, Atul. 2009. "Hellhole." *New Yorker*, March 2009.

Gibson, Thomas. 1985. "The sharing of substance versus the sharing of activity among the Buid. *Man*," N.S., 20 (3):391–411.

————. 1986. *Sacrifice and Sharing in the Philippine Highlands: Religion and Society among the Buid of Mindoro*. London: Athlone Press.

Graeber, David. 2004. *Fragments of an Anarchist Anthropology*. Chicago: Prickly Paradigm Press.

————. 2007. *Possibilities: Essays on Hierarchy, Rebellion, and Desire*. Oakland and Edinburgh: AK Press.

Granovetter, Mark. 1973. "The strength of weak ties." *American Journal of Sociology* 78 (6):1360–80.

————. 1983. "The strength of weak ties: A network theory revisited." *Sociological Theory* 1:201–33.

Grassian, Stuart. 1993. "Psychopathological effects of solitary confinement." *American Journal of Psychiatry* 140 (11):1450–54

Hickey, Gerald C. 1982. *Free in the Forest: Ethnohistory of the Vietnamese Central Highlands, 1954–1976.* New Haven and London: Yale University Press.

Howell, Signe, and Roy Willis, eds. 1989. *Societies at Peace: Anthropological Perspectives.* London and New York: Routledge.

Ingold, Tim. 1999. "On the social relations of the hunter-gatherer band." In R.B. Lee and R. Daly, eds., *The Cambridge Encyclopedia of Hunters and Gatherers,* 399–410. Cambridge: Cambridge University Press.

Ingold, Tim, D. Riches, and J. Woodburn, eds. 1988. *Hunters and Gatherers.* Vols. 1 and 2. Oxford: Berg.

Kemp, Graham, and Douglas P. Fry, eds. 2004. *Keeping the Peace: Conflict Resolution and Peaceful Societies around the World.* New York and London: Routledge.

Kemp, Jeremy. 1991. "Processes of kinship and community in North-Central Thailand." In F. Hüsken and J. Kemp, eds., *Cognation and Social Organization in Southeast Asia,* 91–107. Leiden: KITLV Press.

Leach, Edmund. 1968. "Social structure: The history of the concept." In D. Sills, ed., *International Encyclopedia of the Social Sciences.* Vol. 14, 482–89. New York: Macmillan and the Free Press.

Macdonald, Charles J-H. 1977. *Une Société Simple: Parenté et Résidence chez les Palawan.* Paris: Institut d'Ethnologie.

———. 2007. *Uncultural Behavior: An Anthropological Investigation of Suicide in the Southern Philippines.* Honolulu: University of Hawai'i Press.

———. 2008. "Order against Harmony: Are humans always social?" *Suomen Antropologi: Journal of the Finnish Anthropological Society* 33 (2):5–21.

———. 2009. *The Anthropology of Anarchy.* Occasional Papers from the School of Social Science, no. 35. Princeton, New Jersey: Institute for Advanced Study.

Murdock, George P. 1960. "Cognatic forms of social organization." In G.P Murdock, ed., *Social Structure in Southeast Asia,* 1–14. Chicago: Quadrangle Books.

Needham, Rodney. 1971. "Remarks on the analysis of kinship and marriage." In R. Needham, ed., *Rethinking Kinship and Marriage,* 1–34. London: Tavistock.

Orenstein, Henry. 1968. "The ethnological theories of Henry Sumner Maine." *American Anthropologist* 70 (2):264–76.

Peletz, Michael G. 1995. "Kinship studies in late twentieth-century anthropology." *Annual Review of Anthropology* 24:343–72.

Radcliffe-Brown, Alfred. R. 1952. *Structure and Function in Primitive Society: Essays and Addresses.* London and Glencoe: Cohen and West and the Free Press.

Rosaldo, Michelle Z. 1980. *Knowledge and Passion: Ilongot Notions of Self and Social Life.* Cambridge: Cambridge University Press.

Rosaldo, Renato. 1980. *Ilongot Headhunting, 1883–1974: A Study in Society and History.* Stanford: Stanford University Press.

Sahlins, Marshall. 2008. *The Western Illusion of Human Nature.* Chicago: Prickly Paradigm Press.

Schneider, David M. 1984. *A Critique of the Study of Kinship.* Ann Arbor: University of Michigan Press.

Schryer, Frans J. 2001. "Multiple hierarchies and the duplex nature of groups." *The Journal of the Royal Anthropological Institute* 7(4):705–21,

Sillander, Kenneth. 2004. *Acting Authoritatively: How Authority Is Expressed through Social Action among the Bentian of Indonesian Borneo.* PhD diss., University of Helsinki. Swedish School of Social Science Publications, no. 17. Helsinki: University of Helsinki Press.

Silverberg, James, and Patrick Gray, eds. 1992. *Aggression and Peacefulness in Humans and Other Primates.* New York and Oxford: Oxford University Press.

Strathern, Marilyn. 1989. *The Gender of the Gift: Problems with Women and Problems with Society in Melanesia.* Berkeley: University of California Press.

Wagner, Roy. 1974. "Are there social groups in the New Guinea Highlands?" In M.J. Leaf, ed., *Frontiers of Anthropology*, 95–122. New York: D. Van Nostrand.

Watson, James B. 1970. "Society as organized flow: The Tairora case." *Southwestern Journal of Anthropology* 26 (2):107–24.

Woodburn, James. 1982. "Egalitarian societies." *Man*, N.S., 17 (3):431–51.

———. 1998. "'Sharing is not a form of exchange': An analysis of property-sharing in immediate-return hunter-gatherer societies." In C.M. Hann, ed., *Property Relations: Renewing the Anthropological Tradition*, 48–63. Cambridge: Cambridge University Press.

2

Sources of Sociality in a Cosmological Frame: Chewong, Peninsular Malaysia

SIGNE HOWELL

IN THEIR SEMINAL STUDY *Tribes without Rulers*, whose purpose is to understand the maintenance of "social order where there is no centralized political authority," Middleton and Tait (1958:1) exclude from their consideration those societies, "like that of the Bushmen," where "the largest political units embrace people all of whom are interrelated by kinship so that political relations are coterminous with kinship relations" (2). Seemingly content to accept that all is thereby said about that particular social constellation, they focus on how the segmentary lineage system can be shown to constitute a political system. However, to those who have worked in societies where there truly are no rulers and no segmentary lineages—or any other corporate kinship groups—the brief characterization of the Bushmen type is unsatisfactory for two main reasons. First, while kin relatedness often does, from a certain perspective, constitute the boundary of the practice of sociality, this does not account for why kinship should be given this a priori status or why some people in such societies adhere to a strong egalitarian ethos, with no leaders of any kind, while others do not. Second, the authors fail to take account of the semantics of a lived sense of belonging that is concurrent with high value being placed on personal autonomy. In what follows, I shall try to elaborate on some of these issues with special reference to the Chewong, a group of aboriginal people who live in the rainforest of Peninsular Malaysia that engages in hunting, gathering, and shifting cultivation. As regards my understanding of what constitutes the principles of Chewong social order—and, in terms of this volume, their sources of solidarity—I will base my interpretation on their ontology and the closely related question of morality.

Since the 1960s, the burgeoning literature on hunter-gatherers has addressed the question of what binds people together in the absence of those social institutions with which anthropologists are familiar. This may be because the analytical approach has tended to emphasize a certain set of practices. These range from organized collective activities such as hunting, foraging, or work groups to relationships based on kinship, companionship, or friendship, from the sharing of yield, immediate consumption, trust, and self-deprecation to nonviolent interaction and the performance of ritual. The explanatory locus has been placed more on the special nature of subsistence activities (mode of subsistence) and less on the semantics and moral injunctions (mode of thought) that constitute such activities. Although, typically, hunter-gatherer societies adhere to some form of animistic cosmology, few anthropologists place the sources of solidarity within that frame.[1] I shall suggest that, in the Chewong case, an anthropomorphic cosmology (or rather, chewongmorphic; see Howell 2010a) extends the boundary of society to include humans as well as the nonhuman objects and beings within the environment that are perceived as conscious beings on a par with humanity. As all these conscious beings interact with each other according to a number of mutually constituted prescriptions and proscriptions—which I call cosmo-rules—the field of Chewong sociality is coextensive with this anthropomorphized world. The Chewong "other" are the dominant populations of Malays and, to a lesser extent, Chinese with whom, until recently, they had little contact but whom they feared. Chewong contrast themselves with these populations. "They" are powerful, violent, angry, demanding, fearless, and living in permanent villages with leaders. "We" are constantly on the move, foraging for a living—timid, peaceful, without leaders of any kind that can tell us what to do. Moreover, Malays are Muslims and cannot eat the food that Chewong hunt and love to eat, thereby precluding close social intercourse should this be desired. Thus, Chewong have a clear understanding of themselves as radically different from their powerful neighbors. Other known aboriginal groups (Orang Asli) occupy an intermediate position, but in describing their more relaxed relationship with the Jah Hut and the Temuan they are nevertheless at pains to stress the differences between them as regards their way of life and the details of their cosmology. All these factors contribute to a strong sense of "us" as a wider group beyond the band (cf. Ingold 1999).

Following on from this, my argument will be that it is only by pursuing the complexity of Chewong modes of thought that one may begin to find some answers to the relationship between autonomy and sociality in egalitarian societies. In particular, I am concerned with elucidating their understanding of metaphysics (what is the nature of reality) and their ontology (what types of things exist in the world) and how they relate to each other. An integral part of such an approach is, of course, the indigenous concept of personhood (human nature), which in this case includes the animated conscious beings in the forest. The sources of Chewong ontological knowledge are found in their numerous myths and shamanic songs (Howell [1984] 1989a, 1996). Ultimately, one might argue that it is the interface between nature and culture that is at stake, the handling of which becomes instrumental in the perception of sociality and the moral prerequisites for social life. It is from such a perspective, I suggest, that we should approach our interpretations about the sources of sociality and solidarity. From such a perspective one may, with benefit, examine the challenges and tensions that arise as a result of recent interactions with the external world, which, inter alia, leads to a more settled way of life, increased interaction with the outside world, and the introduction of money into a previous noncumulative sharing economy.

Society or Sociality

In a society like that of the Chewong in which there is no conceptual space for leaders, with no mechanism for coercion, and in which individual agency is highly valued at the same time as a profound sense of communality exists and is regularly acted on, premises for shared knowledge of the world and how to behave within it become highly important for all concerned. Recent theoretical debates about the nature of society, or, indeed, whether there is anything that might usefully be termed "society," have alerted the ethnographers of open-aggregated communities, yet again, to a consideration of the issues involved. Timothy Ingold, a defender of the proposition that "society" has outlived its analytical usefulness, at least as concerns the study of hunters and gatherers, suggests that we are better served by "focusing on the themes of immediacy, personal autonomy, and sharing." A hunter-gatherer way of life, he argues, demonstrates "how it is possible to live socially ... without having to 'live in societies at all'" (1999:400). His critique of society on an earlier occasion is directed at a common anthropological usage of the concept "as a bounded totality that is formed of the sum of its parts" (1996:58).[2] Instead, he argues, with Strathern and Toren (1996), against a reification of society that is dependent for its existence on an understanding of the individual agent. Rather than pursuing the age-old dilemma of the individual-society relationship, they wish to abandon the whole debate and replace it with a different conceptual vocabulary, anchored in the concept of sociality, "by which particular persons come into being through their relationships" (Strathern 1996:64).

Although I have much sympathy for this position and earlier argued along similar lines (Howell [1984] 1989a, 1989a, 1996), I also have some reservations, the most important of which concerns the abandonment of society as a concept.[3] Minimally, the question of whether society exists ought to be an empirical not an analytical one. But the chosen definition of society is crucial. Paradoxically, those employed by Ingold and Strathern appear to be more concerned with the individual than with the whole—the social.

In order to elucidate my argument, I need to clarify my usage of the term *sociality*. In an earlier volume exploring the sources of societal peaceful interaction in Chewong and other societies (Howell and Willis 1989), we argued that these might best be found in the theoretical approach developed by some cognitive psychologists—such as Trevathern (1989) and, later, Bråten (1998)—which emphasizes sociality as an innate, presumably genetically inscribed predisposition in all human beings. Convincing experimental work shows that human infants are, from the moment of birth, aware of themselves in relation to others and define and experience themselves in a relational mode; in other words, humans experience and act intersubjectively. Thus, far from being autonomous, "individuals" are the very opposite: they have a drive to connect—to communicate and relate to others (Bråten 1998).

This approach has wide applicability in the ethnographic study of social forms and allows one to explicate the similarity, or variety, of cultural premises for sociality. It is particularly helpful when trying to understand the premises for a shared experience of belonging in open-aggregated societies. However, while this understanding of sociality collapses the conceptual separation between individual and society, it does not necessarily follow that the analytical usefulness of "society"—or culture for that matter—should be dismissed.

Two further points are relevant in this connection. First, the notion of the bounded individual agent is a product of recent Euro-American political thought and is closely linked to a discourse of rights. As such, it may not have relevance outside that particular intellectual environment. Using the term *person*, and notions of personhood, I wish to show that Chewong indigenous understandings do not correspond to this Euro-American one. The Chewong person is a relational being in his or her very essence—as argued by the psychologists cited above—and they experience a sense of belonging to a shared locality and universe of meaning that constitute practice and link them together in what I choose to call a society.[4]

Second, what constitutes the limits of society in any one case may, as in the case of Chewong, be extended beyond human persons to include the many conscious nonhuman persons that inhabit their environment and with whom they interrelate. In such a case, sociality is intrinsic to a definition of what may be called an extended humanity (see below for details). This further helps elucidate questions of Chewong morality—as I encountered it during my first fieldwork in 1977–79. The extent to which it is changing under new social-economic circumstances will be addressed toward the end of this essay.

Chewong Sociality as Manifested through Sharing

The Chewong are about four hundred people who live in the rainforest of central Peninsular Malaysia.[5] At the time of my first fieldwork they lived in small, temporary settlements scattered throughout the area.[6] They had little interaction with the majority Malaysian society, and few spoke Malay. Although they practiced simple swidden agriculture, their self-perception was constructed around hunting and foraging and they defined themselves as "forest people" (*bi breté*) or "digging people" (*bi bay*). The latter appellation refers to the fact that they dig for wild tubers.

Chewong social organization has little obvious formality, that is, they have no leaders, perform no elaborate rituals, and observe few kinship-based rules. They display an extreme form of egalitarian ethos. People do not evaluate each other's abilities, and adults never tell each other what to do. Children are allowed to roam freely with very little admonition. Within a shared ontology, people are self-sufficient in their daily lives. Unlike some of the other societies discussed in this volume, Chewong do not cooperate in their work. Typically, a single couple performs every task that is required for survival. To hunt with the blowpipe was (and still is) an essential part of male identity. Men hunt alone, and women and men usually forage alone. When people make cassava "bread," they do so in parallel rather than as a communal group. Each woman plants her own tubers, digs, soaks them in the river, grates, and bakes them. Having done so, she will bring one or two bamboos of bread to a nearby house where bread has not been prepared— or she will give one to a casual visitor.

As stated above, Chewong live in an inclusive animated environment in which humans and animated animals, plants, and spirits with consciousness constitute a single moral universe (Howell [1984] 1989a, 1989b, 1996). Their identity is closely linked to place, that part of the forest that they regard as their traditional territory. This is not "nature" in any common meaning of that term. Rather, the animated forest territory constitutes the limits of their cultural world. Here the Chewong and the various species of conscious personages interact according to a set of principles (expressed in named prescriptions and proscriptions—the cosmo-rules) that form the basis for correct behavior and are a prerequisite for the maintenance of order. Existentially speaking, all Chewong—including the nonhuman beings with consciousness—are equal, with identical personal attributes and qualities; their way of life is formally identical, as are their houses and settlements. Each species is distinguished by its "cloak"—that is, its body—and by the quality of its species-specific eyes, which perceive the same object differently albeit with the same intention. Thus, for example, a human sees a monkey's body as potential meat, and a *bas* (harmful being) or a tiger sees a human soul (*ruwai*) as potential meat (Howell [1984] 1989a, 1996). I agree with Descola, in his discussion of Amazonian Indian cosmology, that "the common point of reference for all beings of nature is not humans as a species, but rather humanity as a condition" (Descola 1992:120). Whereas Euro-American thinking gives rise to the idea of one nature and many cultures, in such animistic thinking one may reverse this and posit that there is one culture and many natures (cf. Viveiros de Castro 1998). As regards the Chewong, I find this a relevant assertion and one that helps me understand the workings of their animated environment (see Howell 2010a for a further discussion of these points). At the same time, I argue that, in the Chewong case at any rate, the view of what constitutes cultural and social life is humancentric and, ultimately, anthropomorphic (see Bird-David 1999 for an extensive discussion about the status of animism in anthropological intellectual history).

Every Chewong—man and woman—has free access to knowledge about the workings of the cosmos. It is narrated in a large body of myths and in shamanistic songs (Howell 1982, 1986), and daily life is performed in conformity with this knowledge. It is through action that each and every person continuously confirms his or her adherence to a common ontological understanding—an understanding that, I suggest, is profoundly ethical and becomes the major source for experiencing solidarity. Children learn how to behave from myths, from remonstrations that invoke the cosmo-rules, and from observation of adult behavior. Those who seek to know more about the wider social universe, and seek out the numerous conscious beings that inhabit the environment in order to establish friendly relationships with them, are those who become acknowledged shamanic healers (*putao*). This, however, does not enhance their status outside the context of healing and does not form the basis for political authority.

Having learned the parameters and rules for correct and moral behaviors, each individual is responsible for observing them. The numerous prescriptions and proscriptions that constitute action become the source for diagnosis when something goes wrong, for example, in determining why X became ill. Perhaps he failed to observe the rule that pork may not be cooked on the same fire as monkey. This enabled the tiger (in the flesh or as spirit) to attack the person—either an actual bodily attack or by removing his soul. Everyone knows this is likely to happen. Importantly, no fellow human may perform retribution on another; this is always done by nonhuman beings who are enabled to do so by the human person's infraction. A shamanic séance in which everyone present participates may retrieve the soul. If the shaman's knowledge is not extensive enough, the patient dies.[7]

By the same token, a severe thunderstorm accompanied by strong winds is attributed to someone not observing *talaiden*—a prohibition on expressing levity in the vicinity of an animal or meat or the cooking of meat. The *talaiden* prescription is one that carries strong moral connotations insofar as individual incorrect behavior may directly affect the community. Visible breach of *talaiden* provokes conciliatory action in the form of someone blowing incense, accompanied by invocations that seek to deflect the resulting anger of the thunder deity or his female counterpart—the original Snake—underneath Earth.[8]

These and similar rules help explain how the Chewong theory of causality derives its meaning from their relationship with the forest environment. Two prescriptions above all stand out as important in explaining people's daily social behavior. These are *maró* and *punén*, both of which emphasize the need to share food. Indeed, Chewong sociality is predicated on them; they are the prime sources of their solidarity, and both are invoked by name whenever food, particularly meat or fish, is brought back to the settlement. While there is no myth that accounts for the origin of *punén* (but see below for more details), the consequence of failure to observe it is demonstrated in a number of different myths. The origin of *maró*, and by implication sociality itself, on the other hand, is recounted in the following (abbreviated) myth.

> In the old days people did not know about *maró*. One day Yed went hunting. He shot a binturong (a species of the civet family), butchered it, and cooked it in the forest in order to eat it there and then. In those days people lived by the maxim, "whatever I catch, I eat. Whatever you catch, you eat." Yinlugen Bud (a prehuman spirit being) came by and asked Yed what he was doing. When told that he was eating his catch, Bud remonstrated with him. "If you eat alone, and don't share your meat, you *maró*," he said. "Human beings must never eat alone, but always share." So Yed took his meat and went home and gave some meat to his wife, who was pregnant. Bud followed. The wife was about to give birth, so Yed got ready his knife in order to cut open his wife's stomach. That was how children were born in those days, and how all women died. Bud stopped him and told him that there was an opening and showed him how to press the woman's stomach until the child came out, how to cut the umbilical cord, how to wrap the afterbirth in special leaves and put it in a nearby tree, and how to cover the blood in ash. He showed how the woman could suckle her baby, and how Yed should collect special roots to cook and give her. Then Bud left for his own land. From that time onward women did not die in childbirth, and people no longer ate alone. Men always brought back all game to the camp and shared it with everyone.

This is a typical culture hero myth and is known by all. To *maró* another is the ultimate Chewong moral transgression, comparable only to *punén*. But there are important differences. It is the perpetrator of *maró* who is made subject to some kind of environmental spirit retribution. The person who is *maró* by someone failing to bring home his catch does not necessarily know about the omission, and nothing befalls him. *Punén* gives rise to a somewhat different scenario. *Punén* is committed by failing to share, but only when the victim is aware of it and experiences unfulfilled desire as a result. It is the experience of wanting, but not getting, food or tobacco or any item brought back from the forest that puts the person in a state of *punén* and renders him or her vulnerable to attack by a tiger, snake, or poisonous millipede—in the flesh or manifested as illness. So, whenever game is brought back into the forest, the hunter or his wife will go to every house and touch everyone present (usually on the shoulder or the back of the hand) with the index finger of the right hand and say "*punén.*" This tells the person not to worry about being excluded.

The retributive force of all cosmological rules, including *maró* and *punén*, applies only to those people who are linked through kinship—biological or social—and who constitute the delineated group of people that today call themselves Chewong or "us people" (*bi he*). Visiting Malays, Chinese, or other outsiders do not fall within this circle of responsibility and obligation; the Chewong do not include them in their world of onto-logical sociality.[9] To do so would, I suggest, threaten the meaning of "us people" in a world already fragile in its premises for solidarity.

Both *maró* and *punén* may be interpreted as constituting Chewong sociality through sharing. The *maró* myth is also of considerable interest for another reason. It links the act of sharing explicitly to the emergence of society as it is known today. Before the first humans were taught to share their food, there was no social life, only self-contained individual men (fathers) and children. There were no mothers. Women died giving birth to their first child, and they did so at the hands of their husbands. So to integrate two seemingly unrelated themes—birth and sharing—in one origin myth, Chewong are in fact showing how sharing and living—socially as well literally in the case of women—are inseparable.

Unlike practices described from some other hunting-gathering societies, it would not be correct to call Chewong sharing practice "demand sharing" (Peterson 1993). This term implies a focus on the recipient, whereas the powerful moral responsibility to share associated with *maró* and *punén* lies with the owner. A related fact is the low-key tone that characterizes all social interaction. Chewong do not ask each other for anything, nor do they command anyone to do something. People act of their own volition—

they come and go as the whim takes them, but sharing edible jungle products is one of the few acts that holds no element of choice.[10]

Belonging

Although they live in small groups—sometimes no more than one nuclear family—Chewong nevertheless have a strong sense of belonging to the wider community of "us people" and the animated environment. Integral to their shared metaphysical understanding are a number of social behavior patterns that further contribute to a sense of belonging—and sociocultural uniqueness. Uxorilocality is normal after a marriage, but not prescribed, and settlements are often made up of one old couple and their daughters, sons-in-law, and grandchildren. Sibling attachment is a strong force in organizing settlement patterns after the death of the parents; married brothers or sisters make up settlements, but these form and dissolve at individual decision. There is a clear pattern of groups of brothers marrying groups of sisters and of their children marrying each other. This encourages solidarity on a microlevel but might act as a barrier against including others; to some extent both are the case. However, a sufficient number of marriages are contracted that do not follow this pattern, and ultimately the outer boundary of the Chewong kinship system stops at those defined as "us people." Everyone has an allocated kin position vis-à-vis everyone else. People keep track of births, marriages, illnesses, and deaths, and news about everyone's activities in the forest circulates quickly.

Their cognatic kinship has no preferential or prescriptive marriage rules, but a slight patrifocus is discernible insofar as children of brothers ought not to marry each other. This nevertheless happens fairly frequently and, while frowned on, is not censored, and no spirit attack results from such unions. Sexual relations between parents and children, and between siblings, are prohibited; they are referred to as *tanko*, the name of the thunder spirit who will cause destructive thunderstorms in the wake of such acts.[11] The practice of mother-in-law/son-in-law avoidance (see also Benjamin, this volume), expressed by not referring to each other by name and by addressing each other with the formal third-person personal pronoun, further marks the "Chewongness" of their culture. Finally, the practice of nicknames confirms their separateness from their neighbors. While every child is given a name—often derived from the place where it was born or of some natural nonanimal kind—during their childhood almost everyone receives a nickname, which is known only to the Chewong. Frequently it is the result of some unusual incident in the person's life and provokes amusement. However, the given name is the one that outsiders know a person by, and nicknames are kept to themselves and regarded with some degree of shyness.

Chewong social interaction, like that of other Orang Asli groups (Dentan 1962; Endicott 1979; Robarchek 1979), is marked by its peacefulness (Howell 1989b). There are no reported incidents of violence—either within the group or toward outsiders (Howell [1984] 1989a). Their self-perception is that of timid, fearful people who withdraw rather than confront potential conflict. They characterize themselves as fearful in contrast to the neighboring Malays and Chinese and regard this as a valuable attribute that they inculcate in their children. As a cultural character trait, timidity and self-effacement do not encourage individual aggrandizement, a fact that, combined with the moral injunction to share, contributes to the maintenance of social order without the involvement of authority figures. Timidity is further a characteristic that they share with some categories of especially helpful nonhuman conscious beings, the leaf people, those who most commonly act as spirit guides in séances but are easily frightened and run away. They may be interpreted as the Chewong alter ego, and when Chewong women put sweet-smelling flowers in their hair or leaves in their waistband, they say they look like these "leaf people."

The egalitarian ethos is manifested in almost all Chewong activities. "All men are good hunters," I was told—almost as an admonishment—when I suggested that one particular man was more successful than the rest. No one tells anyone what to do; children are indulged. Sharing of edible forest produce is general, and it is unconditional. It is not useful to characterize it as reciprocity because no thought of gift or return is present. To describe it as exchange may be more appropriate, certainly if one takes a long-term view, but I prefer to use the word *share* because not only is all forest foodstuff brought home, displayed, and shared among all present, but everything is cut into small pieces before being distributed. Large animals such as wild pigs are usually cut into sections for each household, thereafter to be cut into small pieces for individual distribution. If there is too much meat to be eaten straightaway, each individual keeps the meat separately and eats from it whenever he or she feels like it. Individual piles are not shared.

Nowhere is the demarcation of Chewong belonging made more manifest than in the practice of tobacco exchange. On every encounter—including those within a settlement—people exchange (not share in this case) tobacco. They sit down, get out their tobacco pouch, and roll one or two cigarettes, which they formally hand over to all, one by one. They receive rolled cigarettes in return from everyone present. Indeed, tobacco exchange is the act par excellence that confirms and continually reconfirms belonging. It is never engaged in with outsiders, although Chewong are happy to be offered cigarettes by non-Chewong visitors. There is no named prescription that guides this action, but, like *punén*, tobacco exchange is reported in all myths when people meet, including encounters between humans and non-humans—when the latter appear in human guise.

The Political Cosmology of Forest Living

Although *maró* and *punén* are the two prescriptions that are explicitly relational in Chewong premises for sociality, these and the number of other prescriptions and proscriptions that also are predicated on Chewong metaphysical and cosmological understanding produce sociality in its wider sense between humans and nonhuman conscious persons. As such they are an important source of solidarity. Retribution for a transgression can never be performed by another Chewong human being, but always by some being in the forest or the cosmos. By extension, retribution in the various nonhuman worlds is traced to humans. Just as incorrect behavior activates nonhuman beings to attack humans, so also the reverse. In other words, there is no existential distinction between human and nonhuman species of persons in the Chewong world. It is from this position that I elucidate the Chewong form of solidarity.

Theirs is not so much a "giving environment" in Bird-David's (1990) terms, but rather an environment of parallel worlds of animate, conscious people in which the various categories of people interact with, and act on, each other.[12] Human Chewong may harvest what they need without mishap unless they transgress a cosmo-rule. Despite the autonomy of individual Chewong, which permits them to pursue their own inclinations, there is a clear underlying sense of responsibility toward the other "us people." Thus, ideologically speaking, human beings cooperate and share the products they harvest from the forest or swidden, just as all the other species of conscious beings in the forest do the same among themselves—"in their own land." However, interspecies relationships are exchange relationships, not sharing ones. This may be brought back to the species-based differences in the perception of the same object. Chewong eat the flesh of the animals they hunt and kill. They do not skin the animal, but singe the fur before butchering it. The smell of the singed fur goes to the land of the particular species. This is an act of exchange. By returning part of what they have taken they ensure the replacement of the killed animal, not in the sense of any kind of rebirth but as a returned source of future fertility. These relationships between parallel and overlapping worlds display moral connotations and contribute, I suggest, to generating feelings of solidarity. But more than that, humans and nonhumans constitute each other as persons through their exchange activities.[13] From this perspective, Chewong society may usefully be thought of as coextensive with their cosmos: an empirical example of one culture, many natures (see Howell 1996). It is this grammar and syntax of social life that constitute action, the narration of which provides a collective memory on which each person may draw for insight.

Change

The Chewong moral universe can be understood only within the context of this overriding value placed on equality and autonomy coupled with a strong feeling of social inclusiveness and responsibility. My argument, that this mentality makes sense only when we consider the cosmologically informed injunction to interact according to a number of social and cultural norms that demand sharing and discourage individual accumulation, is further enhanced in view of their practice of immediate consumption. Forest produce is not only shared; it is also consumed on being distributed. This immediate-return subsistence economy (see Woodburn 1982), I argue, is extended into an "immediate-spending" practice when they enter the short-term cycle of individual acquisition and spending based on cash-earning activities. So far, this has served to discourage accumulation of wealth.[14]

At the time of my first fieldwork, the forest provided most of what people needed. No one owned much in the way of bought items, and everyone owned much the same: a few knives, machetes, ax heads, saucepans, some sarongs and other clothing. Nothing challenged the egalitarian mode of thought, and the practice of generalized sharing produced no problems.

In the late 1980s things began to change. Logging activities reached Chewong territory and, in their wake, government interest in the seminomadic Chewong. Government officials urged them to move out of the forest and settle permanently in a more accessible forest-fringe village and to engage in cash cropping. The authorities provided some housing and fruit trees. Many Chewong responded to the officials' request—in many cases as much out of timidity as any actual desire—and moved. But the orchards were soon abandoned and became overgrown. Many returned to the forest. People preferred to harvest nontimber forest products for sale rather than become farmers. Nevertheless, in spite of people moving to and fro (Howell 2002), the growing gateway village is today larger than ever with about one hundred inhabitants, many of whom appear to have settled more or less permanently. They recultivate the same fields where they engage in agricultural activities but more for sale than for their own consumption.

With increased monetization, the Chewong are becoming involved in new work practices directed at earning money in order to purchase food and consumer goods. These practices are undertaken at the expense of hunting, gathering, and shifting cultivation, and the previous egalitarian exploitation of the forest engaged in by all for supplying most of their needs is losing its cogency. As a result, some individuals who energetically pursue cash-generating activities are earning more cash than others, although the practice of immediate consumption (spending) prevents large imbalances in wealth from occurring. Unequal wealth represents, of course, a potential for social disequilibrium. So far, however, the growth in short-term cycles of exchange for individual profit is being kept in check by the cosmologically constituted long-term cycles that reproduce society (see Parry and Bloch 1989). At the same time, the new consumption pattern requires an intensification of cash-earning activities and has sent those Chewong who have abandoned deep forest life into a never-ending search for money.

Emerging Inequalities

Previously, the forest provided most of what was needed, and there was no shortage of food for those who went in search of it. There was no need to preserve or keep food for times of shortage, and the sharing ideology ensured that no one went hungry. However, unlike all produce caught or collected in the forest, which has to be displayed and shared among all present, money—and things bought with money—falls outside *punén* and *maró* prescriptions. By not including money into these cosmo-rules, Chewong are, in effect, establishing different "spheres of exchange" (Bohannan 1959), laying open the field for unequal wealth. Bought food occupies an ambiguous position. While those who live inside the forest will always share with others outside the immediate family some of their bought food (though never in equal portions as is done with food from the forest), those who live in the village are very restrictive in the distribution of bought food. Certainly, bought staple food is not shared, and luxury food (and now also caught game), is shared only among close relatives. One no longer hears the earlier daily utterance of "*punén*" whenever food is brought home and waiting to be shared. Consumer items like motorbikes, TV sets, radios, clothing, and so on, belong unequivocally to the individual who has bought them. This development toward individual ownership further manifests itself with regard to land in the settled area around the gateway village. The notion that anyone may clear a field anywhere is, in effect, beginning to be questioned due to a more settled lifestyle. Moreover, a few families have planted rubber fields, the yield of which belongs to them.

Changes in Chewong way of life are leading to more physically aggregated permanent settlements. The organization of living space is affecting social interaction. Modern brick houses with electricity are provided by the authorities. They are built on the ground in long rows. Solid walls and doors shut out the neighbors in ways not imagined earlier. Although tobacco exchange is undertaken as much as before, indications are that the previous loosely stated, but all-important, sense of solidarity is diminishing in force. As people come together (in space), things fall apart (in terms of sociality).

Mode of thought is commonly thought to be resilient in meeting with changes in modes of subsistence (production). However, in societies where the modes of thought have no institutional counterparts, as is the case of

Chewong, changes in modes of subsistence may more rapidly affect modes of thought than in societies where there are clearly defined political, economic, and religious institutions that correspond in some way or other with the mode of subsistence. There are indications that this is the case among Chewong. As life is led more and more outside the forest, the forest-centered cosmology is becoming less relevant. The earlier strong sense of place to which they were bound—indeed, in which they dwelled (Heidegger 1977)—is giving way to a new village space that has little cosmological relevance, space that does not generate the moral authority of forest sociality.

With the arrival of money on a relatively large scale, there arises the potential for two main kinds of inequalities to emerge: that between men and women, and that between individuals and/or kin-based groups (Howell and Lillegraven, n.d.). So far, no dramatic change is occurring, but it is possible to discern some emerging inequalities, especially with regard to gender relations. As the harvesting of nontimber forest products is heavy work, men are the principal cash earners in the gateway village, rendering women passive in new ways.[15] Married women increasingly rely on the efforts of their husbands, and men are gradually taking on the role of decision maker in money matters as well as in household activities. More generally, some men wish to, and are able to, make more money than others—either by the sustained search for salable forest products or by more intense cultivation of cash crops. Through frequent interaction with outsiders both men and women are much less timid than in the past, and fearfulness appears less often as self-description. At the same time, the young generations—especially those who spend most of their time in the gateway village and sporadically attend primary school—are not learning the knowledge of their parents. Myths are not told, and shamanistic songs are not sung. Many of the cosmologically constituted prohibitions and prescriptions are less relevant in the new circumstances that they find themselves in. More disturbing are reports of physical violence of young husbands against their wives.

Despite the practice of immediate spending, manifestations of unequal wealth are appearing. Rather than displaying their wealth, those families that are becoming richer than the rest tend to hide it by removing themselves from the village. It is important to appreciate that high individual status is not desirable or sought after and, therefore, earning lots of money gives rise to ambivalence and uncertainty, not high status. Wealth and property do not form the basis for political influence any more than esoteric knowledge or exceptional hunting abilities did in the past. The Chewong simply do not have a conceptual space for leaders. Outsiders, however—officials, missionaries, and traders—assume there to be leaders and tend to interact with a few individual men who are active in selling forest products who they assume hold such positions.[16] This is creating some tension.

In Conclusion

I started my consideration of the sources of Chewong solidarity from a premise that humans are innately social and define and experience themselves in a relational mode. I argued that Chewong personal and social interaction is predicated on their metaphysical and ontological understanding. With no formal political system, and an egalitarian ethos that values autonomy, they nevertheless display a profound sense of communality—the outer boundary of which coincides with their animated forest environment, in which humans and "spirits" stand in a continuous exchange relationship. Despite living in small and scattered settlements that are moved every other year or so, the actual makeup of the population of any one settlement fluctuates. However, everyone participates in a shared perception of the cosmos and carries out their daily activities according to a number of cosmo-rules. The relevance of the idiom of kin relatedness, the egalitarian ideology of sharing, the practice of immediate consumption and immediate spending, and the forest as a source for all to exploit ensure a continuity of the vital values of equality and autonomy in Chewong society. In the recent engagement with the outside world their sense of belonging and communality is as strong as before, and people still describe themselves as "us people" in contrast to Malays, Chinese, and others. But the implications of that characterization is becoming fuzzy, not least because the larger agglomeration of people means that sharing all food is not viable, and the exclusion of *punén* from bought items means that this prescription is losing its constitutive social and moral force.

The ideology of immediate consumption inhibits long-term planning and sustained economic activities, which, as a result, discourages entrepreneurship (Howell and Lillegraven, n.d.). But failure to save and plan ahead in what is rapidly becoming a money-based economy means that the satisfaction of basic needs is becoming more difficult. This is giving rise to a feeling of being poor. Poverty was not an issue when I first went to live among the Chewong. The forest was there for the harvesting; people had few needs that were not satisfied by the forest. The Chewong existential orientation was toward the forest, and moral authority was vested in the spiritual world of the forest. In other words, the good life was dependent on their relationship with that world, not, as is becoming the case, with the Malay and Chinese traders and officials.

The new situation in which the Chewong find themselves has alerted them to an inequality in "modern wealth" between themselves and their neighbors. Compared to rural Malays and Chinese, they consider themselves to be poor, disadvantaged, and exploited. Ironically, this may contribute to a continued sense of community. As the cosmologically based behavioral rules are losing their pertinence, Chewong no longer (albeit somewhat uneasily) feel obliged to share food and surplus. Put starkly, what they share more than anything today is a feeling of being disadvantaged, exploited, and "stuck at the bottom" (see Kaskija 2007 and this volume). For those Chewong who spend most of their time in the village, the source of their solidarity today springs as much from a constant exchange of complaints about being poor, badly treated, cheated, and despised for being backward and "not having a religion" as from the shared knowledge that used to make their lives meaningful. However, tension and a strong ambivalence concerning the new are detectable. Many regret the passing of the old way of life, and many return to the forest for short or long periods (Howell 2002), where they take up the old practices of hunting, foraging, and sharing.

Notes

1 Barnard, in *The Hunter-Gatherer Mode of Thought* (2000), goes some way toward correcting this lacuna. He seeks to distinguish a hunter-gather way of thinking from that of non-hunter-gatherers by eliciting values in connection with economic activities, political relations, kinship, and perceptions of land. However, he excludes religion (as well as language and art) from consideration on the grounds that the boundaries between hunter-gatherers and others is more difficult to define (9).

2 This was originally Ingold's "Introduction" to the 1989 Manchester debate, "The concept of society is theoretically obsolete."

3 I think Ingold is wrong when he states in the conclusion to his 1999 article that hunter-gatherers' sociality does not imply boundaries of exclusion, that "people

do not define themselves as 'us' rather than 'them' or as members of this group rather than that," and that this is the reason why early visitors failed to elicit a name for the group (1999:408). Certainly, my work with the Chewong contradicts this (Howell [1984] 1989).

4 This does not mean that Chewong do not recognize that personalities differ between actual individual persons. They maintain that each person is attributed with a unique personality, expressed through the quality of his or her liver. Someone might have a lazy liver, a bad-tempered one, or an energetic one. This helps explain his or her actions, but no value judgments ensue from this.

5 For a discussion about the name Chewong, see Howell [1984] 1989a:9.

6 Fieldwork for my doctoral thesis was undertaken for eighteen months in 1977–79. I have subsequently made ten visits lasting between one and three months each. The last visit was in 2010.

7 Shamans have cool eyes—as opposed to the rest, whose eyes are hot—and because of this they may see through ordinary appearances to the reality that is hidden behind other beings' or places' "cloaks."

8 On such occasions in former times, Chewong, like other Orang Asli groups (Endicott 1979; Schebesta [1928] 1973), would perform a form of blood sacrifice by cutting themselves on the lower arm and letting the blood drip onto the ground.

9 Other Orang Asli are somewhat ambiguous. Chewong would normally offer them some cooked game if they happened to be in a house or settlement when it was brought back, but only if they were well known to the hosts would they invoke *maró* or *punén* as a reason for doing so. I was included after I had lived with them for many months, began to speak the language, learned the cosmo-rules and observed normal behavior, and participated actively in daily life (see below on the practice of tobacco exchange).

10 To observe the numerous prescriptions and proscriptions is also not a matter of choice. Although breaches of many of them often have social consequences, *punén* and *maró* demonstrate belonging in no uncertain terms.

11 I was unable to find a link between these different aspects of Tanko except that he is portrayed as highly sexed and performs sexual intercourse with young girls without their knowledge. Menstrual blood is called "Tanko's children."

12 I prefer this term to *perspectivism* as developed by Viveiros de Castro (1998). His work in the Amazonian forest shows a number of similarities to the Chewong situation, but there are also important differences, one of which is that in the Amazon animals are transformed dead human souls. This renders the human-animal relationship more directly entwined than is the case with Chewong understanding. See Willerslev 2007 for a recent discussion on animism and perspectivism.

13 In this interpretation I draw on Bird-David (1999:73), but I do not agree with her that the nonhuman persons become relatives through this interaction. This may be because Chewong exchange rather than share with the other species.

14 It also acts as a brake on serious engagement in settled cultivation of seasonal crops (Howell and Lillegraven, n.d.; Howell 2011).

15 Men respond to demands for forest products expressed by the Chinese or Malay merchants. These products are seasonal and can usually be found some distance away from the settlement. They range from live toads caught in large rivers at night to heavy *dammar*, which must be hacked from trees and carried long distances; certain vegetables that grow in the tops of tall trees; and heavy rattan. Women may go in search of the valuable *gahur* wood or cultivate ginger and other vegetables for sale.

16 The Department of Aboriginal Affairs appoints one man to be the local headman (*batin*). In the Chewong case, the current *batin* is the son of the previous one and is not regarded as in any way the leader of the rest.

References

Barnard, Alan. 2000. *The Hunter-Gatherer Mode of Thought*. Buenos Aires: Annales de la Academica Nacional de Ciencias de Buenos Aires.

Bird-David, Nurit. 1990. "The giving environment: Another perspective on the economic system of gatherer-hunters." *Current Anthropology* 31:183–96.

———. 1999. "'Animism' revisited: Personhood, environment, and relational epistemology." In *Culture: A Second Chance? Current Anthropology*, special issue, 40:67–91. Comments by Eduardo Viveiros de Castro, Alf Hornborg, Tim Ingold, Brian Morris, Gisli Palsson, Laura M. Rival, and Alan R. Sandstrom. Reply by Nurit Bird-David.

Bohannan, Paul. 1959. "The impact of money on an African subsistence economy." *Journal of Economic History* 19:30–42.

Bråten, Stein. 1998. "Introduction." In S. Bråten, ed., *Intersubjective Communication and Emotion in Early Ontogeny*, 1–29. Cambridge: Cambridge University Press.

Dentan, Robert. K. 1962. *The Semai: A Non-violent People of Malaya*. New York: Holt, Rinehart and Winston.

Descola, Philippe. 1992. "Societies of nature and the nature of society." In A. Kuper, ed., *Conceptualising Society*, 107–26. London: Routledge.

Endicott, Kirk. 1979. *Batek Negrito Religion*. Oxford: Clarenden Press.

Heidegger, Martin. 1977. "Building, dwelling, thinking." In D. Krell, ed., *M. Heidegger: Basic Writings*, 334–64. New York: Harper and Row.

Howell, Signe. 1982. *Chewong Myths and Legends*. Kuala Lumpur: Royal Asiatic Society, Malaysian Branch.

———. [1984] 1989a. *Society and Cosmos: Chewong of Peninsular Malaysia.* Chicago: University of Chicago Press.

———. 1986. "Formal Speech Acts as One Discourse." *Man,* N.S., 21 (1):79–101.

———. 1989b. "To be timid is to be human, to be angry is not to be human." In S. Howell and R. Willis, eds., *Societies at Peace,* 45–59. London: Routledge.

———. 1996. "Nature in culture or culture in nature? Chewong ideas of 'humans' and other species." In P. Descola and G. Palsson, eds., *Nature and Society: Anthropological Perspectives,* 127–44. London: Routledge.

———. 2002. "Our people know the forest: Chewong re-creations of uniqueness and separateness." In G. Benjamin and C. Chou, eds., *Tribal Communities in the Malay World: Historical, Social, and Cultural Perspectives,* 254–72. Leiden and Singapore.

———. 2010a. "Seeing and knowing: Metamorphosis and the fragility of species in Chewong animistic ontology." Paper prepared for the panel "Animism in Southeast Asia: Persistence, Transformation and Renewal," European Association of Southeast Asian Studies Conference, Gothenburg.

———. 2011. "The uneasy move from hunting, gathering, and shifting cultivation to settled agriculture: The case the Chewong (Malaysia)." In M. Janowski and G. Barker, eds., *Why Cultivate? Anthropological and Archaeological Perspectives in Foraging-Farming Transitions in Island Southeast Asia.* Cambridge: McDonald Monograph Series, 93–100.

Howell, Signe, and Anja Lillegraven. N.d. "Cash, culture, and social change: Why don't Chewong become entrepreneurs?" Manuscript.

Howell, Signe, and Roy Willis, eds. 1989. *Societies at Peace: Anthropological Perspectives.* London: Routledge.

Ingold, Tim. 1996. "The concept of society is theoretically obsolete." In T. Ingold, ed., *Key Debates in Anthropology,* 57–59. London: Routledge.

———. 1999. "On the social relations of the hunter-gatherer band." In R. Lee and R. Daly, eds., *The Cambridge Encyclopedia of Hunters and Gatherers,* 399–409. Cambridge: Cambridge University Press.

Kaskija, Lars. 2007. "Stuck at the bottom: Opportunity structures and Punan Malinau identity." In P.G. Sercombe and B. Sellato, eds., *Beyond the Green Myth: Hunter-Gatherers of Borneo in the Twenty-first Century,* 135–59. Copenhagen: NIAS Press.

Middleton, John, and David Tait, eds. 1958. *Tribes without Rulers.* London: Routledge.

Parry, Jonathan, and Maurice Bloch, eds. 1989. *Money and the Morality of Exchange.* Cambridge: Cambridge University Press.

Peterson, Nicholas. 1993. "Demand sharing, reciprocity, and the pressure for generosity among foragers." *American Anthropologist*, N.S., 95 (4):860–74.

Robarchek, Clayton. A. 1979. "Learning to fear: A case study of emotional conditioning." *American Ethnologist* 6 (3):555–67.

Schebesta, Paul. [1928] 1973. *Among the Forest Dwarfs of Malaya*. Kuala Lumpur: Oxford University Press.

Strathern, Marilyn. 1996. "The concept of society is theoretically obsolete: For the motion." In T. Ingold, ed., *Key Debates in Anthropology*, 60–66. London: Routledge.

Toren, Christina. 1996. "The concept of society is obsolete. For the motion 2." In T. Ingold (ed.), *Key Debates in Anthropology*, 72–76. Loundon: Routledge.

Trevarthen, Colwyn, and Katerina Logotheti. 1989. "Child in society, and society in children: The nature of basic trust." In. S. Howell and R. Willis, eds., *Societies at Peace: Anthropological Perspectives*, 165–86. London: Routledge.

Viveiros de Castro, Eduardo. 1998. "Cosmological deixis and Amerindian Perspectivism." *Journal of the Royal Anthropological Institute* 4 (3):469–88.

Willerslev, Rane. 2007. *Soul Hunters: Hunting, Animism, and Personhood among the Siberian Yukaghirs*. Berkeley: University of California Press.

Woodburn, James. 1982. "Egalitarian societies." *Man*, N.S., 17 (3):431–51.

3

Cooperative Autonomy: Social Solidarity among the Batek of Malaysia

KIRK ENDICOTT

Hereby it is manifest, that during the time men live without a common Power to keep them all in awe, they are in that condition which is called Warre; and such a warre, as is of every man, against every man.
— Thomas Hobbes, *Leviathan*, 1651

In referring to solidarity I mean reciprocal dependence, the common recognition of a moral duty to help one another, and the consciousness of being at one in interests, sympathies and values.
— Rodney Needham, "Mourning Terms," 1959

WHAT HOLDS TOGETHER SOCIETIES that give individual members the freedom to do whatever they want? A strong theme running through Western social philosophy is the assumption that, because individual interests diverge or conflict, societies must have ways of constraining the actions of individuals or else the society will fly apart and anarchy will ensue. Hobbes's view, quoted above, may be unduly pessimistic, but more moderate commentators also assume that well-functioning societies must have some means of inducing individuals to cooperate for the benefit of the group as a whole, a condition sometimes termed "social solidarity." In theory societies can have different amounts of social solidarity, depending on the number and effectiveness of the mechanisms by means of which it is created, although in practice social solidarity cannot be directly perceived and measured (Durkheim 1964:64). Social scientists who use this concept generally assume that societies that operate harmoniously have a high degree of social solidarity and those prone to strife and dissention have low solidarity. The means by which social solidarity is generated range from authority structures that force individuals to cooperate to ingrained beliefs and values that impel individuals to act with regard for other members of their group.

One intriguing question is how can societies without authority structures induce members to behave in a manner that is beneficial to the group as a whole, that is, how can they generate social solidarity? Since the 1960s anthropologists have recognized a stable type of society in which individuals are autonomous, free to do almost anything they want to, and yet they operate in a cooperative fashion. At first this type of organization was thought to be limited to hunting and gathering societies. The "Man the Hunter" conference at the University of Chicago in 1966 brought together researchers who had studied hunting and gathering peoples from many different regions and environments. The discussions gave rise to a new stereotype of hunting and gathering or band society, one based largely on the characteristics of the !Kung Bushmen (now termed Ju/'hoansi) of the Kalahari Desert in Botswana and Namibia (Lee and DeVore 1968). According to this "generalized foraging model," the quintessential hunting and gathering society depended on plant food more than game, did not store food, did share food, had bilateral kinship organization, lived in nomadic bands with flexible membership, was egalitarian (even between the sexes), had low population density, and lacked exclusive rights over land and resources (Kelly 1995:14–24). Richard Lee and Eleanor Leacock later formulated a Marxist "foraging mode of production" based on those features (Leacock and Lee 1982). However, some hunter-gatherer specialists objected that not all hunting and gathering peoples fitted the generalized foraging model. James Woodburn, in an influential article (1982), distinguished between "immediate-return hunter gatherers," who conformed to the generalized foraging model, and "delayed-return hunter gatherers," who did not. The latter included semisedentary peoples like the Ainu and the Northwest Coast Indians, who stored food and had a social hierarchy, and the Aboriginal Australians, among whom initiated men had authority over women and uninitiated males. Scholars have argued over whether the immediate consumption of food (immediate return) or residential mobility (nomadism), which limits the accumulation of wealth and power, is the primary cause of the emphasis on equality and individual autonomy in immediate-return societies. Robert Kelly simply terms the two types "egalitarian" and "nonegalitarian" hunter-gatherers (1995:293–332). Recently some anthropologists, including those represented in this volume, have pointed out that the emphasis on equality and individual autonomy is not confined to hunter-gatherers. As the articles gathered here show, both hunter-gatherers and some small-scale swidden farmers in Southeast Asia share these social features. Thus, attempts to determine the basic causes of their extreme emphasis on personal autonomy cannot be limited to the social concomitants of hunting and gathering.

The forces promoting social solidarity in these societies can be seen as being of two types: centripetal forces drawing individuals and families together and external constraints preventing them from moving apart. The former include the innate human tendency to live and work together (see the essays by Howell and Eder, this volume), the psychological attachment normally formed between parents and children (see Dentan, this volume; and Bowlby 1980, 1988), and the interdependence resulting from the division of labor (Durkheim 1964). External constraints include danger from wild animals and human predators (e.g., slave raiders), competition with other groups for land and resources, and attempted political domination by governments and powerful outsiders. The particular combination of forces undoubtedly varies from one society to another, but different combinations may lead to the same result, such as egalitarian social relations. Centripetal forces and external constraints favor some degree of unity even in groups that highly value individual autonomy, and this unity may be reinforced by the ethics and values taught to children.

Recently some scholars have questioned whether immediate-return hunter-gatherers and other "open-aggregated" communities can be considered societies at all (Strathern 1988; Ingold 1999). The answer, of course, depends on one's definition of society. Ingold says (1999:400) that the term *society* is used in three senses in current discourse: (1) "a group of people bound by shared history, language, and sentiment"; (2) "the mode of association of rational beings bound by contracts of mutual self-interest, as epitomized by the market, rather than by particularistic relations like those of kinship, friendship or companionship"; and (3) "a domain of external regulation—identified either with the state or, in polities lacking centralized administration, with comparable regulative institutions—which curbs the spontaneous expression of private interests on behalf of public ideals of collective justice and harmony." After considering the characteristics of immediate-return hunting and gathering bands, he comes to the conclusion that "the principles of *immediacy, autonomy,* and *sharing* add up to a form of sociality utterly incompatible with the concept of society, whether by society is meant the interlocking interests of 'civil society,' the imagined community of the ethnic group or nation, or the regulative structures of the state" (408). Thus, he says, "hunter-gatherers show us how it is possible to live socially ... without having to 'live in societies' at all" (399).

I think this analysis unnecessarily exaggerates the distinction between the social relations of hunter-gatherers and people with other types of economies. As Ingold admits, the "familistic" relations that characterize hunter-gatherer sociality exist "even in modern states with industrial capitalist economies" (1999:400), although those societies contain unequal power relationships as well. His conclusion that hunter-gatherers do not form societies depends on comparing their form of social relations with the second or third senses of society mentioned above, which only apply to groups composed of corporate groups bound together by hierarchical power relations. I prefer to use the more general definition of *society*, "a group of people bound by shared history, language, and sentiment" (400). By that definition, immediate-return hunter-gatherers and other open-aggregated communities have one type of society, which can be usefully compared with other types of societies, such as chieftainships and states. Therefore, I would refer to the Batek as an example of an "open-aggregated" or "loosely aggregated" society, not as a people without a society at all.

In this essay I look at some of the beliefs and practices of the Batek, an indigenous foraging-trading people of Peninsular Malaysia, who exemplify the egalitarian "hill tribe" of Southeast Asia, even to the extent of treating the sexes as equals (Endicott and Endicott 2008).Like other such peoples, they emphasize the autonomy of all individuals and married couples while also maintaining a strong sense of community and a certain degree of social solidarity. Karen Endicott and I term this behavior pattern "cooperative autonomy," as distinct from the "competitive autonomy" of such peoples as the New Guinea highlanders or what Americans call "rugged individualism," self-reliance unhampered by obligations to others. In this essay I explore the ethical principles that inform Batek social behavior and discuss the sources of the solidarity of groups of various types and sizes. I end by addressing the questions of how Batek balance obligations to others and personal autonomy and why they practice cooperative autonomy.

The Batek

The Batek De' (hereafter termed Batek) are a linguistically distinct group of about eight hundred Malayan Aborigines (Orang Asli) living in scattered camps in the lowland rainforest in and around the National Park (Taman Negara) in the Malaysian states of Kelantan, Pahang, and Terengganu. In the 1970s their economy was based on hunting and gathering, collecting forest products for trade, and occasional stints of swidden farming. Batek residential groups were highly fluid. Individuals and conjugal families regularly moved from camp to camp, and whole camp groups changed location frequently. Batek had a distinctive set of religious beliefs and rituals that were integral to their relations with their environment and each other (Endicott 1979). They deliberately maintained a degree of physical and social distance from other Malaysian ethnic groups, including the numerically and politically dominant Malays.

Ethical Principles of Batek Social Life

Batek social behavior was influenced—though not absolutely determined—by their ideas about how people *should* behave, a set of ethical principles or moral obligations. These principles were not explicitly articulated as in the Judeo-Christian Ten Commandments but rather were embedded in their religious beliefs, values, norms, sanctions, and everyday practices. For ease of discussion, I distinguish the following ethical principles: the obligation to respect others, the obligation to help others, the obligation to be self-reliant, the obligation to be nonviolent, and the obligation to be non-competitive. Batek themselves did not use these categories and labels, and other categories and labels are possible. But I think that the beliefs and values encompassed by these terms did exist in the minds and actions of Batek people.

The principles behind cooperative autonomy may be thought of as ideals that were not always fully achieved in practice. As in all ethical systems, Batek ethics were not entirely consistent. For example, the obligation to help others sometimes conflicted with the value on personal autonomy. Should a man stay near his parents-in-law to help them or should he exercise his right to move and pursue his personal interests? People tried to balance these conflicting obligations in appropriate ways, but they had some freedom to maneuver. Other peoples' responses helped them gauge whether they had made the right choices. Occasionally people might violate a principle entirely, but in doing so they risked alienating other people or offending the superhuman beings.

Ethical principles were enforced in various ways and to varying degrees. Batek did not have an authority structure that could be used to directly punish wrongdoers. In fact it would have violated the obligation to respect others had anyone attempted to sanction anyone else's behavior directly. However, two sets of prohibitions had a lawlike character: *lawac* prohibitions (against incest, mixing some categories of foods, mocking some animals, etc.) and *tolah* prohibitions (against disrespectful acts). Significantly, these prohibitions were enforced not by humans but by superhuman beings—in cases of *lawac* by the thunder god, Gobar, and the underworld deity, Ya', and in cases of *tolah* by Tohan. Other principles were enforced by diffuse social pressure, such as gossip and criticism, backed up by the implicit threat of the withdrawal of social support. In addition, the process of enculturation (or socialization) was highly effective at inculcating Batek ethics in children. Most people felt a strong commitment to Batek ethical principles by the time they were old enough to understand the difference between proper and improper behavior. My impression is that Batek had strong social consciences, and they generally conformed quite closely to the ideals described here.

These ethical principles can be seen as sources of social solidarity in Batek society. To the extent that people behaved in terms of them, they acted for the benefit of other Batek while also maintaining a high degree of freedom to act as they saw fit. This does not mean that Batek did not cooperate with each other in various ways, but merely that such cooperation was voluntary. For example, if a group of men went out to collect rattan together, they did so because they each wanted to, not because someone forced them to.

Obligation to Respect Others

Batek seem to have regarded all Batek as basically equal in their intrinsic value and therefore worthy of respect. Although some people, particularly shamans, seem to have been held in especially high regard, they neither expected nor received special treatment from others. All Batek felt that they deserved the same consideration as everyone else, and they were not shy in saying so. For example, I found it impossible to give gifts to some people without hurting the feelings of others. I learned to restrict my gifts to such things as rice and tobacco, which could be given to the camp group as a whole and then divided into equal portions for all families and individuals.

An important entailment of respect for others was the idea that no one had the authority to coerce anyone else to do anything that person did not want to do. People could try to persuade others to do something, using every rhetorical device they could muster, but anyone could simply refuse (*ye*?), without any need to explain their refusal. Batek parents could not even force their children to obey them. As children matured they increasingly considered the wishes of their parents and other elders out of respect. But Batek regarded even children as having the right to refuse.

All Batek expected to be treated with respect by all other Batek, regardless of their personal relationships or feelings about one another. They considered it unacceptable to insult or ridicule someone, except in good-natured joking among friends. (But see the discussion of the Batek attitude toward the thunder god below.) To hurt another person's feelings risked causing them to come down with a disease called *kə?ɔy* (Endicott 1979:107, 109–10). *Kə?ɔy* is akin to Western notions of depression, and Batek believed that it could cause physical breakdown and even death. Its main symptom was extreme sadness, often expressed by uncontrollable sobbing. The disease was thought to reside in the heart and to make it hot. *Kə?ɔy* could be brought on by a variety of distressing experiences, including losing something or being frightened, but its most common cause was the sense of being mistreated or misunderstood by other people. When someone had an attack of *kə?ɔy*, all his or her close friends and relatives rushed to that person's aid in a dramatic expression of sympathy and social support. Often they would lightly cut the their own legs, rub some blood on a leaf, and then rub it on the victim to cool his or her heart.

In cases of *kə?ɔy* the onus was on the offender to make amends to the victim. If the offender did not, the rest of the group would be angry at him or her. People's concern about causing someone to contract *kə?ɔy* and getting blamed for it by the whole camp was a powerful sanction against mistreating others.

Batek also believed that some disrespectful acts, called *tolah* (Malay *tulah*), would be punished by the deity Tohan by means of a disease or accident (Endicott 1979:81–82). *Tolah* acts ranged from saying the true name of an in-law to killing someone. People often mentioned spitting on a person as an example of a *tolah* act, possibly because that was something children occasionally did. Tohan's punishments varied in severity, depending on the seriousness of the offense. Minor offenses were usually punished by accidents. I was told, for example, that a man once urinated in a stream above where people were drawing water. A few days later, he fell out of a tree and hurt himself. For a serious offense, such as physically hurting someone, Tohan would send a fatal disease, *ʔaral tolah*, to strike down the offender. Batek expected people to show special respect to their elders and in-laws. It was considered *tolah* to say their true names, so kin terms, outsider names, nicknames, or teknonyms had to be used instead.

Another way Batek showed respect for elders and in-laws was to listen to them, although they might not agree with what was said. For example, older people sometimes took it upon themselves to criticize and offer unsolicited advice to adolescents and young adults. The youths would listen but then make their own decisions. If an elder put too much pressure on a youth, it would infringe on the youth's personal autonomy and might even cause him or her to contract *kəʔɔy*. Thus elders did not have any actual authority over their juniors.

Because no one had authority over anyone else, the Batek had no formal political organization coordinating their activities. Usually husbands and wives jointly decided what activities they would pursue each day, although they often made their decisions after discussions with potential workmates so that suitable work parties could be formed. Their methods of decision making were cooperative without greatly impinging on the autonomy of the persons making up the families and camp groups.

Although Batek had no authority structure, they did have headmen (called *penghulu* in Kelantan), who were appointed by the Department of Aboriginal Affairs. The headmen were supposed to represent vaguely defined groups of Batek in dealings with the department and other outsiders, in particular to convey the government's wishes to the Batek and to get them to do whatever the government wanted done. But as far as the Batek themselves were concerned, headmen had no authority over them. Batek saw the official headmen as like foreign ministers, who would carry their wishes and concerns to the powers that be, but, because the interests of the Batek and the government often clashed, the headmen were usually unsuccessful.

Batek also had what we call "natural leaders," people whom they themselves looked to for guidance. Batek sometimes called natural leaders *penghulu*, although they were not recognized as such by the Department of Aboriginal Affairs. Natural leaders were usually older, intelligent, capable individuals—male or female—who had strong, charismatic personalities. Natural leaders did not seek power or influence; they merely served as a resource for people who wanted advice.

Batek did not vest natural leaders or headmen with the authority to pass judgment on others or settle disputes. The disagreements that came up in the course of everyday life were handled by the persons directly involved rather than by a designated arbiter or judge. Batek used two means of dealing with disagreements. The first was to talk about them, either directly between the persons involved or in the form of campwide discussions. Such discussions might lead to a consensus about who was in the wrong on a particular issue, and the group might try to bring the pressure of public disapproval on the offender to induce him or her to make retribution— emotional or material—to the victim. If tensions persisted, disputants employed their other method of dealing with disagreements: moving away from each other until tensions waned.

The obligation to respect others both undermined and promoted social solidarity. It undermined solidarity by preventing the development of political authority and structures that would have increased group integration and coordination. But I think it also enhanced the social solidarity among campmates by reducing possible sources of conflict and stress that could potentially drive them to split up. "Live and let live" was the unspoken rule of camp life. The obligation to respect others also protected everyone, including women and children, from fear of being coerced or pressured, thus increasing their feelings of comfort, security, and fellowship (see Macdonald, this volume).

Obligation to Help Others

Batek felt a general obligation to help any other Batek who needed aid, although the feeling seemed to be stronger toward close kin and campmates than toward occasional visitors from other areas. This obligation was expressed through numerous casual acts of assistance carried out in passing, with little notice or fanfare, as when someone helped another build a shelter or brought some firewood to another family. Adults felt a special obligation to help all youngsters, not just their own children. Also, all able-bodied adults and adolescents took a hand in helping elderly and handicapped people as needed.

Some obligations to help others were somewhat formalized and were specified in terms of kin relationships. Adult children were expected to make special efforts to help their aging parents in any way needed. In the sharing of food, people gave portions to their parents and parents-in-law before giving them to other families in camp. Men were also expected to make a special effort to help and share food with their wives' parents. At the beginning of a marriage, especially if the wife were very young, a couple might make a point of camping with the wife's parents for a year or so to help them and give them things, a period of informal bride service.

The obligation to share food was a central principle of Batek social life (Endicott 1988:115–18; Lye 2004:13–14). Batek generally considered unharvested resources to be free to anyone for the taking, but once food was harvested or bought from a trader or shop, it had to be shared with other members of the camp. Sharing was done without calculating exact returns for what a person gave and received from the sharing network. The usual procedure was for people to give shares first to their own children and spouse, then to any parents-in-law or parents present, and finally to all other families in the camp. Small amounts of food could be consumed by the procurer's conjugal family alone, but if a family had more than it needed, it shared the surplus with other families, usually families living nearby. Usually food was shared only with other camp members, but sometimes temporary visitors from other areas would be included, especially if they were closely related to a camp member.

Normally the people who obtained the food decided how to share it, but occasionally other people asked them for food or just showed up at their fires at mealtime. Generally speaking, the amounts of food given were roughly the same for each family, although slight adjustments might be made according to the size of the family.

The obligation to share food applied to all foods obtained, but slight differences in the distribution procedure resulted from the different characteristics of the foods and the ways they were obtained. Vegetable foods, especially wild yams, were a reliable food source. Usually anyone who looked for them would get some, although the amount obtained was seldom more than three times the needs of a single family. Thus, there were usually several sources of vegetable food in a camp on any given day, and each source family supplied between one and two other families. Batek obtained meat less regularly than vegetable foods and in sizes varying from less than an ounce to about sixteen pounds. Small animals—such as fish, frogs, birds, and bats—were usually consumed by the family that caught them. However, larger animals, such as monkeys and gibbons, would be shared with the entire camp. Often the hunter gutted and partially roasted the kill in the forest, and he and his companions might eat the tail and internal organs. All food collectors ate some of the foods they obtained if they got hungry, and no one begrudged them that right. Hunters or other camp members cut the animals into a standard number of pieces—for example, thirteen for monkeys—and gave the portions to that many families. Batek shared purchased foods and nonfood consumables, such as tobacco and kerosene, according to the same principles as wild vegetable foods unless they were obtained in unusually large amounts. If someone bought a whole gunnysack of rice (more than one hundred pounds), for example, he or she would usually dole it out to others gradually over a period of days or weeks. Occasionally the buyer would resell portions of the food to other Batek at cost, thus becoming, in effect, the purchasing agent for the group as a whole.

Sharing food was an obligation for Batek, not something the giver had much discretion over. The sharing obligation was enforced by means of strong social pressure. As one hunter said, "If I didn't take the meat back to camp, everyone would be angry at me." Recipients treated the food they were given as a right; no expression of thanks was expected or forthcoming. Supposedly anyone who consistently refused to share food would be excluded from the food-sharing network. Although I did not see this happen in Kelantan in 1975–76, Lye Tuck-Po reports that it often happened during her research in Pahang after 1993 (personal communication). Because food sharing was an obligation rather than a voluntary act, it did not give power to food getters over food recipients.

In theory nonconsumable goods a person made or obtained in trade, including cash, were considered personal possessions that did not have to be shared. In practice, however, the general obligation to help others led to a relatively even distribution of material wealth. Although sometimes people tried to hide their possessions, Batek frequently loaned and gave things to others. People also regularly borrowed other people's possessions, even without asking. When I gave gifts or payment to someone in the form of durable goods, such as clothes, I often saw them later being used or worn by someone else.

Helping others, especially by sharing food, which is vital to people's survival, obviously contributed to the solidarity of Batek kin groups and camps. Although Batek did not have a rigid division of labor, different people contributed different things in different quantities to the general pool of supplies, and the sharing system evened out their distribution. Thus everyone was dependent on everyone else in some degree, one feature of Needham's definition of social solidarity, as quoted at the opening of this chapter: "In referring to solidarity I mean reciprocal dependence, the common recognition of a moral duty to help one another, and the consciousness of being at one in interests, sympathies and values" (1959:80).

Obligation to Be Self-Reliant

The obligation to help others was associated with an expectation that everyone would be as self-reliant as possible, even though they could depend on others to give them food and help if necessary. Although Batek did not make a fetish of working hard or steadily, most seemed to feel guilty if they loafed for very long. Some people said, half jokingly, that if they did not do any work for several days in a row, the ghost *(jərəŋ sarɔʔ)* of one of their dead ancestors would thump them on the back with a forefinger. But there were exceptions. For example, no one expected sick or elderly people to support themselves. The children and children-in-law of elderly people were especially obligated to help them, and elders also benefited from the general sharing of food in camp.

The obligation to be self-reliant was enforced mainly by means of social pressure. Batek generally wanted to be respected by others, and they avoided developing a reputation as lazy or a freeloader. Being a hard worker was often mentioned as a desirable attribute in a spouse, so being regarded as lazy would hinder one's chances in marriage. Batek said they would exclude someone from the food-sharing network if they consistently failed to contribute to it, although people seemed quite ready to offer excuses for individuals who seemed not to be carrying their weight.

Obligation to Be Nonviolent

Batek, like most other Orang Asli, considered all violence, aggression, and physical coercion unacceptable (see, e.g., Dentan 1968). To them being violent was something only outsiders would do. Except for occasional scuffles between small children and the odd swat from a frustrated parent, I never saw any Batek commit a violent act. One man told me that the ancestors had forbidden Batek to engage in war. In former times, when Batek were attacked by slave raiders, they fled rather than fighting back. Batek said that hurting someone was both *tolah*, punished by Tohan, and *lawac*, punished by Gobar and Ya?. I was told that if a person were violent during life, the superhuman beings would refuse to take the offender's shadow soul to the afterworld after death. The offender was doomed to roam the forest as a malevolent ghost. Any human punishment for violence would be superfluous in light of these powerful sanctions from on high. Still, in answer to the hypothetical question about what people would do about a persistently violent person, I was told that the group would abandon that person, fleeing if necessary.

Batek methods of socialization were very successful at curbing violent impulses in children at an early age. Whenever babies or toddlers hit each other, adults immediately separated them and tried to distract each one with a new activity. Often people laughed at children's aggressive behavior, making what seemed important to the child appear trivial and ridiculous. If people saw a child about to hit someone, they would cry out "Stop it!" As children grew older, they became aware that adults did not hit each other, withhold food or possessions from each other, or display explosive anger. The absence of an adult model of aggression for children to follow was probably the greatest factor in socializing children to be nonaggressive.

The tendency for adults to ridicule aggressive acts of young children may be a key to understanding one of the oddities of Batek religion, namely, their numerous stories in which the thunder god, Gobar, is ridiculed and depicted as a buffoon (Endicott 1979:163–68; Lye 1994:116–28, 2004:155). For example, in one story Gobar, in human form, decided to become a honeybee. He climbed a tree and hung from a limb, like a bees' nest. So superhuman beings in the form of bees flew up and burned him with torches, as Gobar had often done to bees' nests when collecting honey. Gobar fell to the ground screaming from the burns, which is why his skin is now covered with welts and his voice, thunder, is so loud. It is possible that these stories ridiculing Gobar constitute an intensified version of the Batek method of sanctioning violent behavior in children by making it seem ridiculous. Gobar, as the main cause of violent and frightening thunderstorms sent to punish human misdeeds, is the epitome of violence, which, being totally unacceptable in Batek society, must be countered by ridicule.

The Batek prohibition on violence contributes to social solidarity by protecting all Batek, including women and children, from aggression and aggressive coercion. It gives everyone the security of knowing that they are safe within Batek society, in contrast to the possibility of aggression by outsiders.

Obligation to Be Noncompetitive

Competition, like interpersonal violence, was almost nonexistent in Batek social life. I never saw people deliberately trying to outdo each other or drawing attention to their accomplishments. Although people seemed pleased when they succeeded at something, Batek etiquette required people to be modest and self-effacing (see also Lye 2004:140). Similarly, children's games were not competitive. In many hours of observing children's play, my wife Karen never saw them playing in a way that created winners and losers.

In a sense the lack of competition was merely a side effect of some of the other principles of social life, including the prohibitions against aggression and hurting the feelings of others. Competition creates winners and losers, and Batek avoided making anyone feel the pain of losing, since it might cause them to contract kaʔɔy. However, I have highlighted the obligation to be noncompetitive as a separate ethical principle—even though it is the mere absence of something they had little experience with—because in some other egalitarian societies, such as those of New Guinea, competition is highly developed.

The lack of competition in Batek social life seems to contribute to social solidarity by helping to maintain a spirit of goodwill and fellowship and by inhibiting the development of disputes and resentments that often result from competition. Absence of competition promotes "the consciousness of being at one in interests, sympathies and values" (Needham 1959:80).

Groups

Batek did not have any corporate groups in the sense of groups that owned property in common and that persisted after the deaths of any particular set of members. But they did have a number of groups in the broader sense, as aggregates of people with a common identity and purpose. These ranged from the temporary work groups that formed every day to conjugal families, which might last for many years. In this section I describe some of the more important groups and discuss the principles by which they formed, their purposes, how they carried out their tasks, and what generated their social solidarity.

Conjugal Families

Conjugal families (*kəmam*), consisting of a married couple and their dependent children, were relatively stable groups in the general flux of Batek social life—despite the ease with which people could divorce—and therefore can be regarded as the component units of camp groups, which split up and recombined throughout the year. A couple was considered a *kəmam* even after their children moved out of the family shelter, but a household without a conjugal pair (e.g., a widow with children) was not. Conjugal families always had separate shelters and cooking fires in forest camps.

To a large extent conjugal families were self-sufficient economically, even though they could count on others to share food with them if their own food-getting efforts fell short. Given the Batek division of labor and people's free access to resources, a man and woman together could perform all the tasks necessary to support themselves, their children, and any elderly parents they might have. Because Batek did not prohibit anyone from engaging in any kind of economic activity, the division of labor was not rigidly defined. However, there were statistical differences in the kinds of work done by husbands and wives in conjugal families, depending on the nature of the work and the demands of child care, which fell predominantly to mothers. For example, men did most of the blowpipe hunting, while women made most of the mats and baskets constructed from pandanus leaves (Endicott and Endicott 2008:69–109).

The solidarity of conjugal families was based in part on the male-female division of labor, which made each spouse somewhat dependent on the other for certain foods, handicrafts, and services such as child care. Single adults could obtain the things normally supplied by a spouse through their own efforts and the help of the camp group, but with more difficulty and uncertainty. Married couples were also held together by mutual affection, the usual basis of Batek marriage choices. Batek marriages were not arranged by parents or other senior relatives of the couple. Children were bound to their parents by dependency, in their early years, and affection, which normally continued throughout the lives of both parents and children (see Dentan, this volume). Because Batek ethical principles ensured the personal autonomy of spouses and children, there was normally little tension among the members of conjugal families. Couples who fell out of love usually divorced and remarried, and stepparents treated children from their spouses' previous marriages similarly to their own.

Camp Groups

Batek always lived in groups of conjugal families and individuals who chose, for their own reasons, to camp together at a particular time. Camp groups changed size and composition constantly, as some families moved into a camp and others left to join other camps or form new ones. When abandoning a campsite an entire group might move to a new location to-gether or split into two or more new camp groups; sometimes only a few families would break away to join other groups. Because of the danger from wild animals, mainly tigers and elephants, people did not like to camp in groups of fewer than three families. At the other extreme, camp groups of over twenty-five families might form when it was easy to find food, as during the height of the fruit season, but such large groups usually could not stay together long, for they quickly depleted the resources in the neigh-borhood. The camps in which I lived in 1975–76 varied in size from four to twenty-five households but usually numbered between five and ten. Camps usually existed for a week to ten days, until the resources in the area had been thoroughly picked over.

People chose their campmates on the basis of common economic inter-ests, kinship ties, and friendships. In theory a person or conjugal family could join any other Batek camp group, but in practice people usually did not join a camp unless they had close relatives or friends in it. Often a camp contained a core of three or four families that were closely related through an elderly parent or grandparent, whom they were supposed to help economically. However, no families or individuals were required to camp together at all times. People could join another camp group if they wanted a change of companions, if they got into a conflict with someone in their camp, or if they decided to join others in a particular economic pursuit. There were no formal criteria for camp group membership or ritual process for joining or leaving a camp. One's presence and participation in the social and economic interaction of the camp was the essence of membership.

Camp groups were not politically unified and coordinated entities. They might or might not contain one or more "headmen" or natural leaders, but, as I have mentioned, such persons did not have any real authority over the other camp members anyway. Decisions were made at the level of the individual conjugal families. Only when a preponderance of the component families decided to do the same thing at the same time did a camp group present the illusion of being a coordinated unit. Few activities involved the camp group as a whole, and those that did took place in a characteristically spontaneous, cooperative fashion.

Although camp groups were transitory, they cooperated economically in a number of ways. Most important, the camp group was the group in which the food-sharing network operated. People were obligated to share food with other camp members, but they had no obligation to send food even to close relatives who were not living in the same camp. In addition, camp group members shared information on the resources of the area, thus making it easier for everyone to find food and trade goods. Only a few economic activities, such as fish poisoning and harvesting rice, mobilized all or most of the adult members of a camp, but the camp group served as a labor pool from which work groups of all sorts were formed. Despite changes in its composition, the camp group was the unit of long-term survival. By cooperating and sharing, camp groups could protect themselves from the dangers of wild animals and could more effectively exploit the resources of an area than if they had done so as separate conjugal families.

Work Groups

Batek carried out their food-getting and other activities in both single-sex and mixed-sex groups. The composition of the work groups depended on the nature of the work being done and the friendships and common interests of the persons involved. People with similar work interests who enjoyed working together did so. Hunting parties, for example, usually consisted of men who liked to hunt together. Gathering parties usually consisted of women who wanted to dig in a particular area together. Rattan-collecting parties often consisted of both men and women, whoever wanted to work rattan that day. There were no rules about who could or could not work together. Every imaginable configuration of workers occurred at one time or another: husbands and wives, adolescents of one or both sexes, old people with young, mothers or fathers with opposite-sex children, married persons with other married or unmarried persons of the opposite sex. Work groups changed in composition from day to day, depending on individuals' changing interests and the changing interests of their potential companions. The only work group that had some degree of stability was the married couple.

The main bases of work group solidarity were common interests and friendship. People who enjoyed each other's company tended to work together, regardless of what kind of work they were doing. Batek, like other groups represented in this volume (see the essays by Gibson and Eder, this volume) carried out some activities in groups, even though they could have done them just as efficiently as individuals or couples. The basic reason was that they simply enjoyed having the company—an expression of innate human sociability (see the essays by Gibson and Howell, this volume)— although safety in numbers was also a consideration in some cases. For Batek such activities included hunting, fishing, and gathering wild yams together; collecting forest products in groups; doing craft work in groups; and performing rituals, such as singing sessions, as groups. The psychologist Peter Gray makes the astute observation that egalitarian hunter-gatherers incorporate a significant element of play into their utilitarian activities (2009). Because of the voluntary nature of participation in a work group, participants could drop out if the activity ceased to be fun, just as in spontaneous play. This certainly applied to Batek social work activities. For Batek, the boundary between work and recreation was not sharp. They viewed such tasks as hunting, fishing, collecting honey, and even gathering wild tubers as fun and exciting, an adventure with an unknown outcome. Like Western recreational hunters and fishermen, they enjoyed the activity for itself, all the more so if done with a group of friends.

River Valley Groups

I use the term *river valley groups* to refer to groups of people who normally reside in the watersheds of particular rivers. In 1975–76 there were two main river valley groups of Batek in Kelantan State: the Lebir River people and the Aring River people. The Batek on both these rivers thought of themselves as distinct groups residentially, economically, and even socially, while simultaneously acknowledging their common identity as Batek. They referred to themselves as "Batek Lebir" and "Batek Aring." Although river valley groups tended to stay in their own watersheds and use the local resources, they did not claim exclusive ownership of the land and its resources or actively prohibit others from camping and foraging there. However, there appeared to be a tacit understanding that each river valley group would exploit the resources of its own watershed as much as possible—especially fruit trees, the only resource to which Batek made a vague group claim.

The social solidarity of river valley groups was based on kinship connections among group members and joint attachment to the land. Most people living in a given river valley could trace consanguineal and/or affinal kinship connections with all other members of their river valley group, sometimes through multiple pathways. Group members also shared detailed knowledge of and emotional attachment to their own river valley. Babies were often named after streams or other landmarks near the place where they were born.

Language Groups

All Batek De'—that is, speakers of the Batek De' language who lived in a contiguous area in Kelantan, Pahang, and Terengganu—thought of themselves as one group in opposition to other ethnic groups, including other Orang Asli groups, such as the Temiar and Batek Teh (Mendriq). Batek De' distinguished themselves primarily by means of language, but they also recognized differences in culture between themselves and other groups. All Batek De' saw themselves as related to all other Batek De', although, due to their shallow genealogies, they did not always know exactly how they were related to any given other person. In Benjamin's terms (this volume), their kinship reckoning was "inclusive" for the Batek De' people as a whole. When individuals met for the first time, they tried to discover whether they had any consanguineal or affinal relatives in common. If they could not find a precise connection, they adopted kin terms appropriate to their sex and age. Batek did have interactions with members of other language groups—even some marriages took place across language group lines—but they regarded the others as different from themselves.

Conclusions

> Why does the individual, while becoming more autonomous, depend more upon society? How can he be at once more individual and more solidary?
>
> —Émile Durkheim, *Division of Labor in Society*, 1964

> Could not one conclude that "individual autonomy" is seriously limited by the feeling of group solidarity? The *obligation* to share is for these societies a principle of law that is the opposite of the 19th-century liberal conception of individualism.
>
> —Alain Testart, "Comment," 1991

How Batek Cooperative Autonomy Worked

This case study of Batek social principles and practices shows that their cooperative autonomy was based on a combination of obligations to the group and protections for individuals against coercion by others. Cooperation, including respecting and helping others, was an obligation that might interfere with an individual's immediate self-interest. For example, a hunter might prefer to eat an animal he killed, but he was obligated to share it with others. However, cooperation benefited the hunter over the long run because the obligation to cooperate was reciprocal and applied to everyone. By contributing meat to the group one day, the hunter ensured that he would have access to meat obtained by other hunters when his own hunting failed. A skilled hunter might never get back as much meat as he gave away, but he gained other foods from others and the security of knowing that he would be helped when he became ill or after he grew too old to obtain his own food. Batek talked about the obligation to share food in this way. But leaving everyone to make such decisions in light of their perceived self-interest would have been too uncertain and unreliable to produce a stable system of individual and group security. Batek preempted a person's decision about whether to help others or not by making it a moral obligation, one that was inculcated in children from an early age. They created a moral community in which members habitually concerned themselves with the welfare of others.

At the same time as Batek ethical principles ensured that individuals would act in the interest of the group as a whole, they also protected individuals from unnecessary interference by other individuals or the group. Batek personal autonomy was not based on independence from others—a precarious sort of autonomy that would require self-sufficiency and the ability to defend oneself from coercion by others. Instead, it was based on protections of their autonomy that arose from their participation in the moral community. In return for refraining from coercing or harming others, people acquired protection from being coerced or harmed themselves. This left them with the freedom to do whatever they wished as long as they did not interfere with the autonomy of others. Every well-functioning society maintains some balance between individual obligations to the group and group obligations to the individual, but Batek cooperative autonomy, by eliminating the possibility of anyone exercising authority over anyone else, tilted the balance markedly toward freedom for individuals.

The solidarity of Batek groups was based on a complex network of weak and strong ties (see Macdonald, this volume), which differed for different kinds of groups. What was unusual about Batek groups was the high degree to which membership and participation in them was voluntary. Of the groups described above, only language groups were ascribed. Individuals had the freedom to join or leave the other kinds of groups at will. Even conjugal families were products of relatively free choices by individual men and women, who might enter or leave a marriage according to their whims. Camp groups and work groups changed composition on a daily basis following the decisions of individuals, and people could even move from one river valley group to another if they wished. Despite the fluidity and ephemeral nature of most groups, they did have some cohesion, which was based to some extent on practical considerations as well as personal preferences. The main difference between Batek groups and those of societies with corporate groups and hierarchical political structures is that Batek groups were mostly voluntary associations and therefore did not constrain the autonomy of individual members.

Why Batek Practiced Cooperative Autonomy

Since the early 1990s, hunter-gatherer specialists have debated why egalitarian (or immediate-return) foraging societies have the social characteristics they do, including their emphasis on personal autonomy (see, e.g., Gardner 1991). Many theories have been proposed, but they can be boiled down to two types: those that see personal autonomy as beneficial to a nomadic foraging subsistence economy ("adaptation") and those that see it as a result of pressures from powerful outside groups ("frontier circumstances") (543–47). Gardner goes on to say that the cluster of social features that includes personal autonomy may be "multidetermined," meaning that more than one causal factor may be promoting it in specific cases (547). He says that we should examine each individual case to find the specific combination of factors in play (558). I think a good case can be made that the Batek practice of cooperative autonomy was a result both of the need for economic efficiency and of pressures from outsiders.

Hunting and gathering economies are based on harvesting naturally occurring resources that are usually thinly scattered, seasonably variable, and somewhat unpredictable. Many scholars study what types of social groups and patterns of movement are most efficient for harvesting the resources of particular environments (see, e.g., Kelly 1995). The main wild foods that Batek depended on were wild yams, honey, seasonal fruit, arboreal game (mostly monkeys), and fish. Yams were available year-round, but they were widely scattered, and it was difficult to predict where mature yams would be found at any given time. Bees' nests and wild fruits were seasonal and varied in their time of availability, location, and abundance from year to year. Monkeys and other arboreal game also varied unpredictably in their location and abundance. The Batek method of harvesting these resources was to continually search for them and to move camp whenever they found promising supplies and after they exhausted the supplies in a particular area. I believe that cooperative autonomy enhanced the success of their subsistence economy by facilitating the movements and adjustments of group size that were necessary for taking advantage of transitory economic opportunities such as the ripening of seasonal fruit in a particular area. Flexibility of work groups also enabled people to form the optimal size and composition of groups for each task. Leaving decisions of what opportunities to pursue to individuals and couples had the effect of diversifying their efforts, thus increasing the chances that someone would have success. Also, individuals were free to concentrate their efforts on pursuits for which they had special knowledge and skills. The alternative of having rigidly defined groups, an authority hierarchy, and centralized planning would probably have been less efficient for harvesting such fluctuating and unpredictable resources.

Other scholars have argued that the basic cultural features of egalitarian hunting and gathering societies result from the societies being "encapsulated" or "enclaved," surrounded and politically dominated by more numerous and powerful people (e.g., Gardner 1966; Testart 1981; cf. Woodburn 1988). Some writers (e.g., Schrire 1984; Wilmsen 1989) contend that the cultures of most if not all contemporary foraging peoples are predominantly shaped by their position in the larger surrounding society. The cultural characteristics of a people such as the Ju/'hoansi of southern Africa, they say, are determined by their position as an impoverished rural proletariat in the class-stratified societies of Botswana and Namibia.

Could it be that the reason the Batek emphasized cooperative autonomy was that they were encapsulated by the Malays who lived in the adjacent lowlands? I think the answer is no. In fact, Malays could never have exercised real control over the Batek as long as the latter were nomadic, were economically self-sufficient, and had a vast empty forest to hide in (see Endicott 1983; and Lye 1997:94). However, the Batek case does support Testart's claim (1981) that abuse or the potential for abuse by a more numerous and powerful people may reinforce the nomadism of some foraging groups. Readiness to move on a moment's notice was probably the most effective defense the Batek and similar peoples had against the slave raiding that went on in some areas into this century (Endicott 1983). More recently, it also protected them from exploitation by forest product traders and interference by government officials and other outsiders. Thus, pressure from outsiders, as well as economic efficiency, favored cooperative autonomy in the form of freedom to move at will.

The probable reasons that the Batek practiced cooperative autonomy would not all apply to the open-aggregated swidden farmers of Southeast Asia. Other combinations of causes must be sought (see, e.g., Rousseau 2006). Although swiddeners also move from time to time and possibly benefit from some flexibility in group sizes and composition, the economic advantages of cooperative autonomy are not so obvious for them. One could easily argue that corporate groups and hierarchies of authority would be *more* advantageous, and, indeed, the majority of tropical forest swiddeners throughout the world have more structured social relations than the Batek do. However, potential interference by outsiders is a common problem for Batek and the open-aggregated swiddeners of Southeast Asia. As Gibson discusses (this volume), the open-aggregated societies of the interior often live in proximity to predatory hierarchical societies in the adjacent coastal regions. It is tempting to see the egalitarianism and emphasis on personal autonomy of the interior peoples as a reaction of some kind to the hierarchical organization of their coastal enemies. However, it is necessary to ascertain the exact causes and nature of that reaction in each case. The Batek's emphasis on nomadism as a means of avoiding aggressive outsiders would not apply to swiddeners, who must stay with their fields in order to survive.

Note

This essay is partially adapted from chapter 3 of Kirk M. Endicott and Karen L. Endicott, *The Headman Was a Woman: The Gender Egalitarian Batek of Malaysia* (Waveland Press, 2008). I thank Waveland for granting permission to republish some material here. I presented an earlier version of this essay at the annual meeting of the Association for Asian Studies, Chicago, March 28, 2009. I thank the participants in the panel and especially Thomas Gibson and Kenneth Sillander for many valuable suggestions. I thank all my Batek friends for their generous hospitality and endless assistance. I also thank the Economic Planning Unit (EPU) of the Prime Minister's Office and the Department of Orang Asli Affairs (JHEOA) for granting me permission to conduct research with the Batek. I gratefully acknowledge financial support for my fieldwork from the U.S. National Institute of Mental Health, the University of Malaya, the Australian National University, the Fulbright-Hays Commission, the American Social Science Research Council, and the Claire Garber Goodman Fund of Dartmouth College.

The fieldwork on which this essay is based took place between 1971 and 1990. The essay refers mainly to the Kelantan Batek in the 1970s, before extensive logging and government-sponsored development projects disrupted their lives. Some Batek still live in the fashion described, especially those living in the National Park, Taman Negara.

References

Bowlby, John. 1980. *Attachment and Loss*. New York: Basic Books.

———. 1988. *A Secure Base: Parent-Child Attachment and Healthy Human Development*. New York: Basic Books.

Dentan, Robert K. 1968. *The Semai: A Nonviolent People of Malaysia*. New York: Holt, Rinehart and Winston.

Durkheim, Émile. 1964. *Division of Labor in Society*. New York: Free Press.

Endicott, Kirk. 1979. *Batek Negrito Religion: The World-View and Rituals of a Hunting and Gathering People of Peninsular Malaysia*. Oxford: Clarendon Press.

———. 1983. "The effects of slave raiding on the aborigines of the Malay Peninsula." In A. Reid and J. Brewster, eds., *Slavery, Bondage, and Dependency in Southeast Asia,* 216–45. Brisbane: University of Queensland Press.

———. 1988. "Property, power and conflict among the Batek of Malaysia." In T. Ingold, D. Riches, and J. Woodburn, eds., *Hunters and Gatherers.* Vol. 2: *Property, Power, and Ideology,* 110–27. Oxford: Berg.

Endicott, Kirk, and Karen Endicott. 2008. *The Headman Was a Woman: The Gender Egalitarian Batek of Malaysia*. Long Grove, IL: Waveland Press.

Gardner, Peter. 1966. "Symmetric respect and memorate knowledge: The structure and ecology of individualistic culture." *Southwestern Journal of Anthropology* 22:389–415.

———. 1991. "Foragers' pursuit of individual autonomy." *Current Anthropology* 32:543–72.

Gray, Peter. 2009. "Play as a foundation for hunter-gatherer social existence." *American Journal of Play* 1:476–522.

Hobbes, Thomas. 1651. *Leviathan, or, the Matter, Form, and Power of a Common-Wealth Ecclesiastical and Civil*. London: Thomas Crooke.

Ingold, Tim. 1999. "On the social relations of the hunter-gatherer band." In R.B. Lee and R. Daly, eds., *The Cambridge Encyclopedia of Hunters and Gatherers,* 399–410. Cambridge: Cambridge University Press.

Kelly, Robert L. 1995. *The Foraging Spectrum: Diversity in Hunter-Gatherer Lifeways*. Washington, DC, and London: Smithsonian Institution Press.

Leacock, Eleanor, and Richard Lee. 1982. "Introduction." In E. Leacock and R. Lee, eds., *Politics and History in Band Society,* 1–20. Cambridge: Cambridge University Press.

Lee, Richard B., and Irven DeVore, eds. 1968. *Man the Hunter*. Chicago: Aldine.

Lye, Tuck-Po. 1994. "Batek *Hep*: Culture, nature, and the folklore of a Malaysian Forest people." MA thesis, Department of Anthropology, University of Hawai'i.

———. 1997. "Knowledge, forest, and hunter-gatherer movement: The Batek of Pahang, Malaysia." PhD diss., Department of Anthropology, University of Hawai'i.

———. 2004. *Changing Pathways: Forest Degradation and the Batek of Pahang, Malaysia*. Lanham, MD: Lexington Books.

Needham, Rodney. 1959. "Mourning terms." *Bijdragen tot de Taal-, Land- en Volkenkunde* 115:58–89.

Rousseau, Jérôme. 2006. *Rethinking Social Evolution: The Perspective from Middle-Range Societies*. Montreal and Kingston: McGill-Queen's University Press.

Schrire, Carmel. 1984. "Wild surmises on savage thoughts." In C. Schrire, ed., *Past and Present in Hunter Gatherer Studies* Orlando, FL: Academic Press.

Strathern, Marilyn. 1988. *The Gender of the Gift*. Berkeley: University of California Press.

Testart, Alain. 1981. "Pour une typologie des chasseurs-cueilleurs." *Anthropologie et Sociétés* 5:177–221.

———. 1991. "Comment on *Foragers' Pursuit of Individual Autonomy* by Peter Gardner." *Current Anthropology* 32:564–65.

Wilmsen, Edwin. 1989. *Land Filled with Flies: A Political Economy of the Kalahari*. Chicago: University of Chicago Press.

Woodburn, James. 1982. "Egalitarian societies." *Man,* new series, 17:431–51.

———. 1988. "African hunter-gatherer social organization: Is it best understood as a product of encapsulation?" In T. Ingold, D. Riches, and J. Woodburn, eds., *Hunters and Gatherers*. Vol. 1: *History, Evolution, and Social Change*, 31–64. Oxford: Berg.

4

Childhood, Familiarity, and Social Life among East Semai

ROBERT DENTAN

> [W]e could not learn all the details of their internal economy, but it seemed to approximate the improved state of association which is sometimes heard of among us; and as theirs has existed for an unknown length of time, and can no longer be considered experimental, Owen or Fourier might perhaps take lessons from them with advantage.
>
> —John L. Stephens, *Incidents of Travel in Yucatan*, 1843

THIS CHAPTER TOOK ROOT IN A TALK that the ever-magnanimous Geoffrey Benjamin arranged for me to give at Nanyang University (Singapore) (Dentan 2006b). That off-the-cuff talk initiated my shift from the theory that Semai peaceability, and their social arrangements in general, resulted from intimidation by particularly ruthless slavers (e.g., Dentan 1992, 1994, 2008b) to the one presented here. E-conversation with the other authors of this book (notably Macdonald, this volume, and 2010) convinced me that (1) in fact Semai live the way that evolution wires people to live (Dentan 2010) and (2) their intimidation stems not merely from their "political ecology" (in the sense of Dentan 1992, 1994) but also from the relative powerlessness that in fact characterizes life among peoples with a fairly limited technological toolbox when they face an environment as fundamentally hostile as tropical rainforest. Whatever its origin—and I still think slaving plays a role (see Gibson, this volume)—this *feeling* of powerlessness has a number of consequences that I have discussed elsewhere (Dentan 2008b), notably what Furedi (2002:170) calls the "precautionary principle—be careful or else— ... a fatalistic outlook whose main aim is to warn rather than direct people. ... The fatalistic sociology of the precautionary principle depicts people as essentially powerless to do very much more than to avoid taking risks."

More specifically, the chapter comes in response to the question of whether the analytical construct "society" discussed in this volume, "problematic in smaller-scale systems" (Rousseau 2006:13), is necessary to understand solidarity among peaceable egalitarian peoples like "east Semai" of central Peninsular Malaysia. That aim requires a preliminary section defining "society," "east Semai," and "peaceable egalitarian peoples." After that comes a section on method. Next, the main body of the essay discusses the centrality of child care in human evolution and in east Semai social life. The conclusion is that child care—and the "familiarity" that develops within the small groups involved in child care—provide enough "social glue" to account for Semai social solidarity without using the concept of society.

The essay reflects long-term theoretical concerns with peaceable egalitarian anarchic peoples (Dentan 1992, 1994, 2008b, 2010). More recently, concern with this issue generated cooperation with west Semai collaborators on essays describing how "modernization" necessitates removing Semai children from their society, disrupting the multidimensional social skills that their quotidian home life requires (Macdonald 2008a), and substituting unidimensional ones that facilitate subordination to the economic benefit of others (Dentan and Juli Edo 2008; Dentan, Williams-Hunt, and Juli Edo 2010). As Piaget noted years ago, among the skills repressed are those required for egalitarian interaction (Cords and Killen 1998:196; Dentan 2010).

This essay does not problematize individual autonomy or the egalitarianism that it implies and engenders. Both seem primordial (Dentan 2010; Rousseau 2006:43–51; Woodburn 1980:431).

> [T]hey're egalitarian because they respect the individual so much, right? And you can't respect other people's individuality in a kind of abstract, isolated way. The point is that you are an individual inasmuch as you exist in a social matrix of others who respect your individuality and your right to make choices. That's ... an individuality that recognizes that it owes its existence to a kind of communal respect on the part of all other individualities, and that it had better respect them similarly.
>
> (Miéville 2003:63; see Endicott, this volume)

Semai say explicitly that coercion is physically and spiritually dangerous, especially for children, whose bodies and souls are "soft." Children learn to choose and act independently, with the one restriction that their parents teach them to fear and flee strangers, one way of inculcating Furedi's "precautionary principle" (Dentan 1978, 2001, 2008b:179–97, 2010; Dentan and Juli Edo 2008:8; Robarchek 1979:559–62; see Endicott, this volume; Furedi 2002:107–26).

The concomitant sociality seems for most such peoples to generate and depend on trying to avoid conflict by fleeing rather than fighting (Dentan 1979, 1992, 2004, 2008a, 2010; Fry 2006; Otterbein 2004; Howell, this volume; and Endicott, this volume). The historically specific experience of remarkably brutal slaving intensified Semai commitment to autonomy, egalitarianism, and peaceability (Dentan 1992, 2008b; Endicott, this volume; Gibson, this volume; cf. Scott 2009). This "negative peaceability," as Macdonald suggests (2009), builds on the evolutionary advantage peaceability confers on small egalitarian groups (for further sources, see Dentan 2008a, 2010).

Society

This paper uses *social* as a descriptive adjective for animals that live in groups and *societal* to refer to the notion of society. I prefer Macdonald's (2008a) term *gregarious* over *social* and would use it if it were more entrenched in the ethological literature. The concept of society (e.g., Strathern 1988) derives from Alexis de Tocqueville's ([1835] 2002) contrast of American "individualism" (a term Tocqueville coined) with more aristocratic European "social conditions." Tocqueville intended his coinage to refer to the sort of atomic individualism he observed in Jacksonian America—with its proliferation of "democratic" ad hoc voluntary groups based on shared goals: "contract" (Maine 1861) or "weak" (Macdonald 2010) relationships in contrast with inegalitarian Old World "status" or "strong" relationships expressed as ascribed kinship and class positions. The sharp distinction between society and individual in this sense seems inappropriate outside mass societies. East Semai reject "the interlocking interests of 'civil society,' the imagined community of the ethnic group or nation, or the regulative structures of the state" (Ingold 1999:408), along with toilet paper, republicanism, and advertising. Throughout Southeast Asia, this rejection is central in the self-definition of peripheral peoples (e.g., Burling 1965; Dentan

1976a; Duncan 2004; Gibson, this volume; Kaskija, this volume; Nobuta 2008; Scott 2009).

In the weaker noncontrastive sense used here a society comprises "corporate groups" and the relations between them (Brown 1976; Macdonald 2008a; Rousseau 2006). A corporate group is one that holds a status, that is, a (usually named) bundle of rights and duties. The status usually refers to property. Thus a common interpretation of the Semai term *tei' saka'*, literally "hereditary lands," is as a geographical area that a particular band of Semai "owns." That "ownership," however conceived, entails construing Semai bands as corporations. That construal seems appropriate for west Semai "settlements" that developed out of traditional bands in Perak State (e.g., Juli Edo, Williams-Hunt, and Dentan 2009a, 2009b; Williams-Hunt 1995, 2007). Indeed, west Semai "settlements" manifest their corporate status more elaborately than merely by owning property. They exist in "presumptive perpetuity" (Brown 1976:20–21, 34–35) and have official headmen (Macdonald 2008a, 2010). But construing east Semai bands as corporate seems problematic (see below). Demonstrating the irrelevance of the idea of corporation would be one way to imply the irrelevance of the idea of society. Another would be to show that social behavior results from autonomous individual choices. Society need not involve ethnic identity or homogeneous culture: while a society cannot exist without people, a society is not the sum of the individuals who constitute it. A society cannot be reduced to individual characteristics; rather, it plays a major role in constituting individuals (Rousseau 2006:12).

If societal/cultural factors do not significantly constrain what people do; that is, if behavior seems "natural" in the sense of resulting from noncultural or nonsocietal factors like natural selection, which generally operate at the individual level, then the notion of society is irrelevant (Dentan 2010). The principle of parsimony (Ockham's Razor) dictates that, of two otherwise equally complex and sufficient accounts of solidarity, the one that omits complex nonempirical postulates like "subjectivity" or ideology is the better.

East Semai

I first met Semai on the Telom River in northeastern Pahang State, West Malaysia, in 1962, the "east Semai" of Dentan 1979. Nowadays there are about thirty thousand Semai, east and west, mostly in the states of Pahang (east) and Perak (west). The term *Semai* is a basically linguistic exonym. In 1962–63, east Semai called west Semai "Malays" (for Semai the ultimate "Other"); conversely, west Semai called east Semai "Temiar," referring to a closely related people whose territory overlaps with Semailand in the north (Benjamin, this volume). Many Temiar family groups lived among Semai on the upper Telom. This "mixed" collocation of Semai and Temiar are the Semai or east Semai of this essay (Dentan 1979, 2008b:68–74; 87–108). The implicit "ethnographic present" is 1962.

As the casual intermixture of Telom linguistic "groups" suggests, applying notions of "ethnicity" in the 1960s to a congeries of east and west Semai bands speaking over forty distinct dialects was tricky (e.g., Dentan 1975, 1976b, 1978:98–99; 1979:1, 4, 15; 1999:417–18). Traditional Semai group identity works as a series of nested contrasts between ego's local group or kindred and a progressively alien series of "Others" ("folks," *maay*) at increasingly great "effective distance," a demographers' measure of how much time and effort it takes to have face-to-face interactions (Dentan 1976a). The distance is also sentimental and social: *hal maay,* "other people's business," is a dismissive phrase for affairs in which one has no stake or interest (see Howell, this volume, contra Ingold 1999:408). Malays are so distant as to be a "contrast culture" so that the standard format for Semai describing their lifestyle is "We do this, Malays do that," a common rhetorical device of peripheral peoples (Dentan 1994; Kaskija, this volume; Lechner 2003; Woodburn 1988). In the case of Semai, long subject to slave raids, the contrast seems to contain an element of "double consciousness," a mild form of identification with and rejection of the aggressor (Dentan 2008b:9, 83–84, 110–12; Du Bois 1979) characteristic of traumatized people (e.g., Saathoff 1996; cf. Scott 2009). They likewise contrast themselves as "poor" versus "rich" Others (Dentan 1999:418, 2008b:7, 31–33; cf. Fei 1980:99; Kaskija, this volume; Frake 1999).

Ethnicity develops as a tactic in the struggle for limited resources (e.g., Barth 1969). That struggle is salient in Semai life today (e.g., Dentan 2003; Dentan et al. 1997; Nicholas 1994, 2000). But, among east Semai in 1962, the irrelevance of "ethnicity" is central to the idea of "familiarity" discussed below.

Peaceable Egalitarian Peoples

The familiar materialist categorization of peoples' lifeways by dominant mode of subsistence (e.g., Murdock 1949, 1981) is misleading here. Recent cross-cultural studies (e.g., Dentan 1992, 1994; Fry 2006; Macdonald 2009; Otterbein 2004) suggest inter alia the following rejiggering (Dentan 2008a, 2010). The category "hunter-gatherers" splits into egalitarian, peaceable, anarchist "foragers" and patricentric, generally feuding "big game hunters," the latter but not the former characterized by statistical virilocality and fraternal interest groups. The "foragers" would blend with egalitarian, generally peaceable "swiddeners-agroforesters" like east Semai and Buid (cf., for Philippine peoples, Frake 1999) and the big game hunters with patriarchal, generally warlike "pastoralists" (cf., for transitional peoples, Qiu 1983). Archaeological and ethnographic evidence suggests that simple swiddening evolves seamlessly and reversibly from agroforestry and husbandry of wild plants by foragers (Ellen 1982). The similarities of social and political structure among small-scale peaceable egalitarians might explain why Semai so often wind up in the anthropological literature as foragers (e.g., Kottak 2009:370), although their traditional subsistence rested on swiddening, agroforestry, and trade. When British counterinsurgency bombing drove east Semai from their settlements in the 1950s, the people were unable to subsist by foraging and came, starving, to the British concentration camps. *Anarchs* (Dentan 2010) is a useful term for the category that lumps swiddener-agroforesters like Semai, Semaq Beri (Lim 2010), Buid (Gibson, this volume), and Palawan (Macdonald 1977 and this volume) with foragers like Batek (e.g., Lye 2004, 2008; Endicott 1979 and this volume; Endicott and Endicott 2008), as well as some fisherfolk like Btsisi' (e.g., Nowak 1987) and Sama Dilaut (e.g., Sather 2004 and this volume).

This lumping obviates certain analyses. For instance, the notion of "immediacy" or "instaneity" (lack of foresight, present orientation) postulated as determining forager social arrangements (e.g., Meillasoux 1973, 1981) loses its economic roots. A Semai epic explicitly contrasts foraging with the "hard work" of agriculture, organized by a temporal cycle signaled by the call of the migratory Indian cuckoo (Dentan 2006a). But Semai social relations still resemble the "immediate" ones that Ingold describes (1999:405–6; cf. Rousseau 2006:19–20; cf. Macdonald 2010) and foraging also follows seasonal cycles. In fact, immediacy may stem from a sense of "learned helplessness" (Peterson, Maier, and Seligman 1993) vis-à-vis one's natural or social environment, resulting in "the precautionary principle" (Furedi 2002) and aversion to long-term plans or striving in the present for hypothetical future benefits. Instaneity recalls the "culture of poverty" construct briefly popular among American social scientists (e.g., Banfield 1970; Lewis 1966). Acceptance of being overwhelmed by circumstances produces a similar orientation, for example, Buddhist "right-mindedness" or the "First Step" of Alcoholics Anonymous (Dentan 1992, 1994, 2008b; Lechner 2003; Macdonald 2008a). Lumping anarch social formations together allows setting the complex empiricist "personalism" of such peoples against the simplistic, abstract, hierarchical, rule-based "universalism" of gesellschaft social relations, whatever the dominant mode of production (Dentan 1992, 1994, 2008b, 2010; Dentan and Juli Edo 2008; Dentan, Williams-Hunt, and Juli Edo 2010; Macdonald 2009, 2010; Maine 1861).

Major disjunctions do occur along the continuum between foragers and swiddeners. For instance, like Chewong (Howell, this volume), east Semai give no sign of regarding their territory as a "giving environment" (Bird-David 1990) nurturing its people "the way adults do children" (Ingold 1999:409). Trekking with east Semai through the woods, I was struck by how much their demeanor resembled that of Americans wandering through a supermarket. They would collect things opportunistically, with no sign of reverence or fellow feeling for "life." For instance, Prwan, a "mature man" (see below) on one trip picked up a couple of horned frogs, carried them for a couple of miles and then, tired of carrying them, smashed them casually against a tree. Young people roasted small rodents and birds alive.

More generally, the complex Semai notion of hunting expresses what Mary Douglas might call a natural metaphor hunter : prey :: lover : lover (Dentan 2008b:75, 87–112), an idea more familiar to European sport hunters than to most foragers (e.g., Luke 1988). Animals are people, *maay*, in their own dimension (cf. Howell, this volume), though not "humans," *snˀooy*. The word for hunting, *-srlooˀ*, refers both to putting something where it belongs and to deceit or betrayal, suffering that, for Semai, can be fatal (Dentan 2008b:124–27, 257). The predatory erotic relationship goes both ways. As some empirical-world humans murder or entrap empirical-world animals in order to devour them, some animals' souls devour or seduce human souls in dreams, causing disease and death. (The east Semai word *janiiˀ*, *nyaniiˀ* in other dialects, refers to such souls and is often Englished as "evil spirit" or "demon.") But in dreams the souls may seduce each other, so that a hunter can get a "hunting wife" or a shaman a demon lover who help the humans hunt down wild animals or *janii'*. Séances, in which shamans sing the dream songs their *janii'* lovers give them, express these relationships, rich with passion and deceit, dependency and betrayal (Dentan 2008b).

But this apparent difference between swiddener and forager ideology has no consequences for the reductive evolutionary analysis this chapter is testing out, in which ideology is a dependent variable or epiphenomenon. Abstractly, whether one's relations with animals feel humanly respectful or humanly dangerous is inconsequential. The point, as Ingold argues (1999: 409), is that "the aim is to maintain proper relationships .... And if no absolute boundary separates relationships that are soci[et]al from those that are not, then what need have we for a concept of the soci[et]al at all?" Semai find relationships with animals as tricky as relationships with people. Furedi's "precautionary principle" applies equally to both. With no "absolute boundary," the difference makes no difference.

Method

The question of whether notions of society are helpful in understanding egalitarian anarchist societies is partly a question about judging "authoritative accounts." This essay argues (in contrast to most of my writing) that the point of explanation is to explain as many social facts as possible in the simplest possible way (Lounsbury 1964). Anthropology has lately turned away from this sort of explanation, preferring to contrive interpretive accounts that reflect the richness of ethnographic facts rather than to abstract and simplify them. But for the purposes of deciding whether or not to use a concept, a formally parsimonious method that discards any concepts that are not literally necessary seems appropriate, despite the sacrifice of complexity. The point of explanation, after all, is to make things easier to understand, not harder. And that requires "abbreviating the singularity of things to ... an orchard seen from the air rather than this gnarled tree" (Kaplan 1999:2).

Besides, the longer I try to understand how Semai life works/worked, the more sensible it seems to me, and therefore the less reasonable it seems to insist on parochial "cultural" explanations (Dentan 2006b, 2007, 2010). Charles Macdonald (2007, 2010d, this volume) likewise suggests that nonsocietal analyses of particular peaceful egalitarian/anarchist societies might shed light on the origins of human social life. Since the first human social aggregates seem to have had similar social arrangements (Dentan 2008a, 2010; Fry 2006; Hrdy 2009; Isaac 1978; Otterbein 2004), it seems useful to begin by recalling the pressures that led to their evolution.

So this essay is a "mental experiment" in logical reductionism of the sort common in the late nineteenth and early twentieth centuries. It begins by listing evolutionary pressures that set the parameters of all human society. (It differs from "evolutionary psychology," which begins with particular modern behaviors and imagines primordial evolutionary conditions that might have encoded such behaviors in the human genome.) It then lists social arrangements that seem logically to follow.

Discussion

"K" Reproductive Strategy and the Centrality of Child Care

The account starts by defining basic pressures on organisms and on the characteristics of the particular organisms (hominines). As the presentation goes along, I will try to indicate how Semai life seems to reflect this interaction of evolutionary pressures and social behavior. The next few paragraphs are a simpler and less empirical version of the opening section of my general essay on practical anarchies (2010).

Evolutionary "success" requires individual organisms to deploy the energy available to them so as to produce a larger number of surviving fertile offspring than their competitors. There are two basic strategies for such differential reproduction: (1) "K," which focuses on filling up the relatively few slots left in an environment near its carrying capacity (K) for the species, as herd ruminants do; and (2) "r" (the symbol for "reproductive capacity," i.e., the maximum possible number of offspring if all survive), which focuses on filling up a suitable environment relatively empty of the species, as many amphibians do. The limited energy available to any organism means that K-strategy invests the available energy in a few offspring; the heavy investment in each allows them to be "precocial," capable of surviving on their own relatively early in ontogeny. In r-strategy, the same amount of energy is dispersed among a relatively large number of offspring, which therefore tend to be "altricial," less mature and less likely as individuals to survive.

Anthropoids tend toward K-strategy. Humans, however, partly as a result of the pelvic changes attendant on upright posture, produce altricial (= neotenous/fetalized) offspring, which require relatively long postpartum protection. Even juveniles remain vulnerable. This requirement is conducive to the development of a caretaking family. The basic human kin tie is between mother and child. The father-child tie develops quite early in human evolution, however, perhaps as a way of dealing with the relative immobilization of human mothers postpartum because of the incompetence of human infants. The father is an especially reliable alloparent (Hrdy 2009). For Semai, the role of midwives, who Semai say remain emotionally close to the infants they deliver, is somewhat similar.

Semai teknonymy and (individually optional) precautionary food restrictions reflect this centrality of children. Both mothers and fathers take teknonyms beginning at the birth of the child and reflecting the fact that, for adults, nurturing children is the focus of their biological lives. Both may avoid certain "dangerous" foods and behaviors (as do midwives). There is little agreement on what to avoid and a lot of variation in scrupulosity, but fathers generally make fewer adaptations. As children get older and need less fostering, avoidances fade away. These avoidances seem to reflect the degree of risk that particular people assess attendant on their personally raising kids (Dentan 1965; Dentan and Juli Edo 2008:8–10; cf. Furedi 2002:73–126). Those risks depend on individual circumstances (Dentan 1975). Although one spouse may complain about the other's choices, no one would try to constrain another person's right to pick and choose.

Semai "age categories" (Dentan 1989:102, 104) also seem to embody the centrality of children. There are three named stages and one unmarked one. The first is "child," with a marked subcategory "new child," that is, infant (Dentan 1978:116–27). Specification of gender, for example, 'aleeh, "girl," is optional and rare, maybe because "children" do not reproduce. A pair of gendered terms, *litaaw* and *mnaleeh*, identify the next stage, pubescent and postpubescent men and women respectively: nubile, old enough to reproduce but more interested in the act of reproducing than in providing the nurture the K reproductive strategy requires. This lack of investiture means that other Semai regard them as flighty, unserious people whose opinion is of little value (Dentan 2008b:211–14, 224–25, 255–56). Next comes the unlabeled category of mature people who have settled down with a family and are raising children. Their opinions are relatively weighty. I venture the guess that this category has no name of its own because it represents a norm, what being a person is all about, a central reality of human life, as linguistically unmarked terms often do. However, Semai "norms" seem more descriptive than prescriptive, post hoc rationalizations of no constraining importance and thus not part of society. Finally, there are "old" (postmenopausal) people, usually referred to generically as "old folk," *maay nraa'*, but optionally by gender as "old men," *(ta)taa'*, and "old women" *(ja)jaa'*. The latter terms connote respect and are cognate with the two terms for one's male and female kinsmen in one's grandparental generation. Another cognate term, *ra'naa'*, refers to "elders," people with political influence.

No ceremony marks entry into or exit from these stages. That flexibility allows the frequent eristic tactic of dismissing opponents as *litaaw, mnaleeh*, or "children," whose opinions don't count because of their inexperience, flightiness, vanity, and avoidance of commitment (Dentan 2008b:145, 224–26, 238–40, 255, 256). Thus the linguistic chopping up of the continuum of reproductive maturation is not authoritative but as gradual as the underlying biological changes themselves.

Kinship terminology is consonant with this "age" (maturation/child-rearing) system. If analysis begins with the idea of a child ego (propositus), then ego's generation consists of older children who function as alloparents, *tnee'*, and younger children for whom ego is an alloparent, *mnaang*. The first ascending generation consists of parents and alloparents. Because adult males and adult females foster children differently, gender distinctions are important in that generation. For example, although east Semai children suckle, albeit with diminishing frequency as they age, almost until puberty, men rarely give suck (but see Williams-Hunt 1952:51). Thus there are terms for "father" (pater, usually genitor) and "mother" (mater, usually genetrix). Because of the importance of relative age in nurture, the terminology splits a parent's siblings into junior versus senior aunts and uncles. (Some Semai avuncular/amital terms mean "father" or "mother" in other Austroasiatic languages, reflecting the complex origins and "mixed" ethnicity of the people.) Senior aunts and uncles have an affinity with grandparents; the reciprocal term (= younger sibling's child) is "grandchild," and the seniors deserve the deference due experience and maturity. Complementarily, junior aunts and uncles, addressed respectively as Wa' and Bah, are relatively immature. Indeed, children, *litaaw* and *mnaleeh,* are all three referred to as Wa' or Bah So-and-So. The reciprocal for "junior aunt/uncle" is "child."

This last usage is internally inconsistent, since, by rule, the child of a "child" is a "grandchild" and the child of a "grandchild" is a *ciciid*; but a *ciciid* is any relative in the third descending generation. The inconsistency seems to pose no problem for east Semai, perhaps because actual usage was pretty ad hoc—people would adjust generational definitions to conform with relative age, for example—and because people almost never lived long enough to have any meaningful relationship with great-grandchildren. But the anomaly seems to have facilitated terminological adjustments among west Semai (Dentan 1970).

To summarize: except in relationship to child care, the Semai kinship system is not particularly "normative." Individuals manipulate it ad hoc according to the sort of relationship they want to have (cf. Macdonald 1977, 2009:9). Instead, kinship terminology seems to reflect patterns that result from the nurture central to K-reproductive strategy, in which the paucity of kids requires focusing attention on them, rather than to embody a set of societal rules.

I think this freedom from ideological constraint is not just an artifact of methodology. Semai organic intellectuals enjoy rummaging in a multiplicity of ideologies but treat them all with skepticism, eclecticism, and pragmatism (Dentan 1979:93–95), a far cry from Muslim/Malay ideas of authoritative customary law encapsulated in the Arabic word *adat*. Malays traditionally say "better your child should die than your *adat*," a thought east Semai would find horrendous. Indeed, when I said in 1962 that I had come to study their *adat*, meaning "culture," people denied they had any. Retrospectively, I think they meant *adat* more specifically in the Arabic-Malay sense of authoritative and constraining customary law, the sense in which west Semai, who assert that they do have *adat*, do use the term (Juli Edo, Williams-Hunt, and Dentan 2009a, 2009b; Williams-Hunt 1995, 2007). Carey Island Btsisi' (= Mah Meri) in the 1970s told me that they lacked *adat:* "We just get up, work all day, and at night go to sleep." Since the politically dominant Malays regard lacking *adat* as symptomatic of de-graded, mannerless savagery (Dentan 1997), and since *adat* is crucial in Malaysian land tenure cases, most indigenous Malaysian peoples now assert that they have always had *adat*. Thus one difference between tradi-tional Austroasiatic-speaking west Malaysian indigenes and their more authoritarian Austronesian Bornean kin is the prominence of authoritative *adat* among the latter (e.g., Rousseau 1990), especially in matters of kinship and land tenure, so that morally constraining kinship rules in Borneo can be "a principle source of self-identification and solidarity" there (Sillander, this volume) as opposed to neighborly familiarity among Semai, which resembles Buid "companionship" (Gibson 1985) based on shared residence and activity.

In conclusion, Semai age and kin relations can be construed as largely the product of the centrality of children and nurture in human reproductive strategy. I want to stress that this centrality is emphatically not ideological or "cultural" in the normal usage of the word. While east Semai often make a fuss over "new children" (babies), older children pretty much fend for themselves unless they are fighting or otherwise in emotional distress (Dentan 1978:125–26; 2008b:192–97, 206–9). That's one of the ways they learn independence and autonomy. Semai also don't talk much about children, although gossip about who is engaging in reproductive activity with whom is pandemic. Although this essay does not treat motives as significant, a different approach (Robarchek 1986:177–78) says of highland west Semai:

> The theme of dependence (including its reciprocal, nuturance) permeates Semai life and constitutes an important structural and emotional dimension in nearly all human social relationships as well as in relationships between humans and the world of supernatural beings.

That is, the parent-child relationship seems to be a folk model, largely unconscious, for most relationships (Dentan 2000a). In short, society, in the literally denatured Franco-British sense, seems irrelevant to the structural centrality of children among east Semai, which develops normlessly and without corporate involvement from the natural conditions attendant on assuring the children's survival to adulthood.

Pairs

Another indication of the centrality of child rearing is that the basic Semai unit is the "pair," *klamin*. In hominine reproductive strategy, as noted above, the basic unit is mother and child(ren) plus father. Participation in a stable pair, with children, marks "mature" status for Semai (cf. the Batek "conjugal family" in Endicott, this volume; and Endicott and Endicott 2008:111–26). Talking of a particular pair, people use the third-person dual pronoun plus the name of one partner, for example, *obaay* Wa' Lang. For purposes of this discussion, it is important to stress that, while people may agree that their sons and daughters should marry, pairs do not usually form by means of weddings but gradually, out of sexual experimenting, almost entirely by "kids," that is, *litaaw* or *mnaleeh*. Shacking up develops gradually into "marriage" and may equally gradually fade into "divorce." Thus Bah Cong, an amiable love-starved teenager, listed silly Wa' Mas as a woman to whom he had been "married." Mas, however, didn't list him. When I raised the contradiction, Mas pondered a moment, then giggled: "O, *that*. That was just fooling around." Similarly, when I was taking my first census Wa' Long said she was "married" to a man doing wage work downstream; on a second census, a few months later, not having seen him in the interim, she ventured, "I *think* I'm divorced now." Children go with whichever parent they prefer and occasionally wind up, after a few splits, living with biologically unrelated people. In short, east Semai "pairs" are informal products of spontaneous reproductive activity by autonomous individuals. Other people eventually come to recognize the pair post facto, if it lasts long enough, as an increasingly stable two-person primary group in the sociological sense. The arrival of the first child or two or three makes neighbors think the pair is likely to endure and the two adults are thus "mature."

Within the pair the roles of men and women tend to be informally complementary, for example, women tend to do the cooking and men the hunting, although men often cook and a few women hunt. *Litaaw* are more likely than young women to seek a mate outside their band (as is common among other terrestrial primates), although Semai explain the difference as due to women's fear of being kidnapped or raped "by Malays." Hence the proverb "men's loincloths are long, women's are short." Men and women have equal but complementary ritual statuses (e.g., women tend to be midwives and men shamans), although men make especially good midwives and women good shamans. Men's "cool" and women's "hot" blood are equally but complementarily powerful (Dentan 1988b). Men occasionally take a couple of wives, but polyandry and multiple polygyny are rare because of individual spousal discontent. The situation of a woman with a child but no partner is unusual enough to warrant amused commentary, but neither women nor child suffers obloquy. Adoption does not make children less loved—more, if anything. A child who feels neglected will move in with more accommodating adults. There are no formal institutions of marriage, legitimacy, or adoption.

Pairing is central to Semai thinking. When, for instance, people apportion (precisely equal) portions of large game, the portions are allocated on banana leaf squares ("leafings," *snlaa'*, from *slaa'*, "leaf") by "pair" rather than by individual. People past puberty who are not in a pair are grouped into twos for purposes of distribution. Similarly, same-sexed pubescent *litaaw* or *mnaleeh,* too old to sleep with their parents, are paired off to occupy vacant sleeping compartments in a longhouse—from which visiting conjugal pairs may displace them.

Semai pairs may form households, which often include siblings or ancestors of the members. People refer to them as the "house of So-and-So" (the man who built the house) or of *obaay* Bah or Wa' So-and-So, referring to the founding pair. In 1962 east Semai households ranged in size from two to fifty-four people, the largest being longhouses inhabited mostly by Temiar. Low walls mark off longhouse floors into cubicles, each assigned to a particular twosome, although teenage boys often sleep in the central common space.

Pairs seem to be the model for *kkasih,* a relationship east Semai say is "like marriage." Normally, each person in one pair becomes the "friend," *kasih,* of his or her same-gendered counterpart in the other, so that the relationship is effectively between two pairs. Like marriage, *kkasih* is voluntary, informal, based on mutual affection and mutually complementary work; but it lacks a sexual component. No ritual marks the beginning or end of the relationship, although people may use the reciprocal address term *kasih* while the relationship lasts. *Kkasih* evolves from and facilitates cooperation. Thus Hukum depended on his *kasih* Mrlooh for market goods, since Hukum didn't do wage work but Mrlooh did. (Both were men too mature to use the title Bah). Conversely, Mrlooh got space in swiddens that Hukum cleared and, if Hukum had several chickens, he would give some to Mrlooh. *Kasih* should speak softly with each other, to avoid disrespect, and may exchange particular goods, for example, a blowpipe for a blowpipe, without consideration of whether the blowpipes are of equal quality. The exchange is, I will argue later, an outward and visible sign of an inward invisible mutual "familiarity." As with marriage, the associated terminology seems exogenous. *Kasih* is cognate with a Malay word for "deep affection," as in the formal Malay phrase for "thank you," *terima kasih,* "receive affection."

Band and Kawaad

> If we compare comparables, we find the ... band of thirty to sixty persons
> larger, to be sure, than the family in urban America, but it is still a family and
> it is still very small-scaled.
>
>   (Service 1966:24)

Tim Ingold (1999:399) argues that questions like those this book addresses turn on the "nature" of "a peculiar collectivity known as the *band*." This essay takes band living as an evolutionary product/requirement of primate terrestrial life, found among baboons and hominines alike, facilitating defense, subsistence and, as part of K-reproductive strategy, safeguarding vulnerable children (Hrdy 2009). An important part of Semai child rearing is teaching children that people from outside the band are dangerous and safety depends on staying near familiar adult band members (Dentan 1978, 2001, 2008b:177–201; cf. Furedi 2002:73–126). A Semai band takes its name from the small river along which that collectivity lives (e.g., *maay Jnteer*, "Jinteh [River] folk"). Geography thus sets the basic group identification for peoples like those in this volume (e.g., Carole Robarchek 1980:90; Kaskija, this volume). Most bands comprise a loosely related set of kinsmen, a few married in, ranging in size in 1962 from about 5 to about 146 individuals, with a mean of 35 to 65 (Dentan 1971:139; cf. Robarchek 1980:91). The band is thus a "primary group" in sociological jargon, one in which people have more frequent face-to-face interactions with every other member of the group than with any people outside the group. Most terrestrial primates live in troops of similar size; the existence of the group does not necessitate postulating a society in any sense discussed here. The term for a member of one's band is *kawaad*, sometimes translated as "friend" (e.g., Luering 1901:97) but better understood as "neighbor."

The core of a band was typically one (occasionally two or three) sets of ambilineal kinsmen plus their affines. The smallest were families that had broken away from larger groups as the result of local disputes, the largest the result of regroupment by the British as part of a counterinsurgency strategy during a Communist uprising. The mean size (about 45 people), the median (38), and the mode (31 to 40) reflect the primary group status of the bands and the resultant mutual familiarity of the people (Dentan 1971:139).

Most larger east Semai bands in 1962 resulted from forced relocation. The aboriginal "normal" Semai band size range was probably more like 20 to 65 people. At the top of the range (e.g., on the Teiw Jnteer where I lived then), these amalgamated bands were unstable and by 1962 were disinte-grating. For example, the group of 130 people among whom I lived broke into three. One stayed; one went back to the Jlaay River in the west, the location from which troops had moved them; and some Temiar speakers drifted back to their coethnics across the border in Kelantan State. Among the reasons for the instability was the difficulty of maintaining ongoing face-to-face relationships with everyone in so large a group and the increasing incidence of quarrels, which Semai blame on forcing people together in unnaturally large groups.

Band life turns familiarity into "fellowship"

> Miracles don't cause faith, but rather
> The scent of kindredness that unites people …
> Faith grows from fellowship.
>
> —Rumi

Territorial band life makes people's relationships with their human and nat-ural environment "familiar" in at least three of senses of the word.

1. People are well enough acquainted with their human and natural surroundings to anticipate pretty much what's going to happen in most situations. Semai are keenly interested in each other's activities; gossip, often wildly inaccurate and malicious, fills the need for entertainment as well as any daytime TV serial in the United States. But they are rarely startled by either environment and indeed lay the blame for "soul-loss" diseases on being "startled" (Dentan 1978, 1988a). Familiarity with one's human and material environment helps minimize risk and facilitates survival, as well as according with the "precautionary principle."

2. Although Semai say other people's emotions are basically unknowable and not subject to amelioration by others—unlike Malaysian foragers (see the essays by Endicott, Howell, and Kaskija, this volume)—they are careful to avoid actions that might cause "psychic trauma," *lukaa' sngii'* (Dentan 2000a, 2000b, 2008b:113–40). This caution, not based on *knowledge* of other people's inner selves nor even on personal affection, preserves the mutual comfort that results from the first kind of familiarity and fosters a sort of relatively stress-free family feeling, the second kind of familiarity:

fellowship (Macdonald 2009 and this volume) or companionship (Gibson 1985 and this volume). This fellowship and respect for each other's individuality lowers communal stress and facilitates cooperation among autonomous individuals (for analysis, see Dentan 2010).

3. The core of the local group becomes an extended *family*, in the sense of a primary group constituted by birth, supplemented by marriage. Interacting with each other oftener than with outsiders, *kawaad* see people in a wider array of contexts and infer a more holistic view of them than is possible for people in contextually limited gesellschaft identities like "cop," "politician," or "mailman." This familiarity (family-like-ness) makes the behavior of group members predictable and thus forefends the supererogatory stress (risk) and expenditure of energy that forming relationships with outsiders requires (cf. Furedi 2002). Social life is "outlined against the gentle twilight of familiarity and comfort" (Gaitskill 2005:28). Remember that conserving energy for differential reproduction is a driving force for evolution (cf. Dentan 2008b:137–40).

The only group members not "familiar" in this sense were people from neighboring groups who had married in. Semai tend to call such people *maay*, "them," in the sense of "not us." But two or three months' familiarizing coresidence, especially when one spoke the local dialect and ate the local food (and thus depended on the local environment), established one as a band member (cf. the essays by Endicott and Howell, this volume) so that, after a month or two, people treat coresident anthropologists like other band members (e.g., "share" with them, consult them about matters that affect the band as a group, and so on). Communities could include both Semai and Temiar speakers, longhouses and nuclear family houses, and even ethnographers, Chinese and Malays, as equally group members because all were *kawaad*, "neighbors."

The term *kawaad* is cognate with a Malay word for "friend," "follower," or "group member" (Wilkinson 1901, I:518, s.v. *kawan*), itself cognate with other Austronesian words for "kinsman." Social psychologists say that one does not hang around with people as a result of their being one's friends; friendship is the product of hanging around with people. The sentiment of affection therefore tends to follow from familiarity and is thus a connotation, though not a denotation, of that word. The resulting fellowship buttresses the group once the group has formed but does not ultimately cause it. Shared experience as a result of group membership further reinforces fellowship. In similar small-scale enclaved anarchist groups like Alcoholics Anonymous, fellowship can become therapeutic (Dentan 1994; Lechner 2003; Macdonald 2008b). Semai major séances, which involve everyone in the band, focus the attention of the group on a few currently needy people and may thus provide similar therapy and stress reduction (Dentan 2008b:87–112). The feeling involved is far more basic and comfortable, and far less ideological and violent, than Christian love or its cognates (Dentan 2010; cf. Kropotkin [1902] 2006:xv–xvi; Žižek 2010:97–109). Perhaps "an unconditional love for the Neighbor *can* serve as the foundation for a new Order ... an egalitarian social order of solidarity" (Žižek 2010:117), but the fellow feeling/neighborliness of Semai fellowship has no ideological pre-suppositions and is therefore considerably less exclusive. As a result, Semai-land was a refuge for lowlanders, including Khmer colonists fleeing Malay incursions, Chinese looking for easy sex and reliable food, losers in the interminable Malay internecine conflicts (like Hang Tuah, the great Malay culture hero, for a while!), British displaced by the Japanese invasion, and pretty much anybody passing through, although one man told me "only ugly, stupid Malays come and live with us." All they needed to do was hang around long enough to become familiar.

Most east Semai have ties with people in adjacent bands and occasionally visit kinfolk there. This attenuated familiarity makes it possible for *litaaw* to seek unrelated *mnaleeh* there, as they often have to, since east Semai (and Temiar) kindreds, the egocentric categories within which one should not marry, extend indefinitely outward, potentially to encompass almost the entire social universe, although such extension in fact becomes more and more optional and fictive as collateral distance increases (Benjamin, this volume). Long residence away from one's own band generates strong feelings of painful *rniaak* homesickness. In 1962 I wrote a letter for one newlywed *litaaw* to his brother, asking the brother to come and visit the longhouse in which he was living with three dozen other people. "I can't stand it here," he said, "all alone by myself." Unfamiliarity was so emotionally painful that individuals preferred band endogamy even with a distant member of one's kindred (Robarchek 1980:91). (As a result, genetic variation between bands used to be striking; see Fix and Lie-Injo 1975.) Ties with other bands, however, make it possible, when quarrels or homesickness becomes acute, for individuals or groups to move from one band to another, following the fission-fusion model characteristic of egalitarian acephalous bands (Dentan 1992; Fix 1977).

Familiarity with a particular physical environment reduces the amount of time and energy that subsistence requires. Traditionally, a Semai band's territory, the *tei' saka'*, was a small river valley basin. The hilly flanks of the basin increased the "effective distance" between bands. (Effective distance is the amount of time and energy it takes to travel between two spots. Thus, for Semai in the old days, the effective distance between small river delta A and small river delta B depended on whether you were traveling downriver, which you could do by lashing two or three stems of huge *Gigantochloa* bamboo together with rattan and letting the current carry you to your destination, or upriver, which required trekking uphill on foot.). Not needing to "learn the territory" meant that one could be relatively stress free and comfortable where one's band lived. Swiddens required about 0.38 acres per capita, and almost everyone knew where the most valued fruit trees were to be found.

What this analysis suggests is that the relationship between a band and its territory was not in any serious sense proprietary but sentimental. Land and band "belonged" to each other in the sense that the territory was "home" to each member of the band. People felt more comfortable at home than away. *Rniaak*—roughly "nostalgia" or "homesickness"—is a powerful Semai emotion, salient in conversation. Strangers should ask permission before intruding into a band's territory, although no band member had the right to refuse such permission, their relationship with the territory being not proprietary but familiar, in the sense just sketched. Lgòòs, a Temiar *tnataa'* who lived his whole life among east Semai, put it this way.

> This is what we call our *tei' saka'*. Perhaps we don't build a settlement, but we bury our children here. I buried my father in this *tei'*; I buried my grand-child; I buried my *tnee'*. When I die my wife will bury me in this *tei'*. After that, she'll pound rice, give it to the people [in a funeral feast] and go wherever she will. All of us have always been buried here from the beginning of time. When I die, my children will replace me. When they die, my grand-children will replace them. I don't want to live in another place. Next time, if war comes, tell them to let us stay here. So we die here. So what? I don't want always to be moving upstream and downstream. I just want to stay here.
>
> (Quoted in Dentan 1979:93)

Note that children are salient even in talking about relations with the land.

The term *saka'* is cognate with Malay *saka,* often glossed as "property" (Wilkinson 1901, II:367). For traditional Malays *tanah pesaka* was "inherited land that one cannot readily alienate" or property of which one has only the usufruct (260). As Wilkinson suggests, for example, the term need not imply alienability. And *pesaka* include "ancestral traits" (367), like a "tradition" of piracy (260), or sayings, taboos, and beliefs handed down from generation to generation (Abdul Jalil 1961). Thus the term, even among Malays, is a good deal less precise than *property* but simply indicates a long and emotional association: familiarity.

So the Semai band is not a corporation vis-à-vis land. Remember, the Ockhammy principle of parsimony forbids introducing the notion of property if we need not. The term *tei' saka'* is a bit of a red herring. Even in English *one's land* does not connote property. The Woody Guthrie song "This Land Is My Land," for example, refers to a sign that said on one side (differently in various versions) "Private Property" or "No Trespassing" but on the other side "didn't say nothing." The blank side "belongs to you and me."

And that raises the question of property in general. Under these circumstances, ownership was a matter of not only familiarity but also the associated use. If you were actually using something—eating a meal, say— that thing belonged to you. If you weren't using it, it didn't. If someone else wanted to use it, good manners required that person to ask whether you were still using it—a field that had lain fallow for a year or two, say—but if the user had no further use in mind, then the response, as already noted, had to be to allow the petitioner to bring it back into use. Thus the "sharing" for which people like Semai are famous (e.g., Endicott, this volume; Fortier 2001; Lye 2004:13–14) is less a matter of generosity than an acknowledgment that one has no rational claim to more resources than one can use. That is, you don't own in principle what you are not using in fact.

The *kkasih* exchange mentioned earlier, I would argue, has nothing to do with property. Semai talk about their bodies as lacking firm borders. Everyone is surrounded by a cloud of *glamòò',* an aura composed of dandruff, scurf, spiritual fragments, fragrances, and so on. *Glamòò'* accumulates in a person's familiar haunts, for example, in his or her sleeping area. Sleeping in another person's area blends *glamòò,* so that people become spiritually and emotionally close, Semai say. The exchange of blowpipes similarly manifests and buttresses mutual familiarity, intimacy, and friendship in the same way; it is not a gift or act of sharing (for exemplary cases, see Dentan 1979:119, 125; and Howell, this volume).

Although the band rarely functions as an action group, it constitutes a category like the kindred from which one can recruit kinsmen, *kkasih,* and neighbors for particular purposes like building a weir across a major river to catch fish when they migrate up- or downstream when the season changes (not a very common activity). There are occasional meetings of the band as a whole, typically inconclusive, to decide on collective responses to government initiatives. And, if someone is very sick, most *kawaad* attend a community séance (Dentan 2008b:87–113). Séances provide an opportunity for *litaaw* and *mnaleeh* to make assignations, people know. The ceremonies almost always focus on puerperal matters, like bathing midwives and/or neonates, or caring for the afflictions so salient in Semai childbirth that men outnumber women at every level of the demographic pyramid.

The other main band activity is the funeral. In 1962 the Semai infant mortality rate in the first year was two out of three. Dead neonates and still-births get an abbreviated funeral. But even so, the prevalence of puerperal problems meant that a disproportionate number of funerals involved new mothers or "new children." Like other foragers (e.g., Cassandra Complex 2008:33; Guenther 1979), Semai express only vague, idiosyncratic, and mutually contradictory ideas about an afterlife. But they worry that the shadows of dead persons, especially those of neglected or abused children, will be drawn back to their familiar surroundings to haunt and devour the survivors, perhaps as ravening dream demons or tailorbirds plaintively calling "Mommy, Mommy, Mommy" in the bushes. So they break and bury familiar things that would recall the dead (= call the ghost back) in the grave and strew foul-smelling lantana on the path to the grave to counteract the fragrances and *glamòò'* of home that draw even the evil dead back to the safe and familiar. Longing for the love and care that a dead child did not receive in life is what allures its soul-devouring ghost, a quite sharp contrast with Malay ghost beliefs (e.g., Kamarul Baharin and Dellios 2003:79–80).

In short, territoriality, medico-religious activity, and funerals also express the centrality of child care in Semai daily life.

Summary and Conclusions

In a Helpless Baby, the Roots of Our Social Glue
           —Headline of a *New York Times* story by N. Angier

This analysis suggests that east Semai life can be understood as a reflex of the hominine K-reproductive strategy. It does not suggest that Semai are *aware* of how vital begetting children and keeping them safe is for their way of life and its survival. Semai don't talk much about or to children, although children are always around. Perhaps understanding the parts of their lives to which they themselves devote more analytical discourse would require a more societal analysis than this one. But I suspect that, in most places, the most fundamental determinants of human life normally go undiscussed and are often unconscious.

Charles Macdonald (2007:138) suggests that analyses like this one can involve "social institutions, moral values, or inner dispositions." This chapter stresses "inner dispositions," by suggesting that east Semai solidarity in 1962 could be understood as basically evolutionary in origin, with a post hoc filigree of local explanations and rationalizations. There is no need, a priori or a posteriori, to deploy notions of society (including social institutions), property (including sharing), marriage (including endogamy) or values (including essentialist nature or postulated nonobservable ethical principles). The principle of parsimony justifies omitting such discussion, and the primacy of individualized *choosing* in Semai life makes societal-institutional analysis seem out of place.

Although I enjoy cognitive analyses, I suspect that Semai, like most other people I know, use their verbal intelligence more for rationalizing, mystifying, and justifying the actions they pursue for unexamined reasons than for actually deciding on particular courses of action. In egalitarian bands, people agree on a few basic assumptions, supplemented by personal experience, with no authoritative "truth" (Gardner 1967; Guenther 1979; Dentan 1979:93–95). This vague consensus is by definition a "total ideology" (Mannheim [1929] 1954). Among peoples like those to which most ethnographers belong, Mannheim argues, sets of ideas become political weapons and thus constitute "partial ideologies," often with loci (sacred documents, popes, etc.) for authoritative truth. Partial ideologies—organized religions, political beliefs, and so on—may actually influence behavior. But I think total ideology is usually a dependent variable. Semai certainly do not talk about the topics of this essay as if the behavior involved had ethical roots.

Although egalitarian people in 1962 had as long a history as any other people of their time, their social conditions seem to have been fundamentally like those of people millennia ago (see Dentan 2010). When people from other ways of life try to create those egalitarian anarchic polities, they usually see themselves as trying to "get back to" much earlier conditions (Cohn 1970; Dentan 1992, 1994; Lechner 2003). Perhaps they are right. Perhaps these conditions are those that evolution wired people to create and maintain. In that case, we need notions like society (or property) not to discuss egalitarian peoples' lives but only the social aberrations of the last twelve thousand years. Whether these relatively short-lived experiments with inequality, forms of marriage, exclusive property, and coercive hierarchy—agricultural, pastoralist, and industrial capitalist societies—prove viable or not, it is they, not band organization, that require explanation by means of concepts like society, corporation, class, and property. Exposure to these societies may indeed intensify Semai egalitarian anarchy, as I have argued elsewhere (Dentan 1992, 1994, 1997, 2008b).

Note

The Jabatan Hal Ehwal Orang Asli allowed me to conduct the research on which this paper rests. The Ford Foundation sponsored the original research. Daniel Cadzow helped make the writing intelligible. And, obviously, Charles Macdonald nurtured this paper to "maturity."

References

Abdul Jalil bin Haji Noor. 1961. *Pesaka orang tua-tua*. Siri Bahasa, no. 7. Singapura: Al-Ahmadiah Press.

Angier, N. 2009. "In a helpless baby, the roots of our social glue." *New York Times*, March 2.

Banfield, E.C. 1970. *The Unheavenly City*. Boston: Little, Brown.

Barks, C., with J. Moyne, A.J. Arberry, and R. Nicholson, eds. and trans. 1995. *The Essential Rumi*. New York: HarperCollins.

Barth, Fredrik, ed. 1969. *Ethnic Groups and Boundaries: The Social Organization of Cultural Difference*. Oslo: Universitetsforlaget.

Bird-David, Nurit. 1990. "The giving environment." *Current Anthropology* 3:183–96.

Brown, Donald E. 1976. *Principles of Social Structure: Southeast Asia.* Boulder: Westview Press.

Burling, R. 1965. *Hill Farms and Paddy Fields.* Englewood Cliffs, NJ: Prentice Hall.

Cassandra Complex, Dr. P.'s. 2008. "Dwelling-while-letting-be." *Green Anarchy* 25:32–34.

Cohn, N. 1970. *The Pursuit of the Millennium.* Rev. ed. Oxford: Oxford University Press.

Cords, Marina, and Melanie Killen. 1998. "Conflict resolution in human and nonhuman primates." In J. Langer and M. Killen, eds., *Piaget, Evolution, and Development*, 193–218. Princeton, NJ: Lawrence Erlbaum Associates.

Dentan, Robert K. 1965. "Some Senoi Semai dietary restrictions: A study of food behavior in a Malayan hill tribe." PhD diss., Yale University.

———. 1971. "Some Senoi Semai planting techniques." *Economic Botany* 25:136–59.

———. 1975. "If there were no Malays, who would the Semai be? In J. Nagata, ed., *Pluralism in Malaysia: Myth and Reality*, 50–64. Contributions to Asian Studies, no. 7. Leiden: E.J. Brill.

———. 1976a. "Identity and ethnic contact." *Journal of Asian Affairs* 1 (1):79–86.

———. 1976b. "Ethnics and ethics in Southeast Asia." In D.J. Banks, ed., *Changing Identities in Modern Southeast Asia*, 71–81. The Hague: Mouton.

———. 1978. "Notes on childhood in a nonviolent context." In A. Montagu, ed., *Learning Non-Aggression*, 94–143. New York: Oxford University Press.

———. 1979. *The Semai: A Nonviolent People of Malaysia.* Fieldwork ed. New York: Holt, Rinehart and Winston.

———. 1988a. "Ambiguity, synecdoche, and affect in Semai medicine." *Social Science and Medicine* 27:857–77.

———. 1988b. "Lucidity, sex, and horror in Senoi dreamwork. In J.L. Gackenbach and S. LaBerge, eds., *Conscious Mind, Sleeping Brain*, 37–63. New York: Plenum.

———. 1989. "Music Semai played for fun." *Echology* 3:100–119.

———. 1992. "The rise, maintenance, and destruction of peaceable polity." In J. Silverberg and J.P. Gray eds., *Aggression and Peacefulness in Humans and Other Primates*, 214–70. New York: Oxford University Press.

———. 1994. "Surrendered men." In L.E. Sponsel and T. Gregor, eds. *The Anthropology of Peace and Nonviolence*, 69–108. Boulder: Lynne Rienner.

———. 1997. "The persistence of received truth: How the Malaysian ruling class constructs Orang Asli." In Robert Winzeler, ed., *Indigenous Peoples and the State: Politics, Land, and Ethnicity in the Malaysian Peninsula and Borneo.* 98–134. Monographs, no. 46. New Haven: Council on Southeast Asian Studies, Yale University.

———. 1999. "Spotted doves at war." *Asian Folklore Studies* 58 (2):397–434.

———. 2000a. "This is passion and where it goes: Despair and suicide among Semai." *Moussons* 101:31–56.

———. 2000b. "Ceremonies of innocence and the lineaments of ungratified desire." *Bijdragen tot de Taal-, Land- en Volkenkunde* 156:193–232.

———. 2001. "Ambivalence in child training by the Semai of Peninsular Malaysia and other peoples." *Crossroads* 15:31–56.

———. 2003. "Ideas redeem but political memories do run short: Islamicization in Malaysia." *Social Justice: Anthropology, Peace, and Human Rights* 3 (3–4):153–89.

———. 2004. "Cautious, alert, polite, and elusive." In G. Kemp and D.P. Fry, eds., *Keeping the Peace*, 167–84. New York: Routledge.

———. 2006a. "How the androgynous bird god brought agriculture to Semai of West Malaysia: Discipline, hard work, and subordination to the cycle of time." In P. Le Roux and B. Sellato, eds., *Les Messagers Divins*, 295–356. Aix-en-Provence and Marseille: IRASEC; Paris: Editions Seven Orients.

———. 2006b. "Ethnocentrism and *kesombongan* in Semai ethnography." Paper presented at the Research Seminar, Sociology/HSS, Nanyang Technological University, Singapore, March 31.

———. 2008a. "Recent studies on violence: What's in and what's out." *Reviews in Anthropology* 37 (1):1–27.

———. 2008b. *Overwhelming Terror: Love, Fear, Peace, and Violence among Semai of Malaysia.* Lanham, MD.: Rowman and Littlefield.

———. 2010. "Nonkilling social arrangements." In Leslie Sponsel and Joao Evans-Pym, eds., *Nonkilling Societies.* 131–84. Honolulu: Center for Global Nonkilling.

Dentan, Robert K., and Juli Edo. 2008. "Schooling vs. education, hidden vs. overt curricula: Ways of thinking about schools, economic development, and putting the children of the poor to work. *Moussons* 12 (1–2):3–35.

Dentan, Robert K., Kirk Michael Endicott, Alberto G. Gomes, and M. Barry Hooker. 1997. *Malaysia and the Original People: A Case Study of the Impact of Development on Indigenous Peoples*. Boston: Allyn and Bacon.

Dentan, Robert K., A. Williams-Hunt, and Juli Edo. 2010. "They do not like to be confined and … told what to do." In K. Adams and K. Gillogly, eds., *Everyday Life in Southeast Asia*. Bloomington: Indiana University Press.

DiMaggio, Anthony. 2010. "Suburban sprawl and the decline of social capital." http://www.truth-out.org/suburban-sprawl-and-decline-social-capital62465.

Du Bois, W.E.B. [1903] 1979. *The Souls of Black Folk: Essays and Sketches*. New York: Dodd.

Duncan, Christopher R., ed. 2004. *Civilizing the Margins*. Ithaca: Cornell University Press.

Ellen, R.F. 1982. *Environment, Subsistence, and System: The Ecology of Small-Scale Social Formations*. Cambridge and New York: Cambridge University Press.

Endicott, Kirk M. 1979. *Batek Negrito Religion: The World-View and Rituals of a Hunting and Gathering People of Peninsular Malaysia*. Oxford: Clarendon Press.

———. 1983. "The effects of slave raiding on the aborigines of the Malay Peninsula." In A. Reid, ed., *Slavery, Bondage, and Dependency in Southeast Asia*, 216–45. New York: St. Martin's Press.

Endicott, Kirk M., and Karen L. Endicott. 2008. *The Headman Was a Woman: The Gender Egalitarian Batek of Malaysia*. Long Grove, IL: Waveland Press.

Fei Xiaotung. 1980. "Ethnic identification in China." *Social Sciences in China* 1:94–107.

Fix, Alan G. 1977. "The demography of the Semai Senoi." Anthropological Papers of the Museum of Anthropology, no. 62. Ann Arbor: Museum of Anthropology, University of Michigan.

Fix, Alan G., and Luan Eng Lie-Injo. 1975. "Genetic microdifferentiation in the Semai Senoi of Malaysia." *American Journal of Physical Anthropology* 43:47–55.

Fortier, Jana. 2001. "Sharing, hoarding, and theft: Exchange and resistance in forager-farmer relations." *Ethnology* 40 (3):193–212.

Frake, Charles O. 1999. "How to be a 'tribe' for the Subanon." Paper presented at the ARNOVA Meetings, Arlington, VA, December 9.

Fry, Douglas. 2006. *The Human Potential for Peace: An Anthropological Challenge to Assumptions about War and Violence*. New York: Oxford University Press.

Furedi, Frank. 2002. *Culture of Fear: Risk-Taking and the Morality of Low Expectation*. Rev. ed. New York and London: Continuum.

Gaitskill, M. 2005. *Veronica*. New York: Vintage.

Gardner, Peter. 1967. "Symmetric respect and memorate knowledge: The structure and ecology of individualistic culture." *Southwestern Journal of Anthropology* 22:389–415.

Gibson, Thomas. 1985. "The sharing of substance versus the sharing of activity among the Buid." *Man,* new series, 20 (3):391–411.

Guenther, M.G. 1979. "Bushmen religion and the (non)sense of anthropological theory of religion." *Sociologus* 29:102–32.

Hrdy, S.B. 2009. *Mothers and Others: The Evolutionary Origins of Mutual Understanding*. Cambridge: Harvard University Press.

Ingold, Tim. 1999. "On the social relations of the hunter-gatherer band." In R.B. Lee and R. Daly, eds., *The Cambridge Encyclopedia of Hunters and Gatherers*, 399–410. Cambridge: Cambridge University Press.

Insieme, S. 2008. "Connecting to place in the land of the lost: Questions for the nomadic wanderers in all of us." *Green Anarchy* 25:8–11.

Isaac, G. 1978. "The food-sharing behavior of protohuman hominids." *Scientific American* 238 (4):90–108.

Juli Edo, A. Williams-Hunt, and R.K. Dentan. 2009a. "'Surrender,' peacekeeping, and internal colonialism.".

———. 2009b. "'Surrender,' peacekeeping, and internal colonialism." *Bijdragen tot de Taal-, Land- en Volkenkunde* 165 (2–3):216–41. Abridged version of 2009a.Kamarul Baharin, A. Kasim, and P.V. Dellios. 2003. *Katalog Pameran Terokai Hantu*. Kuala Lumpur: Jabatan Muzium dan Antikuiti Malaysia.

Kaplan, R. 1999. *The Nothing That Is: A Natural History of Zero*. Oxford: Oxford University Press.

Kottak, C.P. 2009. *Anthropology*. 13th ed. New York: McGraw-Hill.

Kropotkin, Peter. [1902] 2006. *Mutual Aid: A Factor of Evolution*. Mineola, NY: Dover.

Lechner, Thomas. 2003. "Surrender without subordination: Peace and equality in Alcoholics Anonymous." PhD diss., Department of Anthropology, State University of New York at Buffalo. .

Lewis, Oscar. 1966. "The culture of poverty." *Scientific American* 215:19–25.

Lim Chan Ing. 2010. "The sociocultural significance of Semaq Beri food classification." MA thesis, Department of Anthropology, Universiti Malaya, Kuala Lumpur.

Lounsbury, Floyd. G. 1964. "A formal account of the Crow- and Omaha-type kinship terminologies." In W.H. Goodenough, ed., *Explorations in Cultural Anthropology*, 351–93. New York: McGraw-Hill.

Luering, H.L.E. 1901. "The Sakai dialect of Ulu Kampar, Perak." *Journal of the Straits Branch of the Royal Asiatic Society* 35:91–10.

Luke, B. 1988. "Violent love: Hunting, heterosexuality, and the erotics of men's predation." *Feminist Studies* 2 (3):627–53.

Lye Tuck-Po. 2004. *Changing Pathways: Forest Degradation and the Batek of Pahang, Malaysia*. Lanham, MD.: Rowman and Littlefield.

———. 2008. "Being forest peoples." *Moussons* 12 (1–2):35–48.

Macdonald, Charles J.-H. 1977. *Une Société Simple: Parenté et Résidence chez les Palawan*. Mémoire de l'Institut d'Ethnologie, M15. Paris: Institut d'Ethnologie, Museum National d'Histoire Naturelle.

———. 2007. *Uncultural Behavior*. Honolulu: University of Hawai'i Press.

———. 2008a. "Order against harmony: Are humans always social?" *Suomen Antropologi: Journal of the Finnish Anthropological Society* 33 (2):5–21.

———. 2008b. "Joyous, equal, and free." Paper presented at the Anthropology Club, State University of New York at Buffalo. https://sites.google.com/site/charlesjhmacdonaldssite.

———. 2009. *The Anthropology of Anarchy*. Occasional Papers from the School of Social Science, no. 35. Princeton, New Jersey: Institute for Advanced Study.

———. 2010. "Can anarchism be a critical point in the new anthropological imagination?" Paper presented at the annual meeting of the European Association of Social Anthropologists, Maynooth, August.

Maine, Sir H.J.S. 1861. *Ancient Law*. London: Murray.

Mannheim, Karl. [1929] 1954. *Ideology und Utopia: An Introduction to the Sociology of Knowledge*. Trans. L. Wirth and E. Shils. New York: Harcourt Brace.

Meillasoux, Claude. 1973. "On the mode of production of the hunting band." In P. Alexandre, ed., *French Perspectives in African Studies*, 187–203. London: Oxford University Press.

———. 1981. *Maidens, Meal, and Money: Capitalism and the Domestic Community*. Cambridge: Cambridge University Press.

Miéville, C. 2003. *Perdido Street Station*. New York: Random House.

Murdock, George Peter. 1949. *Social Structure*. New York: Macmillan.

————. 1981. *Atlas of World Cultures*. Pittsburgh: University of Pittsburgh Press.

Nicholas, Colin. 1994. "Pathway to dependence: Commodity relations and the dissolution of Semai society." Monash Papers on Southeast Asia, no. 33. Clayton, Vic., Australia: Centre of Southeast Asian Studies, Monash University.

————. 2000. *The Orang Asli and the Contest for Resources: Indigenous Politics, Development, and Identity in Peninsular Malaysia*, IWGIA Documents, no. 95. Copenhagen: International Work Group for Indigenous Affairs.

Nobuta, Toshihiro. 2008. *Living on the Periphery*. Kyoto: Kyoto University Press.

Nowak, B. 1987. "Marriage and household." PhD diss., State University of New York at Buffalo.

Otterbein, Keith. 2004. *How War Began*. College Station: Texas A&M University Press.

Peterson, C., S.F. Maier, and M.E.P. Seligman. 1993. *Learned Helplessness*. Oxford: Oxford University Press.

Qiu Pu. 1983. *The Oroqens: China's Nomadic Hunters*. Trans. Wang Huimin. Beijing: Foreign Languages Press.

Robarchek, Carole. 1980. "Cognatic kinship and territoriality among the Semai-Senoi." *Federated Museums Journal* 25:89–102.

Robarchek, Clayton A. 1979. "Learning to fear: A case study of emotional conditioning." *American Ethnologist* 6 (3):555–67.

————. 1986. "Helplessness, fearfulness, and peacefulness." *Anthropological Quarterly* 59 (4):177–83.

Rousseau, Jérôme. 1990. *Central Borneo: Ethnic Identity and Social Life in a Stratified Society*. Oxford: Clarendon Press.

————. 2006. *Rethinking Social Evolution: The Perspective from Middle-Range Societies*. Montreal: McGill-Queens University Press.

Saathoff, G.B. 1996. "Kuwait's children: Identity in the shadow of the storm." *Mind and Human Interaction* 7 (4):181–91.

Sather, Clifford. 2004. "Keeping the peace in an island world." In G. Kemp and D.P. Fry, eds., *Keeping the Peace*, 123–48. New York: Routledge.

Scott, James. 2009. "The art of not being governed: Hill peoples and valley kingdoms in Mainland Southeast Asia." Golay Memorial Lecture, Cornell University, April 23.

Service, Elman. R. 1962. *Primitive Social Organization*. New York: Random House.

————. 1966. *The Hunters*. Englewood Cliffs, New Jersey: Prentice-Hall.

Stephens, John L. 1843. *Incidents of Travel in Yucatan*. 2 vols. New York: Harper.

Tocqueville, Alexis de. [1835] 2002. *Democracy in America*, 2 vols. New York: Bantam Dell.

Wilkinson, Richard. J. 1901. *A Malay-English Dictionary*. 2 vols. Singapore: Kelly and Walsh.

Williams-Hunt, A.P. 1995. "Land conflicts: Orang Asli ancestral laws and state policies." In Razha Rashid, ed., *Indigenous Minorities of Peninsular Malaysia: Selected Issues and Ethnographies*, 36–47. Kuala Lumpur: Intersocietal and Scientific Sdn. Bhd.

————. 2007. "Semai customary land law." Paper presented at the annual meeting of the American Anthropological Association, Washington, DC, November 28.

Williams-Hunt, Peter D.R. 1952. *An Introduction to the Malayan Aborigines*. Kuala Lumpur: Government Printing Office.

Woodburn, James. 1980. "African hunter-gatherer social organization." In T. Ingold, D. Riches, and J. Woodburn, eds., *Hunters and Gatherers*. Vol. 1: *History, Evolution, and Social Change*, 31–64. Oxford: Berg.

————. 1988. "African hunter-gatherer social organization: Is it best understood as a product of encapsulation?" In T. Ingold, D. Riches, and J. Woodburn, eds., *Hunters and Gatherers*. Vol. 1: *History, Evolution, and Social Change*, 43–64. Oxford: Berg.

Žižek, Slavoj. 2010. *Living in the End Times*. London and New York: Verso.

5

Kinship and Fellowship among the Palawan

CHARLES MACDONALD

RELATEDNESS, AMONG THE PALAWAN people who are the focus of this contribution, must be accounted for using various approaches. One is kinship. Kinship and kinship-related matters have spurred a spate of publications in recent years (see, among others, Carsten 2000; Franklin and McKinnon 2001; Godelier 2004; and Dziebel 2007) and have thus reopened and renewed questions that once were of central concern to anthropologists. Some of these questions, like kin classification and kin recognition, the conjugal family and parenthood, are relevant to communities examined in this volume. Looking at the ethnographic literature describing these communities, one is easily convinced that, *pace* Jérôme Rousseau (1990), kinship matters a lot. Ethnographers, more or less undeterred by the vagaries of theoretical fashions, kept paying attention to kinship terminologies, to the values and types of behavior attached to kin relations, to groups or aggregates based on or defined in kinship terms, and to kinship institutions like marriage, divorce, and adoption. Glancing at the ethnographic literature, the reader is easily convinced that kinship matters to the people concerned. It matters a lot in most cases but in different ways. It operates at different levels and through various channels. I will thus offer in the coming pages two different kinship-based models, one for the dynamics of aggregation in residential sets, the other for basic behavioral norms.

Kinship, however, does not explain everything, and no matter how pervasive the idiom of kinship, with its many attention-catching metaphors (see Carsten 1995), other factors are at play. Observation shows that in the cases examined below, determining considerations in community building and social activities are not solely based on kin relations. Residential and marital choices are dependent on personal preferences; criteria of engagement belong to a larger moral universe than one solely defined in kinship terms.

Another important topic that must be attended to is cooperation. Humans need to cooperate for economic reasons but also for cultural, cognitive, and psychological reasons. Each sector of activity has its specific kind of cooperative activity. It is necessary to determine to what extent a need for cooperation in each sector of activity is responsible for creating and maintaining social ties, as well as the extent to which these various forms of joint activities influence and shape sociality.

In this presentation two related concepts are found useful to account for the final aggregative outcome of kin-based and non-kin-based choices and for modes of cooperative activities. One is the concept of weak tie, and the other is that of fellowship, two concepts that will be defined in due course below.

Palawan Kinship

Among the Palawan people, an indigenous cultural community inhabiting the southern section of Palawan Island in the Philippines, kinship is very important, but there is one thing it does not do, that is, create corporate groups. Since, in any given residential area, everybody is located somewhere in the overlapping kinship networks of more or less everybody else (kinship tends to be inclusive in Benjamin's sense, this volume), whenever two or three people get together they generally form a group of kinsmen, not a kinship group: a group of fellows, companions, or neighbors who happen to have kin ties. Some kinship links, however, are conducive to the formation of small collective entities in a way I have described in previous publications (Macdonald 1977, 2007). The clusters created by these links are central to the formation of local groups or "neighborhoods." Cognatic kinship does not automatically—as with automatic assignment of group membership at birth in unilineal descent systems—create fixed collective entities with clear boundaries. It always keeps a number of options open, and the final choice is based on factors that may be purely personal, not normatively and narrowly premised on kinship principles alone. Palawan kinship, however, fosters the emergence and formation of a certain limited kind of aggregate —what I have called the "residential atom" or "core group" (see below). It does something else as well: it provides a formal grid of status ascription. These functions are distinct and should be treated separately, but they operate in association. Kin classes are defined toward ego with unequal deference values. These values in turn play an important role in structuring and cementing a minimal form of residential and economic association.

1. Kinship as a Substantive Device for Group Assignment

I shall examine two different and complementary aspects of the susbstantive properties of kinship: the way they create core groups and the way these core groups or nuclei combine into larger sets.

Core Groups

After a year of fieldwork in the highlands of southern Palawan Island, I was given by my Palawan collaborator and tutor in things Palawan, M. Jose Rilla, the key that unlocked the organization of the local community and made sense of the spatial arrangement of people and families in small local groups, which are the locus of interaction, activities, and community life in every major aspect of its operation. This key is the concept of *pinemikitan,* from the root *pikit,* which, interestingly enough, means "glue." The *pinemikitan* is the one who one "adheres to," "follows," "stays near to," or "sticks to"; typically, the *pinemikitan* is the father-in-law, and those who follow him—those "stuck to him"—are his sons-in-law. Uxorilocality is the rule, at least in the first few years, during which a couple gets established and raises its first two or three children. The core of this little collection of glued individuals is the predominantly female sibling group. I call it a residential atom. It looks like figure 5.1.

This particular arrangement has important effects on the internal life of this core nucleus, or residential atom of kinship. The moral authority of the senior in-law, *pinemikitan,* to whom the junior in-marrying in-laws must defer, is what holds things together. The economic aspect of this arrangement is the circulation and distribution of food types, of which there are basically three.

1. Rice, the preferred food type: scarce, individually owned within the domestic family

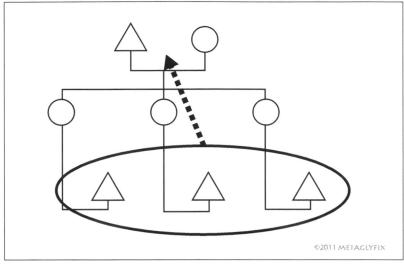

©2011 METAGLYFIX

Figure 5.1 The Palawan core kinship group.

2. Vegetables, particularly tubers like cassava and yams: abundant, collectively owned, and distributed within the sibling group

3. Meat (game and fishes): scarce, shared within the core residential group, not individually owned (see Macdonald 2007:54)

The most essential food type—the one on which survival is conditional —type 2, is shared and circulated within the female sibling groups (and by extension their respective domestic families). Type 3 food, very much sought after but rare, is procured usually through activities of men who, as dutiful sons-in-law, bring their catch to the father-in-law, who then apportions (shares) it among all families in and beyond the local residential nucleus. Rice (type 1 food) is stored in granaries owned by individual families and is kept in these inviolate sanctuaries.[1] In sum, then, three major categories of food match three fundamental categories of ownership and three spheres of distribution. The internal structure of this atom of kinship and residence is thus multifunctional and provides a blueprint for basic day-to-day, face-to-face interpersonal relations, as well as for crucial economic transactions.

Local Groups (Neighborhoods)

Settlements or local groups, "neighborhoods" (*rurungan, senkerurungan*) as the Palawan call them, are usually comprised of a number of such "atoms" or core groups, two to five, or more in certain areas.

Figures 5.2–5.4 illustrate an actual instance of how a core group (consisting of the family of Tuking, the leading elder, that of his son, and that of his grandson-in-law) maintained itself in a central position over thirteen years in an otherwise changed group composition.

Decisions—usually made by the senior in-law, *pinemikitan*—in the choice of residence are open to a great many personal options. As land was neither scarce nor privately owned, one could easily secure the agreement of another neighborhood for the right to cultivate a piece of land in the vicinity—or one just had to walk one more hour to go to one's field. Even within the residential atom or nucleus, there was also a certain amount of possible choices as the senior in-law, or guardian of the married women, could be chosen from among an array of real or classificatory uncles and aunts, grandfathers and grandmothers. As long as the relation was not too distant (second degree and more) and the guardian was deemed to be a responsible senior person related to the bride's mother or father, negotiation

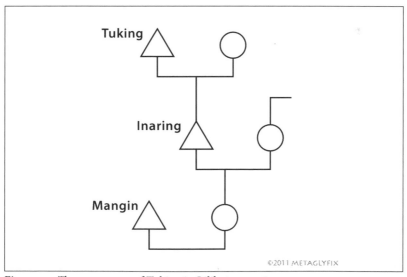

Figure 5.2 The core group of Tuking in Lilibuten, 1976.

was possible and viri- or neolocal options were acceptable. However, strict uxorilocality was a strong preference, and tensions resulted from a reluctance to abide by it.

The Palawan neighborhoods are simple aggregates. They are not formed according to the preceding rule of *pinemikitan* but rather around multiple choices made by individuals and domestic families. Among these choices is a preference to live near someone who knows how to adjudicate disputes and settle quarrels, a "pacifier" or arbiter, expert in speaking the language of customary law, *adat*, adept at spinning the yarn of judicial matters, restoring peace, and healing the community. Healing is another very much sought after capacity, and people also congregate around such experts. At times the healer of bodies (*memimiriq*), the ritual specialist (*belyan*), and

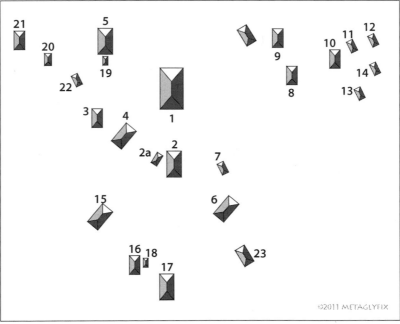

Figure 5.3 The neighborhood of Lilibuten, 1989. 1 = Tuking, 2 = Ulpin, 2a = Kilsu (*pupuq*), 3 = Intin, 4 = Ubinu, 5 = Utun, 6 = Limpungan, 7 = Dendi, 8 = Rusente, 9 = Alisa, 10 = Rupinu, 11 = Inaring, 12 = Simpung(an), 13 = Kering, 14 = Pirmin, 15 = Mangin, 16 = Turing, 17 = Umaring, 18 = *pupuq*, 19 = *pupuq*, 20 = Buntaliq, 21 = Tutuj, 22= Miling, 23 = Perdisju

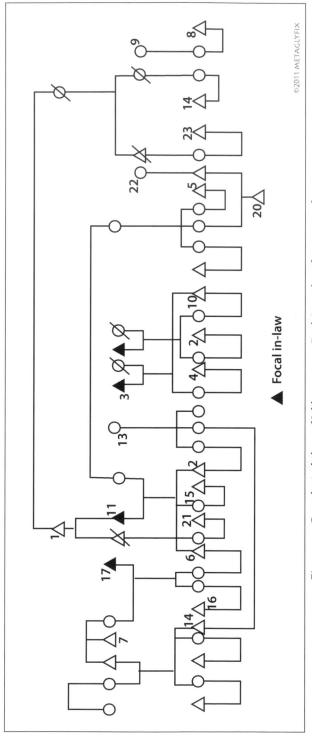

▲ Focal in-law

Figure 5.4 Genealogical chart of Lilibuten, 1989. For house identification, see figure 5.3.

the healer of communal peace (*memimitsara*) are one and the same person. In such a felicitous case the group that aggregates around him tends to be bigger and more permanent. When people disagree too much with their neighbors; find themselves unhappy with the general ambiance of the group; change their minds about their choice of residential area; want to explore other little valleys better provided with fish or sago palms, closer to good hunting, nearer a market, or closer to an orchard or coconut grove they own; want to associate with other members of their kinship networks; or are dissatisfied for any other reason, they move out. I do not suppose that Palawans are more finicky or choosy than Parisians or New Yorkers; they tend to contend with their circumstances as long as possible but are nevertheless on the lookout for better opportunities, a change of environment, or more congenial neighbors. Also, as practitioners of shifting agriculture, they stay in somewhat isolated field huts near their swiddens for a good part of the year, thus alleviating the strain incurred in small and stuffy communities rife with gossip.

In the long run, as domestic units grow and parents become older, younger in-laws regain a certain autonomy vis-à-vis their senior in-laws and in their turn become the focus of new kin-residential nuclei. This happens when the daughters marry and bring in their spouses. Having married uxorilocally, a man often goes back to his birthplace when his daughters or nieces come of age and he and his wife become new centers for core residential units.

2. Kinship as a Formal Grid of Status Assignment

Kinship is used also as a formal grid for a definition of interpersonal relationships. This is best observed when kinship is employed as an address system. To that extent it defines dyadic relationships in the simplest and most elementary way as being symmetrical or asymmetrical. In the language of hierarchy one would be subordinate, superordinate, or equal. In behavioral terms that are more adequate to the Palawan situation, one is more deferent, less deferent, or just deferent. It is best, perhaps, to use the metaphor of "valence" as defined in chemistry. Each relation (or term) combines with a different number of potential others and does it with a different combining power. Seen in this perspective, kinship provides a grid of interpersonal status ascription and can be used in different circumstances and with different valences attached to it. Affinal relations (with close in-laws) are restricted to a close range of in-laws while consanguinity is used to weigh dyadic relations in a larger field of interaction measured by collateral distance.

Whether affinaly or consanguinealy related, nobody is mathematically equal to another. Seniority in the same or adjacent generations and affinity (whether spouse's consanguine or consanguine's spouse) give the relationship its factor of asymmetry.[2] Collateral distance adds a factor of graded symmetry (the more distant the more equal). In other words, asymmetry is asymptotically reduced to zero as one moves farther and farther away. Strangers only can be completely equal.

These formal rules do apply—let us note this very carefully again—to dyadic relations. They qualify dyadic ties but do not result in a vertical system of ranks. We are facing a situation here in which generalized equality is a paradoxical outcome of a network of dyadic asymmetrical ties.[3] The reason for this lies in another formal property of the kinship system. This property is its nontransitivity. The formula *if* A > B *and* B > C, *then* A > C is *not* true because collateral distance tends to asymptotically reduce asymmetry to zero; in other words, the more distant the more equal. Let us say that A is a superior in-law to B because A is B's spouse's father or uncle. Let us say B is in the same position vis-à-vis C (C is the son-in-law of B). So A > B and B > C. But A and C are unrelated, and therefore no asymmetry obtains between them. It is noteworthy that this situation is exactly the opposite of what avails in unilineal descent systems based on a tree paradigm with transitivity as a defining function of the system.

The formal properties of kinship terminologies to be universal codifiers of relatedness explain why, in many different kinship systems, kin terms are used as general address terms. It is thus correct to gloss the kin term *maman*, "uncle," as "Mister" or "Sir" and *minan*, "aunt," as "Mrs." or "Madam."[4]

Weak Ties and the Autonomous Subject

We have seen that Palawan collective organization rests on a formal grid of status, which enables people to evaluate the nature and degree of their interrelatedness. It is also premised on substantive rules of membership in functional and residential groups while leaving a lot of space for individual freedom of choice in selecting partners. Groups, especially the maximal residential units or "neighborhoods," are best described as impermanent aggregates not endowed with transcendence (they do not survive their members and are not seen as embodying a collective personality).

As in neighboring cultures (see the essays by Dentan, Gibson, and Howell in this volume), personal autonomy is a given, something that is valued and fostered and most conspicuous in the way parents treat children (see Dentan 2008). Autonomy, however, is a tricky question, and when defining it one ends up meeting intractable logical and philosophical difficulties (see the discussion in Gardner 1991). I therefore choose to limit my discussion to the notion of weak and strong ties and to speak of autonomy and individual freedom in terms of those ties.

Granovetter's contribution (1973, 1983) has been justly recognized as seminal and immensely useful (e.g., Ikegami 2005) by showing that essential processes in human collective life happen through the agency not of strong ties (like friendship) but of weak ties (like simple acquaintance) because weak ties cross barriers of small, tightly knit groups and carry information, as well as other wanted or unwanted items (like diseases), in much wider circles. Maryansky, a paleoanthropologist, and Turner, a sociologist, have also fruitfully used the concept of weak ties to help explain an important aspect of early humanoid sociality, the fact that, unlike Cercopithecinaes, the first ancestors of Homo sapiens, learned to be individually autonomous and freed themselves of strong ties binding them to small, tightly knit groups (Maryanski and Turner 1992; Maryanski 1994). This allowed them not only to disassociate themselves from conspecifics but to reassociate themselves with them at will. It also made macrogroups possible. A weak tie, in other words, is not only a tie that is not strong (and thus disposable); it is a tie that is always available (or, rather, reusable). It is a transferable tie. Weak ties may be a fundamental characteristic of human gregariousness. People passionately want the company of others, but at times they want with an equal passion to terminate it. In usual circumstances they just want to keep connections alive but at low voltage, with the option of activating them when necessary or terminating them when they prove detrimental to their interests. I therefore use the concept of the weak tie in a more restricted sense than Granovetter's to mean a tie that can be severed or terminated at will by either party, as opposed to a strong tie, which cannot. In this restricted meaning of the word, citizenship is a strong tie because it cannot be terminated unless a third party (the state) gives permission;

friendship is a weak tie because it can be terminated at will by one of the parties only.

Palawan organization, and I suppose that of the Buid, Chewong, Semai, and many others, tends to use weak ties, not strong ties, in order to create aggregates bigger than the domestic family. One could object that strong ties exist, since they exist within the Palawan domestic family: one cannot ever deny a relationship to one's parents. A mother will always be a mother. This statement, however, is not true in all respects. Palawan and Semai people share with North American Indians and Inuits a belief in the autonomous agency of very small children, including infants. Actually the Inuit people (Saladin d'Anglure 1986) and some Indian cultures like the Mohave (Devereux 1961) perceive of agency and autonomy in unborn babies.[5] Against this ideological backdrop one understands better why Palawan people may consider a baby's repeated illnesses as expressing a rejection of the baby's parents. New parents are then selected and will become the baby's true parents. The saying that one does not choose one's parents is not true in this case. The fact that a mother-child tie can be denied is proof that even the strongest possible kinship tie (the only one, with same mother sibling, predicated on a tangible biological reality) can be culturally contingent. Another widespread institution in this culture area that points to a similar idea is adoption. The notion that a strong tie (mother-child) can be *transferred* is very much like saying that the tie is weak in the sense defined above. This, let us note, is not only compatible but congenial with the importance of babies as a social glue as argued by Dentan (this volume).

There is a need to pause briefly at this point. Paradoxically, I have strived so far to highlight factors and dimensions that tend to reduce solidarity rather than promote it. If ties are weak, individual agents completely autonomous, choices purely personal, and kinship nothing but a formal cognitive construct, then what compels people to stay together and cooperate? Rather than explaining solidarity—as I was supposed to do—I have undermined it. To make matters worse I have contended that relations between any two persons tend to have a degree of asymmetry, thus precluding a state of equality among all. I have then to look at the other side of the picture. More generally speaking, one has to face anarchy and egalitarianism as strange creatures. After all, what better social glue than obedience? What better cohesive structure than hierarchy?

Cooperation

Apart from the atom or core kinship-residential unit, which might be considered a microsociety in the sense of having a "structure," I consider that Palawan people have no "social" organization (see Macdonald 2008a, 2008b). They do, however, cooperate. But why? If we look at the different reasons that cause Palawan people to cooperate or induce a desire to cooperate in a circle beyond the domestic unit, I can see three areas where cooperation is either useful or necessary.

1. Utilitarian and Economic Reasons

As horticulturalists, foragers, hunters, and occasional fishermen, Palawan people do not depend on a whole lot of cooperation. For the time being I will put aside the question of sharing (see Macdonald 2008b), which is one of the main forms of cooperation and one that is most consonant with an egalitarian and gregarious ethos, as Howell reminds us (this volume).

Cooperation in agriculture is profitable at three stages: (1) cutting a new field in primary forest—with the special requirement of felling large trees with a workforce of several adult males, (2) planting rice, and (3) harvesting.[6] Cooperative parties in the first and third instances are small in size but more permanent (two families will decide to build field huts side by side and cooperate all year long or a few individuals will help in the harvest). In the second instance work parties are large (the entire population of the settlement will get together) but last for only one day at a time. Single families can actually perform all tasks, although it is more difficult in the first instance and less fun in the second: planting is followed by a communal meal and is performed in highly festive spirits. During these occasions boys and girls, men and women, engage in a mock battle and smear each other with mud and charcoal.

Hunting is mostly a solitary pursuit, although a couple of hunters with their dogs might decide to participate in a joint hunting party occasionally. Stunning fishes with the root of the *tuba* vine (*Derris elliptica*) in the pool of a stream, or on the reef at low tide, is done collectively Fishing expeditions on the reef, and on the part of the beach that is left bare at low tide, once a month usually involve groups of several families, but not always.

Small trade implies markets and marketplaces, and a certain amount of cooperation or at least a collective agreement is necessary, but traders make their trips and manage their little stores individually and markets are actually "owned" by single individuals. A market is where cockfighting and gambling take place, and where people meet and socialize.

It would require a whole article to list all the activities that engage people to act cooperatively at some stage or other. People exchange services and goods in various ways and expect help from neighbors and kin in times of crisis. Opportunities or needs for cooperation are numerous and make it a useful if not necessary institution. My point, however, is that cooperation requiring a large workforce is needed to a very limited extent as far as basic procurement activities are concerned. You can fish, hunt, gather wild plants, and cultivate your cassava and other crops without help. The basic husband-wife team is sufficient. Cooperation is not a survival requirement as far as these activities are concerned.

2. *Relational Reasons*

As noted above, two major activities, planting rice and going to market, are more fun than hard labor or at least involve as much play as work. There is another area where cooperation is necessary, permanent, and depends on extensive participation: traditional justice or *adat* law. The implementation of it requires public hearings with as many people as possible from the same or different local groups. Legal processes and litigations involve many discussions between many different parties and require the attendance of a large public without which the judge's decisions are void and without validity. *Adat* law and *bitsara* (litigation, public negotiations) are essential to Palawan culture and collective life. They combine politics, law, and entertainment and are framed in an ethos of peace and nonconfrontational interpersonal relations. Because of their frequent instantiation, one could say that the Palawan people engage in permanent, communitywide, legal cooperation.

The same kind and amount of cooperation is required in marriage transactions, not only because of the amount of the brideprice—which is paid by the groom's relatives—but because of the time and public attendance it requires as one of the main events in the life cycle of individuals and as a ritual event (Macdonald 1972, 1974). Weddings (*bulun, tinahag*) are probably imported cultural artifacts of Malay-Islamic origin, and their performance in contact areas show clear Islamic influences. They are important social rituals in any case; the establishment of a new couple and the crucial decision as to its location in the uxorilocally formed core group is of prime importance to the life of the community. Its performance includes ritual elements and a lengthy discussion, *bitsara*, with playful and entertaining, and sometimes downright comic, aspects (Macdonald 1972).

3. Ideological and Ritual Reasons

The domain of activity that mobilizes the biggest crowds and sets up the most important communitywide forms of cooperation is ritual. Several large ceremonies of the *tambilew* type (Macdonald 1977), *panggaw* type (Macdonald 1997, 2007), and *sinsin* type (Macdonald 1990) require the cooperation of several families in preparation of a feast during which large amounts of rice wine and food are consumed and involve much work for the construction or repair of a large house where the ceremony will take place and guests accommodated. Many smaller ritual events may also lead to cooperative action. In one coastal community where I did long field studies, Punang, ritual activities are more frequent and intense than elsewhere. I was struck there by the spontaneous cooperative endeavors of the people whose dynamic associative life seemed to rest on their readiness to engage in all sorts of "invented" ritual events, mostly ceremonies based on revelations received in dreams by self-appointed ritual leaders. These ceremonies, it must be noted, included a liturgy with music and poetry and were actually artistic performances. Choreographies and chants were performed by a group of families whose members were enlisted as choir members and ballet dancers (Macdonald 1984).

In the Kulbi-Kenipaan river valleys the *panggaw* ceremony is the only event that endows the concept of regional area with a measure of concrete reality. People from both valleys flock to the place where the earth is cleansed in a ritual performed annually or biannually (Macdonald 1997). It was there also that I could witness the rather exceptional emergence of a central figure of authority over an entire regional area.

I therefore agree with Howell's contention (this volume) that a sense of belonging from which autonomous individuals draw an inspiration to act together can derive from ideological concepts related to the cosmic order (as the Palawan rituals in Punang so clearly exemplify) wherein the general cooperation of all humans, both the seen and the unseen, is called for.[7]

I would like to conclude this very brief discussion on cooperation with three remarks. The first is that, inasmuch humans are gregarious, they must be cooperative. The simplest form of linguistic interaction is a cooperative endeavor. Rules of conversation need to be followed, and a common language must be learned. From the most conspicuous forms of activities engaging large parties to minimal and sporadic interactions, cooperation is present in one form or another. The need for cooperation is a given. However, and this is my second remark, it need not assume a hierarchical structure, as in military activities, which the peoples discussed in these pages reject. Hierarchical cooperation, or what sociologists call rational hierarchy, can cause the whole social body to adopt such an organizational pattern. Of course Semai, Buid, and Palawan alike will not engage in warfare, and the reason for this is, I hypothesize, that they would have to adopt the hierarchical style of social life they resist. My third and final remark is paradoxically that cooperation is not needed primarily in materially useful activities (like food procurement, agricultural tasks, hunting, etc.) but in the pursuit of cultural, ritual, ideological, religious, and artistic goals. Culture is the glue there: people cohere and act together with a deep sense of belonging and solidarity when their spirits are united. Music rather than work is the metaphor of their collective life.

Fellowship

In this last section, I need to reassess my general argument. My central concern is the conspicuous absence of groups endowed with what the French call *personne morale*, which is an explicit gloss for the notion of corporateness: "a group that is like a person." I submit that this notion, so totally central to our understanding of "society" (whether as ethnic, national, professional, religious, business, financial, or domestic), is mostly absent among the communities we are studying in this volume, in spite of occasional and, I may add, questionable occurrences.[8] What takes the place of corporate groups as central constructs is a form of fellowship, similar to the "companionship" suggested by Gibson (1986), or "familiarity," suggested by Dentan (this volume). It refers to an aggregate, from an informal gathering of people having an interest or goal in common to a more formally structured group. The word *fellowship*, better than *companionship*, which refers to a disposition rather than a group, points to an impermanent and open aggregate, which can change and morph into a harder and more stable, more closed entity. Workers unions or Oxonian colleges were fellowships, bands of equals who strived for a common goal. A college today, of course, does not look very much like its ancestor, an open monastic hall, and unions are political and economic machines with powerful leaders. Over time a fellowship can transform itself from a loose open group to a closed, hierarchical, corporate group.

The Palawan suggest a case in which, instead of a society, we have a large and loose fellowship, or, rather, several overlapping fellowships. What makes these fellowships cohere, the essence of their solidarity, consists of three different processes. The first is the accumulation of weak ties. The second is the working of asymmetrical ties not resulting in an overarching hierarchy of ranks. The third belongs to an ethical and normative framework of values and deeply internalized norms.

While the invention of strong ties is, I suppose, historically determined, its heyday just preceding the birth of empires, when persons of rank and renown were followed in the grave by a retinue of slaves, companions, and spouses (see Testart 2004), weak ties that can be terminated at will by either party were and still are the rule. The strength of a relationship conducive to solidarity as a mutual obligation is thus an accumulation of weak ties, so that the relationship is like a hank or skein of fine strands. In other essays I have tried to reflect on what these ties were, how they originated; I have suggested the notion of "conditions of felicity" (Macdonald 2008), which refers to a situation obtained when interaction is desirable to all parties involved. This situation is what lies at the heart of gregariousness: a sense of belonging, happy and serene equality, safety, and balanced and somewhat uncommitted relationships to other persons. Anthropologists have used words like *grace, intimacy, immediacy, harmony,* and so on. Although a Durkheimian sociology tends to reject these notions as too psychological, I do believe they are of the essence in the kind of sociality or gregariousness that I am discussing here. Sharing of food (Carsten 1995); sharing of healing words (as in Alcoholics Anonymous [see Lechner 2003]); coresonance in the form of laughter and humor (see Macdonald 2008); or participation in religious (Amish, Hutterites), aesthetic (Japanese tea ceremony [see Ikegami 2005]), festive (medieval carnivals [see Bahktin 1970]), or communal activities (Rainbow Family [see Niman 1997]) create not only dyadic but multiple horizontal links (see Ikegami 2005) and cause people to experience feelings of shared identity or, at a minimum, enable them to appreciate each other's company. They create a collective mental state on which maintenance of community life is conditional (Macdonald 2008a, 200b).

The other main characteristic of dyadic links in Palawan fellowships is asymmetry (see above). There are essentially two kinds of asymmetric relations: age and seniority, on the one hand; and affinity (relation through marriage) on the other. This may not be a general situation, and cognatic kinship systems differ in the way they distinguish or merge consanguineal and affinal kin.[9] As a formal grid of status, Palawan kinship prevents the spread of asymmetrical relations in a treelike (taxonomic) fashion, so that strong asymmetrical ties exist for ego with a very limited number of partners who are in his immediate collateral circle. The weak asymmetry prevailing between distant collateral kin and strangers is comparable to the formal and respectful manners that people in Europe or America adopt with adult strangers. The use of asymmetrical ties is a wise policy, and a limited formal inequality is an expedient device with which to regulate interpersonal relations. The art of limiting its application and parsimonious use must have been honed by many generations of gregarious egalitarianists.

Norms of conduct, moral values, rules, and normative propositions may actually be nothing but the conditions on which a gregarious and anarchic way of life is premised. The most important and most often quoted vernacular notion regarding interpersonal relations is that of *ingasiq*, which may be translated as "giving disposition, empathy, sympathy, compassion, pity." *Ingasiq* is close in meaning to "sharing" (*beginen, bagibagi*) in the sense of partaking of one's resources (even in the stricter sense given to the latter term as a nonreciprocal transaction [see Woodburn 1998, Macdonald 2008]). *Ingasiq* is thus eminently an expression of solidarity (see Kaskija, this volume, for Punan *mai'*). During my last stay in the highlands of southern Palawan, somebody told me, "If I have food and others [neighbors, family] don't, if I live and they die, what is the point of it? All must survive." The idea that those who live together must share is so engrained in the conscience and habits of the people that whenever I gave a cup of coffee to someone during a gathering it was distributed among the entire assembly, each person receiving a few drops. Neighbors and fellows are like companions (etymologically "bread mates") and comrades (etymologically "roommates"). Following Gibson's apt statement (1985), sharing of space, activity, and food is thus one of the most important founding principles of this form of collective life.

There is no rule for accepting or rejecting someone on the basis of a superior collective authority embodied in the person of a chief or representative of the group. This I have termed "subjective membership," conditional on the will of the member, not on the permission of the group or any higher authority, no matter how counterintuitive this notion appears to us.[10] Such unspoken acceptance entails no long-term commitment. Faced with a threatening individual people would take evasive action. In older times incestuous couples who thus physically threatened the rest of the community, or dangerous and insane individuals, were murdered, not as form of punishment, but as a protective action.

Conclusion

I and the authors of these collected essays are trying to find sources of solidarity in arrangements that would seem to foster selfish individualism rather than altruistic behavior, and we are asking the question of how and why people might be persuaded to help, cooperate, collaborate, share, give, defend, guard, protect, comfort, assist, and even please and indulge each other. The ultimate answer may lie in some predisposition or behavioral template we have inherited from our ancestors. It may be that the gregarious cline of humans fosters cooperation. But for fellowships to develop and endure in an adaptive way, producing small communities of equals, some measure of status asymmetry must remain possible. Kinship in this respect has a mediating role in allowing status differences to create a manageable equality. The day-to-day management of volatile humans requires a modicum of control, and asymmetrical ties are convenient in this respect. But control in itself cannot produce cohesion, punishment does not give birth to virtue, and I have my doubts that a rational calculation of pure self-interest will generate solidarity, in spite of robust equilibria found in game theory.

Fellowships have no transcendence; they are not persons. They are aggregates, and in this sense they do have something in common with heaps of sand. For the grains to stay together they need to constantly readjust themselves and reconfirm their multiple but tenuous links to their immediate neighbors. Fellowships are very dynamic and solidarity-seeking units producing random, shifting, and unpredictable arrangements. The constant is not the group, which never appears as an entity with a transcendent, personlike dimension.[11] The constant is a desire for community. People belong to a community, but the community never owns people.

Kin ties (parents-children and siblings) remain seminal and prototypical ties for other human ties inasmuch as they are learned at the earliest stage of ontogenesis and remain as a template for all others. But kinship plays a different role within social systems, on the one hand, and within gregarious and anarchic communities on the other. With the former, kinship becomes a subsystem immersed in a bigger system in which it is contained. With the latter, and inasmuch as kinship is inclusive, it is the linguistic and cognitive medium of all interpersonal and collective relations. In a manner of speaking, kinship is then the form taken by human gregariousness.

Notes

1 It is forbidden, or at least considered extremely bad manners, to even peep inside someone else's granary, *legkew*, which in the highlands is a sturdy little building with thick walls made out of tree bark. Individual or family ownership thus manifests itself clearly.

2 In the Palawan kinship system I do not count gender among the factors of asymmetry.

3 Cognatic systems are thus best understood as heterarchical (Crumley 1995), not hierarchical (partial orders).

4 In Vietnamese, kin terms are used as pronouns.

5 The theme of intrauterine awareness and memories is highly developed in Inuit culture (Saladin d'Anglure 1986), and Mohave people think that stillborn babies are infants who, in the fetal stage, have *decided* not to be born. They are then counted as *suicides* (Devereux 1961)!

6 Harvesting rice can be done cooperatively, but it is not as ritualized as planting and is done on an individual basis.

7 In the Palawan language spirits and supernatural beings are called "humans" or "persons," *taw*.

8 Corporate groups exist among the Iban (the *bilek* family), Temiar (ramages), west Semai (settlements), and Dusun (villages). I used to consider the Palawan residential group, or neighborhood, as some sort of corporate entity until I realized that I was just foisting my Western preconception of society on an altogether different reality.

9 As an indication, kin terms for "father-in-law" or "mother-in-law" and "uncle" or "aunt" are merged in various languages of the region. The Palawan terminology, by making a clear distinction between "in-laws" and consanguineal kin, is very consistent in that respect. Again, this is not the case everywhere (see Benjamin, this volume).

10 As a foreign visitor, when I took up residence in a local neighborhood or community, nobody ever dictated that I was or was not part of the community. Being a human with a name, and staying there, gave me automatic membership, as long, of course, as I did not threaten their lives or harm them in any way. In the society in which I live, I can hardly belong to anything if I am not a duly accepted, card-carrying, fee-paying, duty-bound, and time-committed member.

11 To be committed, to pledge one's loyalty to a group as a *personne morale*, is radically alien to the Palawan ethos This is why Palawan people cannot really commit themselves to any program, leader, or cause, a situation that baffles indigenous rights advocates (Macdonald 2008b).

References

Bakhtin, Mikhail. 1970. *L'oeuvre de François Rabelais et la culture populaire au Moyen Age et sous la Renaissance*. Trans. A. Robel. Paris: Gallimard.

Carsten, Janet. 1995. "The substance of kinship and the heat of the hearth: Feeding, personhood, and relatedness among Malays in Pulau Langkawi." *American Ethnologist* 22 (2):223–41.

Carsten, Janet, ed. 2000. *Cultures of Relatedness: New Approaches to the Study of Kinship*. Cambridge: Cambridge University Press.

Crumley, Carole L. 1995. "Heterarchy and the analysis of complex societies." In R.M. Ehrenreich, C.L. Crumley, and J.E. Levy, eds., *Archeological Anthropological Association*. Paper No. 6. Washington: American Anthropological Association. 1–5.

Dentan, Robert K. 2008. *Overwhelming Terror: Love, Fear, Peace, and Violence among the Semai of Malaysia*. Lanham, MD, Boulder: Rowman and Littlefield.

Devereux, George. 1961. *Mohave Ethnopsychiatry and Suicide: The Psychiatric Knowledge and the Psychic Disturbances of an Indian Tribe*. Washington DC: Smithsonian Institution Press.

Dziebel, German V. 2007. *The Genius of Kinship*. Youngstown and New York: Cambria Press.

Franklin, Sarah, and Susan McKinnon, eds. 2001. *Relative Values: Reconfiguring Kinship Studies*. Durham: Duke University Press.

Gardner, Peter M. 1991. "Foragers pursuit of individual autonomy." *Current Anthropology* 32 (5):543–72.

Gibson, Thomas.1985. "The sharing of substance versus the sharing of activity among the Buid." *Man*, new series, 20 (3):391–411.

————. 1986. *Sacrifice and Sharing in the Philippine Highlands: Religion and Society among the Buid of Mindoro*. London: Athlone Press.

Godelier, Maurice. 2004. *Métamorphoses de la Parenté*. Paris: Fayard.

Granovetter, Mark. 1973. "The strength of weak ties." *American Journal of Sociology* 78 (6):1360–80.

————. 1983. "The strength of weak ties: A network theory revisited." *Sociological Theory* 1:201–33.

Ikegami, Eiko. 2005. *Bonds of Civility: Aesthetic Networks and the Political Origins of Japanese Culture*. Cambridge: Cambridge University Press.

Lechner, Thomas M. 2003. "Surrender without subordination: Peace and equality in Alcoholics Anonymous." PhD diss., Department of Anthropology, State University of New York at Buffalo. .

Macdonald, Charles J-H. 1972. "Le mariage Palawan." *L'Homme* 12:5–28.

————. 1974. "Une discussion de mariage Palawan: Texte traduit et commenté." *Asie du Sud-Est et Monde Insulindien (ASEMI)* 5:81–139.

————. 1977. *Une Société Simple: Parenté et Résidence chez les Palawan*. Paris: Institut d'Ethnologie.

————. 1984. *Mythes et Rites Palawan*. Paris: Université de Paris Sorbonne, École Pratique des Hautes Etudes.

————. 1990. *Sinsin, le Théâtre des Génies*. Paris: Editions du Centre National de la Recherche Scientifique (CNRS).

————. 1997. "Cleansing the earth: The *panggaris* ceremony in Kulbi-Kanipaqan, southern Palawan." *Philippine Studies* 45:408–22.

————. 2007. *Uncultural Behavior: An Anthropological Investigation of Suicide in the Southern Philippines*. Honolulu: University of Hawai'i Press.

————. 2008a. "Order against harmony: Are humans always social?" *Suomen Antropologi: Journal of the Finnish Anthropological Society* 33 (2):5–21.

————. 2008b. "Indigenous peoples as agents of change and as changing agents." *Palawan State University Journal* 1 (1):63–96.

Maryanski, A. 1994. "The pursuit of human nature in socio-biology and evolutionary sociology." *Sociological Perspectives* 37 (3):375–89.

Maryanski, A., and J. Turner. 1992. *The Social Cage*. Stanford: Stanford University Press.

Niman, Michael I. 1997. *People of the Rainbow: A Nomadic Utopia*. Knoxville: University of Tennessee Press.

Rousseau, Jérôme. 1990. *Central Borneo: Ethnic Identity and Social Life in a Stratified Society*. Oxford: Clarendon Press.

Saladin d'Anglure, Bernard. 1986. "Du foetus au chamane: La construction d'un 'troisième sexe' inuit." *Etudes Inuit* 10:25–114.

Testart, Alain. 2004. "Les morts d'accompagnement." *La Servitude Volontaire I*. Vol. 1. Paris: Editions Errance.

Woodburn, James. 1998. "Sharing is not a form of exchange: An analysis of property-sharing in immediate-return hunter-gatherer societies." In C.M. Hann, ed., *Property Relations: Renewing the Anthropological Tradition*, 48–63. Cambridge: Cambridge University Press.

6

Kinship and the
Dialectics of Autonomy and Solidarity
among the Bentian of Borneo

KENNETH SILLANDER

THIS ESSAY EXPLORES THE DYNAMICS of negotiating kinship ties among the Bentian, a small group of some 3,500 swidden cultivators who inhabit a thinly populated upriver area in the province of East Kalimantan in Indonesian Borneo. Like many swidden cultivators and hunter-gatherers in Southeast Asia (e.g., Atkinson 1989; Benjamin 1968; Chan 2007; Endicott 1988; Geddes 1954; Gibson 1986; Hagen 2006; Macdonald 1977; Needham 1959; Rosaldo 1980; Schlegel 1998) and beyond (e.g., Bodenhorn 2000; Fajans 1997; Myers 1986), the Bentian are simultaneously characterized by extensive individual autonomy and social solidarity. This condition is consistent with the mode of open-aggregated organization characterizing these societies, which enables flexible association and dissociation of individuals with social units, and flexible initiation and termination of interpersonal relationships within and beyond them.

The purpose of the essay is to explore the role of Bentian kinship as an integral aspect of this organization with particular reference to how it is conducive to this condition. I argue that kinship, understood broadly with an emphasis on its social and processual constitution (Carsten 2000; Franklin and McKinnon 2001; Strathern 1992), provides a principal source of self-identity and solidarity among the Bentian and as such plays a central role in what I call the dialectical constitution of autonomy and solidarity. The importance of kinship in this connection pertains especially to kinship as an idiom and ideology but also to how the egocentric bilateral kinship system forms an open-aggregated classificatory system.

Bentian Residence and Social Organization

Most Bentians subsist on the cultivation of rice and a great variety of other food crops in biannually planted swidden gardens complemented by hunting, fishing, and the rearing of domestic chickens, pigs, and water buffalos, which are consumed in connection with remarkably frequent rituals. Cash income is principally obtained from the sale of rattan grown in the swiddens as an integral part of the system of swidden cultivation, and, to a lesser extent, from the collection of nontimber forest products such as *gaharu* (*Aquilaria* sp.) and wage labor for timber, mining, and forest plantation companies.

The organization of the Bentian in social and residential units is complex and characterized by flexibility and frequent rearrangements. Like many swidden cultivators, most Bentian maintain dual residence in small villages (*desa*) and single-family farmhouses (*blai ume*) rebuilt and relocated every few years. Several farmhouses associated with adjacent or closely located swiddens typically form a cluster (*teming*). The swidden family represents the principal agricultural production unit. Its standard composition is that of a relatively young married couple with small children or that of a senior couple or a divorced/widowed elder with a married child and her or his spouse and children. Residence in the villages takes several forms. Some families stay in small, modern-style single-family houses (known as *rumah pembangunan*, "development houses") while others reside in multifamily houses (*lou*), some of which are essentially larger versions of the modern single-family village houses, and some of which are traditional longhouselike structures. Residence in *lou* represents a heritage from an earlier period predating government-imposed settlement in nucleated villages at the turn of the twentieth century, when the Bentian alternated residence between farmhouses and small, frequently moved, one-room multifamily houses dispersed in the forest. In today's *lou*, and sometimes in the smaller houses as well, several swidden-cultivating families often merge into larger households, forming extended consumption units sharing food and other resources and expenditures. Families are often associated with different families in the villages and on the swiddens, although in both cases they are often connected through sibling ties, following the pattern of association between families in traditional *lou*. Beyond these associations, individuals often maintain relationships with other, residentially unaffiliated relatives and friends, within and beyond village communities.

As these practices and arrangements suggest, the organization of individuals and families in Bentian society is predominantly egocentric and associated with considerable personal and family autonomy rather than structurally organized through membership in descent or other groups beyond the household (albeit flexible membership in *lou*, which has become progressively less important after village integration, represent a partial exception to this). Yet, despite this situation, both swidden clusters and villages represent closely knit social conglomerates in which families engage extensively in visiting, cooperation, and various forms of informal and formal distribution and exchange of resources and services. An ethos of kin and neighbor solidarity, as well as a more generalized spirit of communality, is prominent, expressed in public discourse through references to general ideals and specific precepts of *adat* (customary law) and the government-sanctioned concept of *gotong royong* (mutual assistance, community cooperation), especially during frequent collective meetings, rituals, and speeches by the elders (*tuha*).

On this basis, the Bentian, and particularly those of the smaller, non-Christian upriver villages where this pattern was especially salient, enjoyed during my fieldwork in the 1990s a reputation for greater *adat* orientation and greater respect for their kin than their downstream neighbors, a reputation that in turn influenced their own self-understanding. Malay traders and forest product collectors staying among the Bentian would often note, for example, that "if you go to the Bentian, you don't need to pay for rice," and downstream Dayak neighbors would speak about the Bentian's more strictly prescribed application of kinship terminology and its more inclusive extension to remote relatives and nonkin. *Adat* and kinship orientation here notably signified essentially the same thing—adherence to the principles of a moral economy, defined in opposition to the market economy— and this association of *adat* and kinship testifies to the two institutions' emically perceived shared purpose of promoting respectful and solidary interpersonal relations.

Definition and Meaning of Bentian Kinship

The principal question posed in this essay is to what extent and in what ways forms of aggregation and social ties in Bentian communities are influenced by kinship or other principles or practices in combination with kinship. I use the term *kinship* to refer to relatedness in a broad sense, transcending narrowly defined genealogical kinship. This understanding is motivated by Bentian notions of relatedness. Kinship provides the basic idiom in which local social relations are perceived, including relations with affines and unrelated consociates, recognized as kin through the use of kinship terminology on the basis of perceived unity or closeness arising from practical association.

This understanding of kinship is consistent with that of Janet Carsten (1997) and Robert McKinley (2001), who, like David Schneider (1984), reject the sharp conventional distinction between "biological kinship" and "social kinship" in anthropology, but who, unlike Schneider, do not "reject the validity of kinship as a cross-cultural category" (Carsten 1997:290). Like them, I am concerned with establishing a closer fit between analytical and local conceptions of relatedness by taking as the starting point not an a priori analytical understanding of kinship but "the relatedness that people act and feel," whether or not it is centrally based on notions of procreation as in Western societies (290). However, this does not entail that I will stretch the term beyond recognition to signify all conceivable kinds of relatedness, altogether depriving it of precision and usefulness as a cross-cultural tool. Following McKinley (2001), I reserve the term for relatedness that is couched in the "genealogical idiom," thus maintaining an analytical distinction between kinship and other forms of relatedness.

This essay is thus about relatedness *expressed* through the use of kinship terminology—and an associated kinship ideology—but not restricted to kinship based on "shared substance," to refer to a more conventional criterion used in another open-aggregated society by Thomas Gibson (1985) to distinguish kinship from what he labels "companionship" and defines as based on "shared activity." Perhaps partly reflecting these different conceptual understandings, some of my findings regarding the symbolism and sociological significance of Bentian kinship are diametrically opposed to Gibson's on the Buid of Mindoro. Bentian kinship is largely based precisely on shared activity, and instead of signifying negatively valued relations and undesired forms of behavior undermining community solidarity, kinship—in the sense of affirmation of kinship relations and kinship obligations—is one of the most highly valued ideals in Bentian society and is regarded, together with *adat*, as the foundation of social solidarity in it. Thus, a basic symbolic meaning of Bentian kinship is amity, and, unlike the situation among the Buid, for whom kinship has "positive implications for social behaviour only in so far as the roles of immature dependent and mature provider are concerned" (404), it provides a generalized source of interpersonal and community solidarity beyond relations within domestic families.

Bentian Kinship Terminology

Bentian kinship is bilateral and typical of cognatic kinship systems in Borneo and western insular Southeast Asia, exhibiting a combination of Eskimo and Hawaiian characteristics. Kinship terminology emphasizes generation and relative age. Siblings are referred to and addressed as younger sibling (*ani*) or elder sibling (*tuke*) regardless of sex. Siblings can be distinguished terminologically from cousins of different degrees, but the latter are usually addressed and often referred to as younger or older siblings or with the all-purpose term *peyari*, variously denoting sibling, cousin, or same-generation companion. In the first ascending generation, father (*uma*) and mother (*ine*) are distinguished on the basis of sex, but other consanguines of the same generation are referred to as parent's younger sibling/cousin (*burok*) or parent's elder sibling/cousin (*tuo*), although they are often addressed as "father" or "mother," especially in the case of a parent's same-sex siblings or if they are socially close to ego. Consanguineal relatives of the second ascending generations are all referred to and addressed as grandfather (*kakah*) or grandmother (*itak*), while consanguines of higher generations are referred to as *kakah datu,* or *itak datu*. In the first descending generation, children (*anak*) are distinguished from nephews/nieces (*aken*), but the latter are also referred to as *anak* in the case of same-sex siblings' children or if they are close. Grandchildren and collateral grandchildren are lumped together as *opo* and great-grandchildren as *inking*. These terms are also extended to lower-generation descendants, for which there are vaguely recognized but rarely used specific terms (*piyut, alep*).

Affines of ego's generation, including sibling's/cousin's spouse and spouse's sibling/cousin, are reciprocally referred to and addressed as *ayu* (in the case of cross-sex or male-to-male relations) and *ongan* (in the case of relations between female affines). Parents-in-law and their siblings are referred to as *tupu* but addressed with the same consanguineal terms used by one's spouse. Consanguineal terms are also extended to other affinal relatives, including to *ayu/ongan* and child's spouse/sibling's child's spouse (*benantu*), who become *peyari* and *anak/aken*, respectively, if they are perceived to have become close. Second and more distant ascending and descending generation affines are addressed only with consanguineal terms.

Inclusiveness and Classificatory Kinship

Bentian use of kinship terminology is thus characterized by a classificatory tendency to extend a limited number of primary terms for close consanguines to affinal as well as more distant cognatic relatives. This tendency, associated with the extension of kinship terminology to unrelated consociates, is widespread in societies with similar kinship systems (see, e.g., Banks 1974; Bloch 1971; Kemp 1983; Sather 1996; Tsing 1984; Waterson 1986; and Yengoyan 1973). Geoffrey Benjamin (this volume) refers to it as "inclusive kinship" and identifies it as a characteristic of the northern Orang Asli. Among the Bentian, it is consistent with a general tendency toward inclusiveness pertaining also to moral obligations and practical association (Sillander 2004). As one example of this tendency, egocentric action groups are not, *pace* Freeman (1961), restricted to the cognatic kindred, but usually include affines and classificatory kin as well (see King 1991 and Sather 1996 for similar observations in other Borneo societies). A cognate (*kaben*) of the term *kaban*, taken by Freeman and other observers of bilateral Southeast Asian societies (e.g., Yengoyan 1973) to designate members of the kindred, is found also among the Bentian, and, as among the Iban, it may be used both in a restricted sense to refer to consanguines and in a broad sense to designate "kith and kin," cognatic and affinal kin as well as friends and neighbors (Freeman 1960:70).

Designations for kin groups and other social units are also similarly flexible, such as the term *aben*, which most narrowly denotes conjugal families but is also emphatically invoked for extended households, house groups, and village communities. Carsten (1997:162) proposes that the similarly elastic Langkawi Malay term *kampung* "expresses through its generality an unwillingness to differentiate people from each other, and ... thereby stresses the unity of the community." Similar considerations also motivate the polysemy of Bentian kin group and relationship terminology. A general reluctance to make explicit distinctions between categories of people within a local society is, at any rate, strongly characteristic of the Bentian, as of various other, typically egalitarian and "encapsulated" peoples in the so-called peripheries of the region (e.g., Carsten 1997; Schrauwers 1999; Tsing 1993). This reluctance may reflect a desire to maintain internal solidarity in the face of external threats of aggression or incorporation—and internally generated strain and discord arising from conflicting demands and complexly entangled relationships in small, endogamous communities. However, more important than stressing ethnic or communal unity, the inclusive use of kinship and kin group terminology probably serves to enable the extension of moral ties within society for the benefit of its individual members, motivated more by the nature of internal than external societal relations and, in particular, by an often lamented endemic scarcity and erratic accessibility of social capital, ensuing from conditions such as small population size, extensive personal autonomy, low level of social control, and lack of juridically effective and explicit rules defining rights and obligations toward particular categories of kin.

A basic, and sometimes consciously strategic, purpose of using Bentian kinship terminology is indeed to invoke obligations, and the tendency for inclusiveness—which notably itself contributes to the open-aggregated character of the societies in which it is found—obviously serves this purpose, too. Given an ideology in which relatedness entails closeness, and closeness obligations, this usage stresses, as Waterson (1986:94) has argued for figuratively used Toraja sibling terms, "an ideal of closeness of relation-ship and the sort of affection and co-operative behaviour expected within such a relationship." The classificatory and inclusive tendencies character-izing Bentian kinship—the tendencies to extend terms for close relatives to distant ones, and some form of relatedness to almost everyone—thus testify to the significance of the genealogical idiom as a device for creating and multiplying social ties and obligations, for drawing people into personal social networks and inducing them to provide assistance.

Kinship as the Attribution of Respect

The aspirations motivating this usage are not only strategical, however, but also to an important extent ethical, in that its desired outcome is valued for its own sake and represents an idealized state of affairs. The principal rationale for applying kinship terminology acknowledged by the Bentian is that it expresses interpersonal respect. Consistent with this explanation, the use of kinship terms is correlated with rules of avoidance of personal names (for both address and reference), sanctioned by notions of supernatural retribution (*bunsung*), for those relatives for whom the most respect is prescribed, that is, ego's parents and other consanguineal relatives of ascending generations and ego's parents-in-laws and other affinal relatives of ascending or the same generation. These relatives are addressed by kinship terms, and referred to by kinship terms, teknonyms, or nicknamelike pseudoteknonyms (see Sillander 2010).

An important effect of this differential prescription of kinship terminology and name-avoidance rules is that it signals expectations of greater respect, and formality, in some relationships than in others. The two categories of relatives to which these expectations pertain are elders and affines. By prescribing respect to elders, including affinal elders, this usage emphasizes the asymmetrical character of intergenerational relations and the authority and responsibility of elders over juniors, as opposed to the ideally symmetrical relations of moral equivalence and reciprocity expected to inform intragenerational relations (see McKinley [1979] 1983:355–56; and Myers 1986:214–16). In accordance with a widespread Austronesian pattern, seniority is a central structural principle of Bentian kinship. It is expected that elders should regulate social affairs, provide guidance, and take responsibility over juniors, and that the latter in return defer to them. This ideal pertains particularly to relations between the generations, though in a milder form also to intragenerational relations between elder and younger siblings (in which complementary notions of companionship and equivalence usually take precedence, however). It expresses an understanding of the social world, shared by the Pintupi of western Australia, as consisting of "a succession of generations, each 'holding' or 'looking after' … the ones that follow" (Myers 1986:217), an understanding that kinship terminology, especially through its Hawaiian bent, provides a concrete basis for through its consistent division of communities into generational layers, between which intermarriage is prohibited. These principles also take expression in the prominent discursive and ritual importance of the ancestors as an anonymous collectivity of predecessors (*ulun tuha one*) and in the practice whereby people maintain a personal relationship with one or several consanguineal or affinal elders, recognized as their "trunks" or "sources" (*puun*), to whom they may turn with requests for support or guidance (cf. the Palawan institution of *pinemikitan* discussed in Macdonald, this volume).

The attribution of respect to affines, on the other hand, is more complexly constituted. It is informed both by the symmetry and asymmetry respectively pertaining to intra- and intergenerational relations and hence is differently constituted in intra- and intergenerational affinal relations (with the effect that affinal elders receive special respect), as well as by the fact that initiating affinal relations, even with prior consanguines, involves investing extensively in them and hence subjecting them and relations between families to special strain. In affinal relations, the prescribed kinship term use and name-avoidance practices are motivated by a concern for preserving equality and harmonious relations between families (including, not least importantly, between co-parents-in-law, *sanget*), a concern expressed also by the practice of arranging double weddings, one by the bride's family and another by the groom's, and alternating uxori- and virilocality, designed to balance the expenses, statuses, and resources of the bride's and groom's families (see Carsten 1997; Peletz 1988; and Sather 1996). Because of this concern, it is appropriate that affinal relations are, at least initially, more strictly regulated and balanced, and informed by greater formality and respect, than relations with consanguines, between whom greater intimacy and a more uncalculated give-and-take is presumed to prevail.

However, the attribution of respect to affines is also tempered by an ideal—signaled by the substitution of affinal with consanguineal terms of address for them—that they should gradually become like consanguines, which affines in fact often are from before, because of the preference for endogamy. This expresses the fact that affinal relations are additionally informed by a third general ideal, namely, that of closeness, entailing affection and amity, which ideally pertains to all kinship relations. It may perhaps be taken to indicate that the basic function of rules of address and reference, over and above emphasizing different but complementary codes of ideal behavior for different categories of relatives, is to provide an encompassing code for relation-affirming, integration-promoting behavior.

The Generalized Character of Bentian Kinship Ideology

As this indicates, Bentian use of kinship terms not only serves to express special respect in specific categories of relationships. In fact, it is pervasive and frequently used for others than those whose names are tabooed. This reflects an understanding that use of kinship terminology is generally expressive of an idealized, "roundabout" (*mengkelotes*), and "refined" (*halus*) code for responsible and respectful social behavior. In this respect, the Bentian resemble the Punan Bah of northern Borneo, among whom kinship terms are seen "not simply as an expression of a harmonious world, but as the very means by which such a world is maintained" (Nicolaisen 1998:376–77). Conversely, they contrast markedly with the Buid, among whom "only kinsmen in senior generations, and elder siblings, are addressed with the appropriate kinship terms," illustrating the restricted symbolic significance of Buid kinship as an idiom for hierarchic relations of dependency within the domestic family (Gibson 1985:403). For the Bentian, kinship terms, and their function of expressing respect, are perceived to promote a generalized moral ideal of close and harmonious relations.

This ideal basically pertains to all relatives—whether cognatic or affinal, close or distant. Relatives are not ranked and differentiated in any detailed manner other than through the above-mentioned name-avoidance rules, which attribute special respect to some *categories* of relatives, and through some notions that close relatives, such as siblings, children, and parents, are obliged to provide special support, including financial assistance for curing and costly primary and secondary mortuary rituals, and are entitled, if accessible, to receive shares of distributed game, invitations to rituals, and information about important events and affairs. The generality of this ideal results in a fair degree of variation in the degree to which it is invoked in any *particular* kin relationship—at least beyond the circle of the closest relatives—and enables relationships to be initiated and selectively invested in on the basis of other considerations than relative closeness. As elsewhere in Borneo, this indicates a rather "nebulous realm of expectations and moral obligation, in which there is *considerable choice* in co-operating with kinsmen and others" (King 1991:18, emphasis in original). Because of the system of inclusive bilateral kinship, in combination with a high rate of endogamy in most communities, people could not in fact invest equally or extensively in all of their kinship relations even if they wanted to.

There are, in fact, few rules or norms of conduct pertaining specifically to particular kin relations. As in much of Southeast Asia, "social action is thought of as being continuously constructed on the basis of certain shared rules, and not as being defined in advance by a rigid code of conduct prescribing correct behaviour between an individual and structurally defined others" (Gibson 1986:65). *Adat* does not prescribe positive kinship rules or marriage preferences; it only negatively sanctions unacceptable behavior (which generally pertains also to nonrelatives) and proscribes illicit sexual relations (intergenerational marriage and marriage between parallel cousins). Thus, what there is in the way of kinship rules are generalized ideals, unsanctioned by *adat*, such as that relatives should share food and resources and provide mutual help and services, not fight or sue each other or accept monetary compensation for assistance, maintain relationships through visits and ritual participation, and not allow them to be forgotten.

The Authority of Kinship Obligations

This generality of kinship ideology does not mean that it is uninfluential. As among the Pintupi, "being a relative" is important, even though "defining what sort of kin one is" often is not (Myers 1986:107). Notwithstanding that they are more or less selective in investing in the totality of available kin relations, most Bentians regularly go to considerable lengths to help at least some of their relatives and often make substantial material contributions to them (even contributing water buffalos for their rituals). Consciously violating the norms would make most of them more or less uncomfortable unless they had some good excuse to do so, such as illness or unfulfilled obligations on their relatives' part. At the least, no one would readily admit to transgression of them or be indifferent toward accusations of it. In these respects, kinship obligations represent an authoritative imperative, which frequently influences social action.

The reasons for this authority of kinship obligations are complex and impossible to grasp without locating them in the specific social and cultural contexts in which they are invoked. A crucial factor contributing to their authority is certainly that by living in Bentian society one is constantly reminded of them. They are repeatedly expressed in informal, everyday discussions and formal contexts such as customary law negotiations, speeches given at rituals and weddings, and the elders' regular evening monologues (during which a variety of family and other concerns are addressed, work tasks of the next day scheduled, etc.). As a consequence, they are salient in practice and indeed appear to be rather effectively inculcated. In part, their appeal and force no doubt derive from a genuine internalization of kinship values, from the fact that "being a relative" can be consonant with people's self-identity or visions of who they want to be.

This is not to say that the reasons for kinship authority are simply ethical or altruistic, however—even though they may *indirectly* reflect a hegemony of sociocentric values in Bentian society. As is typical in the dual social economy of precapitalist societies, disinterestedness and interestedness are virtually indistinguishable (Bourdieu 1977:191–96). People also affirm kinship obligations because they want to appear to be "good people" (*ulun buen*); because their social status as adults, elders, or relatives in general is contingent on it; and because the presence and demands of kin make it impossible to dismiss them all and still maintain good kin relations and the expectation that others will respond affirmatively to one's requests. The importance of these considerations is made more compelling by the fact that most people in practical life receive recurrent requests for help and material contributions from a wide range of relatives. Like visiting, including both close-range (*koteu*) and long-range (*ngonga*) visiting, "asking someone for something" (*sake*) or "ordering someone to do something" (*siu*) are central social institutions in Bentian society and frequently the purpose of visiting. Furthermore, adding to the authority of kinship obligations is fear of *tapen*, of becoming spiritually weakened and vulnerable to supernatural sanctions for rejecting social connections, the local equivalent of *kempunan* or *punén*, which in the Bentian case is seen to endanger both perpetrator and victim (cf. the essays by Dentan, Endicott, and Howell in this volume).

The Bentian term *tapen* is most paradigmatically invoked in cases of not sharing or accepting food (e.g., by not inviting people present to eat or not accepting, or at least symbolically partaking of, offered food through *sintep* by putting a few grains of rice to one's mouth) but also for not affirming requests for things (e.g., small items of personal property) or services (e.g., ritual participation). It applies not just to relatives, but since most people with whom one is involved are relatives it usually does in practice, thus in effect sanctioning kinship relations. Demonstrating the central cultural significance of *tapen*, it is the most commonly reported reason for soul loss and ensuing performance of curing rituals (*belian*). My informants often said that if there is no *tapen* nothing bad may happen.

The Practical Constitution of Relatedness

The importance of relatedness not merely reflects the importance of principles and obligations, however, whether theoretical or contextual. Indeed, people go through much trouble to maintain kinship relations even in the absence of applicable principles or people making demands. An important expression of this is endogamy, which is not prescribed but strongly preferred and to an extent even practiced in violation of explicit rules proscribing it (i.e., with parallel cousins, necessitating payment of a fine and ritual purification). Bentians tend to marry within a range of second or third cousins, and first-cousin marriage is common. In part, this reflects the fact that most available marriage partners are relatives, entailing that whoever they, or their elder relatives, end up choosing, will often be a relative, even if there may be other considerations than kinship that more primarily motivate this decision (friendship, residence, economic concerns, etc.). This is consistent with an often-made observation in bilateral societies, namely, that "social isolates [i.e., groups] may contain only kin by default" (Appell 1976:151; see King 1978:10; Macdonald, this volume). Endogamy, or cooperation with relatives, indeed sometimes only *appears* to reflect the importance of kinship—an illusion caused by relatives being companions in disguise. However, this is not, I argue, the whole story.

Endogamy, and choice of swidden cluster neighbors, for example, are also positively motivated by the desires to be with one's relatives and not allow ties to weaken. As among the Iban, endogamy serves to "consolidate kindred ties" (Sather 1996:94), and choice of swidden neighbors is similarly often motivated by desires to maintain or reenact preestablished relationships with particular relatives, often siblings. The latter is notably true even for the Buid, for whom Gibson notes that siblingship forms an exception to a stated "total irrelevance of kinship ties among members of the adult generation" (1985:410). However, rather than a concern with genealogical kinship, this reflects a desire to maintain relations with concrete people that are close in a practical sense, that is, with whom one *feels* related as a result of a shared history of interaction characterized by the ideal qualities of kinship: amity, closeness, cooperation, sharing, and reciprocity. This also appears to hold true for the Buid, among whom it is because siblings are "long-term companions that they are bound to one another, not because they share a common substance" (Gibson 1986:99). Siblings are, of course, in a special position of concrete closeness because of their shared childhood, an important factor in making kinship important, together with the ideological significance of siblingship as the ideal type of interpersonal solidarity, whose aptness the former factor also helps explain, together with the "greater moral density" (98) of siblings.

A principal reason why people invoke kinship and maintain kinship relations is thus to strengthen their social networks and build them on a foundation of practically experienced close relations. This suggests that a basic function of Bentian kinship, besides establishing bonds and compelling obligations between people, is to serve as what McKinley ([1979] 1983:360) has called a "framework of mutual trust," and that a sense of trust is most solidly established through personal experience of habitual familiarity and cooperation in everyday life. A similar situation also prevails in other bilateral Southeast Asian societies, including the Ilongot: "Because Ilongots experience kinship as the basis of cooperative support—and frequent contact is considered a prerequisite of true kinship—no man wants to live further than necessary from his relations" (Rosaldo 1980:186).

The reason that Bentians trust kin is thus not so much that they are genealogical relatives but rather that the people they know and are most involved with are relatives. In other words, they prefer to deal with kin, not because genealogical relatives in some respect would be fundamentally distinct per se but because they have practically experienced kin relations to provide support and security, and they generally expect—albeit with some caution and a similar experience-based awareness of the possibility of exceptions—kinspersons to be well-disposed toward them because they assume the sense of obligation to be reciprocal.[1]

The importance of this practical as opposed to genealogical constitution of kinship is substantiated by the fact that the kind of kinship that matters most to the Bentian is typically acquired as opposed to ascribed. Bentians single out those that they perceive belong to the sphere of what Yengoyan (1973) calls the "effective kindred," as opposed to the "complete kindred," by referring to them as *kaben bene*, "true relatives" or "true companions." "Effective kinship," involving solidarity, is defined and constituted by networks of shared activity. It is those relatives who are unified through practical association that most often invoke notions of relatedness, and it is among them that these tend to be most effective. Here again the Bentian are remarkably similar to the Ilongot, who "experience their bonds in terms of the cooperative orientations that unite them and lend substance to the claim that they are kin" (Rosaldo 1980:10).

Conversely, this suggests that Bentian kinship, like egocentric bilateral kinship generally, is not automatic. It has to be enacted. That one is related to someone is not quite enough to make that person important. It is those relatives with whom one has much to do—or that have much to do with oneself—that become important. Those who move away tend to become distant not only physically but also emotionally—if not occasionally visited.[2] Those who never give anything in return tend to be avoided—if possible. Those who are one's neighbors, however, are difficult to ignore and tend to become important whether one likes them or not. Interaction, reciprocity, and proximity thus emerge as crucial factors shaping "true" relatedness. Together these factors define and give shape to a social field of "immediacy" in which sociality itself functions as the principal source of relatedness (Bird-David 1994).

Such a practice-based understanding of relatedness, constituted in this way through sociality, appears to be common—and often still more pronounced—in many open-aggregated societies, especially among hunter-gatherers (e.g., Bird-David 1994; Bodenhorn 2000; Guemple 1988; Myers 1986; Storrie 2003). No doubt, like inclusiveness, it is also an important feature contributing to their open-aggregated character by way of stressing emergent as opposed to structurally predetermined relatedness as a basis for relationships. Nurit Bird-David (1994:598–99) identifies as its foundation a special form of sociality, typical of small groups such as hunter-gatherer bands, which is characterized by what phenomenologists Alfred Schutz and Thomas Luckmann (1973) called "immediacy" and a "we relationship," involving sharing of common space and time, and an unmediated "vivid" experience of consociates "in person" rather than as types. In Bird-David's understanding, enculturation in societies in which such sociality is dominant creates a cultural preference for "an (ethno)sociology that understands 'to relate' in a pragmatic sense" (1994:594), typically expressed through vague and inclusive egocentric concepts designating "kindred" or "family" in a generalized respect (e.g., Nayaka *sonta*, Pintupi *walytja*, or Bentian *kaben, aben*).

This understanding of relatedness is inimical to extensive objectification and theoretical elaboration of kinship roles and obligations—to what Pierre Bourdieu (1977) called "official kinship"—which imposes "distance" through mediation and relatedness of a different order. Thus it helps to explain the typically weak development (or at least the practical unimportance) of these attributes of kinship among open-aggregated peoples (see Dentan, this volume; Guemple 1988; Myers 1986; and Storrie 2003) and the converse preference among them for what Fred Myers (1986:294) calls a "phenome-nological" as opposed to "structuralist … approach to cultural forms." It also contributes to explaining the prominence in open-aggregated societies of what Renato Rosaldo (1993) calls "social grace," a propensity for mutual coordination and adaptive responsiveness to changing courses and contin-gencies in social interaction and a capacity for creative manipulation of such "social indeterminacy." These qualities struck me as conspicuous in facilitating flexible negotiation of social ties among the Bentian (Sillander 2004:141–47), including, as among the Ilongot, in the context of multi-purposed and open-ended visits, which were often excessively prolonged and liable to turn into more or less permanent moves.

The quality of social grace is advantageous for sustaining practical co-existence in small communities with dense and tangled social relationships tending to entail burdensome obligations and difficult balancing with limited social and material resources. It points to the importance of societal scale or community size as an important factor shaping Bentian and other open-aggregated peoples' kinship. Maintaining amity, and conditions enabling smooth cooperation and essentially voluntary provision of resources and services in such a social setting, is contingent on this quality of social interaction and the generation of sentiments of "true" relatedness, which themselves arise in and contribute to facilitating these processes.

Bentian Solidarity

An important characteristic of practically constituted relatedness, as well as bilateral kinship in general, is that its establishment is the result of continu-ous achievement. As Barbara Bodenhorn (2000:143) reports for the Inupiat of Alaska, "[K]inship bonds must be renewed and kept viable through a myriad of reciprocities: shared tools, food, labour, political alliance, ceremonial participation, and simply company." A similar situation is typical of open-aggregated societies and consistent with their social organization, according to which people are not connected "from above" by virtue of ascribed membership in groups as much as "from below" through acquired personal networks and dyadic ties.

The general pattern of Bentian social, or structural, organization, exemplified by the residential pattern described earlier in this essay, is essentially egocentric and as such associated with considerable personal autonomy. In societies organized in this way, individual and society do not simply represent opposing forces. Networks and groups, typically more or less temporary in character, come into being as a result of individual initiative, and ambition is a prerequisite of a covert but important Bentian ideal of self-sufficiency on which not only people's relative material well-being and relative statuses as adult community members among equals depend but, ultimately, the survival of society. This ideal, along with that of personal autonomy, also promotes the tendency for residential dispersal associated with swidden cultivation, which notably enables both, thus motivating the preference of many Bentians for staying more or less permanently in their swiddens, beyond what is motivated by subsistence concerns. As is typical in Borneo (e.g., Geddes 1954; Helliwell 2001), individualism is not suppressed among the Bentian but rather quite salient: idiosyncratic habits abound and personalities vary widely, with no single uniform actual or ideal social character being dominant. People interact, in Rodney Needham's words, in a capacity "as individuals rather than as members or representatives of groups" according to a pattern identified by him as typical for "segmentary" (open-aggregated) peoples (1959:86–87), and that of person-to-person interaction associated with immediacy-based band sociality described by Bird-David.

However, solidarity is achieved in open-aggregated societies not just because it has to be enacted and mediated by individuals but also in that it must be established and sustained through *interaction* to enable the construction of egocentric networks, and development of practical association, and thereby common interests and a sentimental basis for relatedness. Especially significant in this respect is, it seems to me, interaction that involves what Gibson (1985) and Myers (1986:92) call "shared activity."

Gibson argues that Buid communities are "bound together by the sharing of speech, food, labour, and ritual, and by their potential sharing of residence and sex" (1986:218). This observation is equally valid for the

Bentian and many other open-aggregated societies, in which similar activities are instrumental in generating bonds and a sense of unity, but also, unlike among the Buid, perceptions of relatedness and closeness expressed in the genealogical idiom (see Bodenhorn 2000; and Myers 1986). Given such characteristics as vague kin roles and obligations and principles of group affiliation and associated conditions of extensive personal autonomy and limited social control, shared activity is a fundamental prerequisite of solidarity in them. In the Bentian case, examples of social practices involving shared activity are participation in and commensality during a variety of rituals and meetings; sharing ritual work and expenditures; ceremonial distribution of plates and domestic animals sacrificed only during rituals; speeches delivered by elders during rituals and meetings and at other times; sharing game and occasionally fish; adoption or temporary "borrowing" of children and sharing their services; visiting and telling news; framed, institutionalized forms of asking for resources and services and commanding, instructing, and fetching people; community work and agricultural labor exchange; and informal, everyday cooperation and giving of food, things, and economic assistance.

Such social activities represent integrative forces that complement open aggregation and egocentric organization and counteract ever-present tendencies of division and strain inherently associated with life and resource management in small communities of complexly related and associated consociates. They indeed entail *situational* solidarity, integrating people in interaction, but they also create solidarity beyond the situation of interaction. One way in which they engender more enduring solidarity, besides by facilitating the establishment of dyadic interpersonal ties and obligations, and the development of practical association enabling experience-based relatedness is by embodying, through their form and organization, some elementary sociocentric values and life experiences such as affirming relations and sharing resources.

By expressing these fundamental aspects of Bentian ideology and ontology, shared activity can be at once exemplary and compelling. Like Balinese cockfights (Geertz 1972), the above-mentioned Bentian social practices communicate, by virtue of their symbolic form (and actual content), something fundamental to its practitioners about themselves, and this continuously enacted "tacit," as opposed to "didactic," form of communication (Rousseau 1998:118) complements, and likely affects people more profoundly than, the equally frequent invocations of the same messages in discourse.

The importance of shared activity as a source of solidarity is, of course, not limited to open-aggregated communities, even though its importance may, for the reasons indicated, be especially fundamental there. Its general importance in modern society and beyond is highlighted by one of the most prominent sociological theorists of solidarity today, Randall Collins, who on the basis of Durkheim's theory of the ritual production of moral solidarity, and Goffman's extension of it into ritualized everyday encounters, has developed the concept of "interaction ritual" to designate basically the same phenomenon and mechanisms generating solidarity discussed here (Collins 1988, 2005). Interaction rituals include what Collins calls "intentional ceremonies" and "natural rituals," the latter consisting of conversations and various forms of gatherings and encounters, "any form of interaction which can be characterized by some degree of co-presence, common focus, and common mood" (1988:227). Collins thus also understands solidarity to be produced in practice through shared activity and its reproduction as contingent on the existence, in at least some pockets of society, of activities qualifying as "interaction rituals."

In addition to its importance for enabling solidarity and familiarity-based relatedness, an elementary factor in motivating shared activity is an inclination toward sociality, a "desire of people to be with others rather than alone" (Geddes 1954:16). This factor profoundly informs Bentian social life and interaction with relatives in ways poignantly summarized by William Geddes.

> Sociality is probably the most powerful of all community forces, and it is hard to say where its influence in Dayak society begins and where it ends. It is the blood of kinship, and it nurtures many other groups which have an obvious practical purpose but not one sufficient to explain them."
>
> (Geddes 1954:16)

Even though sociality among the Bentian is not always as merry as Geddes (1954) described it for the Bidayuh in the 1950s, and generally not very aptly characterized by the term *gregarious* used by Macdonald and Sather in this volume—many people being quite introverted, restrained, and inclined toward formality in their interactions and voluntarily living quite isolated in often remote swiddens—they nevertheless perceive that company is essential for a good life (*bolum buen*), and they are especially concerned with not having to stay, or having their relatives stay, alone. This, they recognize, would entail a hard life and starvation (*senur*).

The significance of this economically and sociologically motivated need for sociality is expressed through an important general ideal that "no one should be left out" (i.e., of a household or sexual union) (see Gibson 1985:396; and Schlegel 1998:114–15, 125–26). There is also a related ideal that close relatives should stay together in one house, contributing to the relative persistence of residence in larger houses designated *lou*. These ideals are especially motivated by the fact that the Bentian are "few people" (*putik unuk*), an often-lamented condition that consciously informs many attempts to organize social life and motivates frequent adoption and forms of marriage such as polyandry, polygyny, sororate, and levirate and a general flexibility in the composition of residential and other social units.

My data on the Bentian suggest that having no one stay alone and maintaining previously established relations are principal reasons, along with infertility, for the now highly stigmatized institution of polyandry (and polygyny, which used to be practiced by leaders also for different, status-related, reasons). Polyandry is rare outside the Himalaya, but it occurs in several societies in Borneo (Lumholtz 1920:440; Rousseau 1990:227; Sellato 1994:156; Tsing 1993:130), Peninsular Malaysia (Dentan 1993:238; Endicott 1993:235; Howell 1989:28), and the Philippines (Eder 1999:296; Gibson 1986:89). Interestingly, all these societies consist of either hunter-gatherers or dispersed swidden cultivators, which has led some observers to conclude that the institution, and polygamy more generally in these societies, may reflect concerns with optimizing their reproductive potential while maintaining local endogamy (Sellato 1994:156; Knapen 2001:126). This suggests that the demographic conditions of open-aggregated peoples, together with ideals such as having no one stay alone, and a pragmatic attitude toward social organization, may explain the incidence of this practice among them.

The demographic conditions of the Bentian also motivate a hegemonic position of sociocentrism in public discourse, as well as frequent and salient attempts by elders to organize cooperation and other social activities, thereby adding legitimacy to the asymmetry of intergenerational relations. By the same means, it enforces the status of kinship (of which seniority is a central aspect) and contributes to explaining the salience in practice of kinship ideology, which is perhaps best understood as a vehicle of sociocentric cultural integration balancing egocentric social organization.

Dialectic of Autonomy and Relatedness

> Autonomy and relatedness emerge from ethnography not as two opposing forces but as part of a dialectical relationship in which the manifestation of one provokes the assertion of the other.
>
> —Jane Fajans, 2006

The importance of both egocentric agency and shared activity as bases of relatedness and solidarity among the Bentian suggests that neither "individual" nor "society" reigns supreme in any conclusive respect. People are not fully free to do what they want, and certainly not uninfluenced in their actions, but they remain autonomous enough to act at odds with dominant social values at times, and it is only as a result of the reproduction of the latter through individual agency that they retain their dominance. Clearly, individual and society are inseparable in some respects, and clearly neither can do without the other. Indeed, the relationship between them is essentially dialectical. In many ways Bentian social life revolves around a dialectic of "autonomy and relatedness" (Fajans 2006; Myers 1986) or "autonomy and communalism" (Benjamin 1994), borne out, for example, in oscillation between dispersal and concentration, self-reliance and shared activity, introversion and extroversion, division and amity, and informality and formality.

These tendencies do not, of course, in any simple sense follow suit, so that dispersal and introversion, for example, necessarily entail division and autonomy. But they all testify to the general importance of a dialectical pattern in social life, and there is a tendency for correlation, conversely expressed in such a way that amity and relatedness tend to be promoted by concentration and shared activity and so on. Elaborate formalization, for example, together with prominent public negotiation, is a conspicuous characteristic of attempts to affirm relationships and impose collective over individual interests, while situations in which relationships are renounced or interpersonal affairs resolved in contravention of kinship ideology, community interests, or the authority of the elders tend to involve considerable exercise of "social grace" and typically take the form of invisible, low-profile nonevents that just seem to happen, or slowly and furtively "transpire"—suggesting that formality and social grace serve to ease the frequent initiation and termination of relationships enabled by open aggregation.

One context in which a dialectic of autonomy and relatedness operates among the Bentian is in the process of growth and maturation in the life cycle. Here, autonomy and self-sufficiency, on the one hand, and relatedness and dependency, on the other, are essentially dialectically constituted in that the one is largely achieved through the other. In contrast to the Buid, for whom Gibson (1985:398–400) describes maturity as attained through an ability to engage in sexual intercourse and cultivate a swidden and an achieved state of independence from specific others, especially from one's parents, becoming an adult among the Bentian is understood more in terms of developing new relationships outside one's household and natal family and an increasing ability to act responsibly (by performing kinship obligations) and take responsibility over others (by acquiring children and later grandchildren or other dependents).

Among the Bentian, the process of maturation involves not just growing autonomy but both growing autonomy *and* relatedness, and the autonomy one acquires (by becoming economically independent and later socially mature) is quickly countered by new responsibilities—and only maintained through their performance—as well as transposed into dependency on the part of others (for similar findings, see Myers 1986:238–39; and Tsing 1984:517–19). This difference with the Buid reflects the different role of kinship as an idiom and ideology among them and the Bentian and especially the fact that being a relative, by acting as one, represents an integral aspect of Bentian personal and social identity.

Among the Bentian, as among the Ilongot and Pintupi, kinship represents, as McKinley has argued more generally, a "philosophy … about what completes a person socially, psychologically, and morally, and how that completeness comes about through a responsible sense of attachment and obligation to others" (2001:143). Hence, it is, as among the Ilongot (see Rosaldo 1980:68, 182), especially adults who "know of kinship," and I was told that "immature people" (*tia*, a category including children and youths until the age of about thirty) need the guidance of their seniors (and occasional explicit instruction, *matek*) because they "do not know how to act as siblings-in-law" (*beau tau mayu, beau tau mongan*), an expression often used to metonymically designate failure to comply with kinship obligations.

Becoming a mature social person in Bentian society is seen to be not only about acquiring the material resources required for this—although it is important and the vitality of young people enabling them to make large swiddens in primary forest is a source of special prestige for them—but also about adopting proper kin behavior and investing one's resources in this process. Similar, dialectically constituted orientations of autonomy and relatedness like those referred to by the Ilongot as *beya* (knowledge) and *liget* (passion) thus also operate among the Bentian, among whom they are associated with differential generalized roles attributed to old and young people and the principles of intergenerational hierarchy and intragenerational equality structured by the encompassing idiom of kinship.

Conclusion

> And kinship itself, like other aspects of Ilongot social discourse, tends to minimize acknowledgment of enduring differences, permitting people who— for whatever reason—come to see themselves as related to express at once equality, independence, common interests, and cooperative concerns.
> —Michelle Rosaldo, *Knowledge and Passion*, 1980

This essay has addressed a problem noted by Gibson, namely, that ethnographers of bilateral Southeast Asian swidden cultivators lacking descent groups have often "been content to describe the lack of permanence in social group composition, and the weakness of ties between specific categories of kin, without going on to describe the mechanisms by which new and temporary group solidarity is continuously being constructed" (1986: 67). I have offered an answer to this question by describing how kinship functions as a source of solidarity among the Bentian. This is not because it automatically generates organized groups through the application of a simple principle of descent, as classical kinship theory once led us to expect. As in other bilateral societies, Bentian kinship does not operate this way (see Macdonald, this volume).

In the most general sense, Bentian kinship ideology promotes amity, closeness, and the recognition of obligations among all relatives, including genealogical, affinal, and classificatory kin, and facilitates the flexible and selective creation of effective ties based on practical association within a wide range of potential ties. More specifically, it extends an ideal of symmetrical sibling solidarity widely across intragenerational relations, and an ideal of asymmetrical respect and responsibility in intergenerational relations, and provides a personal incentive for compliance with social obligations. The key to bilateral kinship as a source of solidarity in anarchic societies is how it dialectically conjoins the recognition of generalized moral obligations within the local community with the practical cultivation of specific moral relations by autonomous individuals.

Notes

The writing of this chapter and the editing of this volume were enabled by funding from the Academy of Finland for a three-year postdoctoral research project entitled "Sources of Solidarity in an Indonesian Society." The empirical research, on which this article is based, was financed by the Academy of Finland, the Ella and Georg Ehrnrooth Foundation, the Finnish Ministry of Education, the Nordic Institute of Asian Studies, the Nordenskiöld Society, the Swedish School of Social Science at the University of Helsinki, and the Oskar Öflund Foundation. It was carried out under the auspices of Universitas Indonesia and Lembaga Ilmu Pengetahuan Indonesia.

1 An expression of the importance of kinship for providing trust, illustrating that endogamy is not just incidental, is the important institution of "following your kin" (*nyang kaben*) in the context of increasingly frequent village exogamy, meaning that those who marry out tend to marry in villages where their "kin" have already married, and often, to marry affines of their consanguines there. Thus kinship enables people to go (for visits or in search of work opportunities, *usaha*) where they would not otherwise go. Most cases of village exogamy are with people from a quite limited number of other villages.

2 As is common in Southeast Asia (see, e.g., Carsten 1995; and Dumont 1992), "forgetting kinship" plays, notwithstanding ideological injunctions to the contrary, an important part in many Bentians' kinship experiences, thus providing additional testimony to the practical constitution of kinship.

References

Appell, George N. 1976. "The Rungus: Social structure in a cognatic society and its symbolism." In G.N. Appell, ed., *The Societies of Borneo: Explorations in the Theory of Cognatic Social Structure*, 66–86. Special Publications, no. 6. Washington, DC: American Anthropological Association.

Atkinson, Jane. 1989. *The Art and Politics of Wana Shamanship*. Berkeley: University of California Press.

Banks, D.J. 1974. "Malay kinship terms and Morgan's Malayan terminology: The complexity of simplicity." *Bijdragen tot de Taal-, Land- en Volkenkunde* 130 (1):44–68.

Benjamin, Geoffrey. 1968. "Temiar personal names." *Bijdragen tot de Taal-, Land- en Volkenkunde* 124:99–134.

———. 1994. "Danger and dialectic in Temiar childhood." In J. Koubi and J. Massard-Vincent, eds., *Enfants et Sociétés d'Asie du Sud-Est*, 37–62. Paris: L'Harmattan.

Bird-David, Nurit. 1994. "Sociality and immediacy, or, past and present conversations on bands." *Man*, new series, 29 (3):583–603.

Bloch, Maurice. 1971. "The moral and tactical meaning of kinship terms." *Man*, new series, 6 (1):79–87.

Bodenhorn, Barbara. 2000. "'He used to be my relative': Exploring the bases of relatedness among Inupiat of Northern Alaska." In J. Carsten, ed., *Cultures of Relatedness: New Approaches to the Study of Kinship*, 128–48. Cambridge: Cambridge University Press.

Bourdieu, Pierre. 1977. *Outline of a Theory of Practice*. Cambridge: Cambridge University Press.

Carsten, Janet. 1995. "The politics of forgetting: Migration, kinship, and memory on the periphery of the Southeast Asian state." *Journal of the Royal Anthropological Institute* 1 (2):317–35.

———. 1997. *The Heat of the Hearth: The Process of Kinship in a Malay Fishing Community*. Oxford: Clarendon Press.

Carsten, Janet, ed. 2000. *Cultures of Relatedness: New Approaches to the Study of Kinship*. Cambridge: Cambridge University Press.

Chan, Henry. 2007. *Survival in the Rainforest: Change and Resilience of the Punan Vuhang of Eastern Sarawak, Malaysia*. Research Series in Anthropology. no. 12. Helsinki: University of Helsinki Press.

Collins, Randall. 1988. *Theoretical Sociology*. San Diego: Harcourt, Brace, Jovanovitch.

———. 2005. *Interaction Ritual Chains*. Princeton, N.J.: Princeton University Press

Dentan, Robert. 1993. "Senoi." In P. Hocking, ed., *Encyclopedia of World Cultures*. Vol. 5: *East and Southeast Asia*, 236–39. Boston: G.K. Hall.

Dumont, Jean-Paul. 1992. *Visayan Vignettes: Ethnographic Traces of a Philippine Island*. Chicago: University of Chicago Press.

Eder, James. 1999. "The Batak." In R.B. Lee and R. Daly, eds., *Cambridge Encyclopedia of Contemporary Hunter-Gatherers*, 294–97. New York: Cambridge University Press.

Endicott, Kirk. 1988. "Property, power, and conflict among the Batek of Malaysia." In T. Ingold, D. Riches, and J. Woodburn, eds., *Hunters and Gatherers*. Vol. 2: *Property, Power, and Ideology*, 110–27. Oxford: Berg,.

———. 1993. "Semang." In P. Hocking, ed., *Encyclopedia of World Cultures*, Vol. 5: *East and Southeast Asia*, 233–36. Boston: G.K. Hall.

Fajans, Jane. 1997. *They Make Themselves: Work and Play among the Baining of Papua New Guinea*. Chicago: University of Chicago Press.

———. 2006. "Autonomy and relatedness: Emotions and the tension between individuality and Sociality." *Critique of Anthropology* 26 (1):103–119.

Franklin, Sarah, and Susan McKinnon, eds. 2001. *Relative Values: Reconfiguring Kinship Studies*. Durham: Duke University Press.

Freeman, Derek. 1960. "The Iban of Western Borneo." In G.P. Murdock, ed., *Social Structure in Southeast Asia*. Chicago: Quadrangle.

———. 1961. "On the concept of the kindred." *Journal of the Royal Anthropological Institute of Great Britain and Ireland* 91 (2):192–220.

Geddes, W.R. 1954. *The Land Dayaks of Sarawak: A Report on a Social Economic Survey of the Land Dayaks of Sarawak Presented to the Colonial Social Science Research Council*. London: Her Majesty's Stationery Office.

Geertz, Clifford. 1972. "Deep play: Notes on the Balinese cockfight." *Daedalus* 101:1–37.

Gibson, Thomas. 1985. "The sharing of substance versus the sharing of activity among the Buid." *Man*, new series, 20 (3):391–411.

———. 1986. *Sacrifice and Sharing in the Philippine Highlands: Religion and Society among the Buid of Mindoro*. London: Athlone Press.

Guemple, Lee. 1988. "Teaching social relations to Inuit children." In T. Ingold, D. Riches, and J. Woodburn, eds., *Hunters and Gatherers*. Vol. 2: *Property, Power, and Ideology*, 131–49. Oxford: Berg.

Hagen, James. 2006. *Community in the Balance: Morality and Social Change in an Indonesian Society*. Boulder: Paradigm Publishers.

Helliwell, Christine. 2001. *"Never Stand Alone': A Study of Borneo Sociality."* Phillips, ME: Borneo Research Council.

Howell, Signe. 1989. *Society and Cosmos: Chewong of Peninsular Malaysia*. Chicago: University of Chicago Press.

Kemp, Jeremy. 1983. "Kinship and the management of personal relations: Kin terminologies and the axiom of amity." *Bijdragen tot de Taal-, Land- en Volkenkunde* 139 (1):81–98.

King, Victor. 1978. "Introduction." In V. King, ed., *Essays on Borneo Societies*, 1–36. Oxford: Oxford University Press.

———. 1991. "Cognation and rank in Borneo." In F. Hüsken and J. Kemp, eds., *Cognation and Social Organization in Southeast Asia*, 15–31. Leiden: KITLV Press.

Knapen, Hans. 2001. *Forests of Fortune? The Environmental History of Southeast Borneo, 1600–1880*. Leiden: KITLV Press.

Lumholtz, Carl. 1920. *Through Central Borneo: An Account of Two Years of Travel in the Land of the Head-Hunters between the Years 1913 and 1917*. Vol. 2. New York: Charles Scribner's Sons.

Macdonald, Charles. 1977. *Une Société Simple: Parenté et Residence chez les Palawan (Philippines)*. Paris: Institut d'Ethnologie.

McKinley, Robert. [1979] 1983. "Cain and Abel on the Malay Peninsula." In Mac Marshall, ed., *Siblingship in Oceania: Studies in the Meaning of Kin Relations*, 335–87. Lanham, MD: University Press of America.

———. 2001. "The philosophy of kinship: A reply to Schneider's 'Critique of the study of kinship.'" In R. Feinberg and M. Ottenheimer, eds., *The Cultural Analysis of Kinship: The Legacy of David M. Schneider*, 131–67. Urbana: University of Illinois Press.

Myers, Fred. 1986. *Pintupi Country, Pintupi Self: Sentiment, Place, and Politics among Western Desert Aborigines*. Berkeley: University of California Press.

Needham, Rodney. 1959. "Mourning terms." *Bijdragen tot de Taal-, Land- en Volkenkunde* 115:58–89.

Nicolaisen, Ida. 1998. "Ancestral names and government names: Assessing self and social identity among the Punan Bah of Central Borneo." *KVHAA Konferenser* 42:361–82.

Peletz, Michael. 1988. *A Share of the Harvest: Kinship, Property and Social History Among the Malays of Rembau*. Berkeley: University of California Press.

Rosaldo, Michelle. 1980. *Knowledge and Passion: Ilongot Notions of Self and Social Life*. Cambridge: Cambridge University Press.

Rosaldo, Renato. 1993. "Ilongot visiting: Social grace and the rhythms of every-day life." In S. Lavie, K. Narayan, and R. Rosaldo, eds., *Creativity/Anthropology*, 253–69. Ithaca and London: Cornell University Press.

Rousseau, Jérôme. 1990. *Central Borneo: Ethnic Identity and Social Life in a Stratified Society*. Oxford: Oxford University Press.

———. 1998. *Kayan Religion: Ritual Life and Religious Reform in Central Borneo*. Leiden: KITLV Press.

Sather, Clifford. 1996. "'All threads are white': Iban egalitarianism reconsidered." In J. Fox and C. Sather, eds., *Origins, Ancestry, and Alliance: Explorations in Austronesian Ethnography*, 70–110. Canberra: Australian National University.

Sellato, Bernard. 1994. *Nomads of the Borneo Rainforest: The Economics, Politics, and Ideology of Settling Down*. Honolulu: University of Hawai'i Press.

Schiller, Anne. 1997. *Small Sacrifices: Religious Change and Cultural Identity among the Ngaju of Indonesia*. New York: Oxford University Press.

Schlegel, Stuart. 1998. *Wisdom from a Rainforest: The Spiritual Journey of an Anthropologist*. Athens: University of Georgia Press.

Schneider, David. 1984. *A Critique of the Study of Kinship*. Ann Arbor: University of Michigan Press.

Schrauwers, Albert. 1999. "Negotiating parentage: The political economy of 'kinship' in Central Sulawesi, Indonesia." *American Ethnologist* 26 (2):310–23.

Schutz, Alfred, and Thomas Luckmann. 1973. *The Structure of the Life-World*. Evanston: Northwestern University Press.

Sillander, Kenneth. 2004. *Acting Authoritatively: How Authority Is Expressed among the Bentian of Indonesian Borneo*. Swedish School of Social Science Publications, no. 17. Helsinki: University of Helsinki Press.

———. 2010. "Teknonymy, name-avoidance, solidarity, and individuation among the Bentian of Indonesian Borneo." In Zeng Yangwen and C.J.-H. MacDonald, eds., *Personal Names in Asia: History, Culture, and Identity*, 101–27. Singapore: National University of Singapore Press.

Storrie, Robert. 2003. "Equivalence, personhood, and relationality: Processes of relatedness among the Hoti of Venezuelan Guiana." *Journal of the Royal Anthropological Institute* 9:407–28.

Strathern, Marilyn. 1992. *After Nature: English Kinship in the Late Twentieth Century*. Cambridge: Cambridge University Press.

Tsing, Anna Lowenhaupt. 1984. "Politics and Culture in the Meratus Mountains." PhD diss., Stanford University.

———. 1993. *In the Realm of the Diamond Queen: Marginality in an Out-of-the-Way Place*. Princeton: Princeton University Press.

Waterson, Roxana. 1986. "The ideology and terminology of kinship among the Sa'dan Toraja." *Bijdragen tot de Taal-, Land- en Volkenkunde* 142 (1):87–112.

Yengoyan, Aram. 1973. "Kindred and task groups in Mandaya social organization." *Ethnology* 7 (2):163–77.

7

Egalitarianism and Ranking in the Malay World

GEOFFREY BENJAMIN

THIS VOLUME FOCUSES on the highly egalitarian ethos, linked with a high degree of personal autonomy-cum-communality, that has proved characteristic of many minority populations of insular Southeast Asia. Some commentators have suggested that this dialectical configuration reflects an original human propensity that has been suppressed elsewhere by the emergence of interfering (hierarchical) modes of consociation. Others have emphasized the psychological or cosmological underpinnings peculiar to each of these populations. Yet others have seen this societal pattern as a strategic response to depredation or the threat of incorporation by neighboring populations. Each of these views captures an important aspect of the reality. However, we must also acknowledge that the populations in question are (or were until recently) *tribal*. This means that we are dealing not with social isolates but—in Southeast Asia especially—with populations that have long perfected what James Scott (2009) calls "the art of not being governed." In other words, such populations are tribal precisely *because* they have developed techniques for keeping the state off their backs.[1] If they had not succeeded in this, they would have become peasants—which is indeed what happened to many Southeast Asian populations over the past two millennia, following the extension of state power. Tribal society therefore cannot be properly understood except with reference to the wider social framework of which it forms a part and in which ranked centralized social formations dominate. Consequently, the "autonomy, equality, and fellowship" of this volume's title must be seen as characterizing just one path among the several alternative paths that have been taken in Southeast Asia.

The distinction between egalitarian/tribal and ranked/centralized is not a simple two-way contrast. Studies in other parts of Southeast Asia have shown that social ranking—inherited differences of prestige—emerged from within egalitarian populations prior to the imposition of centralized states. Anthropologists have examined this process in detail for upland areas of northern mainland Southeast Asia, where unilineal descent structures have been the norm.[2] My own investigations suggest that this also happened in the Malay World, among populations that have remained in continuous contact with each other but in which cognatic kinship patterns have been much more usual than unilineal ones. Despite their many differences in language and way of life, these populations have long shared the same cultural pool, thereby constituting an interconnected regional array rather than an assemblage of distinct "societies." Thus—in contrast to the situation in upland northern Southeast Asia—state, peasant, and tribal patterns in the Malay World, and probably more widely in island Southeast Asia, arose by differentiation from within essentially the same cultural matrix. It is all the more important, therefore, to view occurrences of equality and fellowship in the Malay World as a choice made from within an array that also includes less equal societal patterns.

As used here, the term Malay World corresponds to what many Malays (*Orang Melayu*) themselves call the *Alam Melayu*. It refers to those parts of Insular and Peninsular Southeast Asia in which Malay-speaking, Islamic sultanates have historically held sway: southern Isthmian Thailand, Peninsular Malaysia, Singapore, the central east-coast parts of Sumatra, and parts of coastal Borneo (including the still extant sultanate of Brunei). In this essay, however, attention is paid primarily to the Malay Peninsula.

From prehistoric times the peoples of the Malay World have variously followed every known tropical way of life (except transhumant pastoralism), namely:

- ➤ Nomadic hunter-gathering (forest, strand, and maritime)
- ➤ Forest and maritime collecting-and-trading
- ➤ Hill-dwelling swidden farming
- ➤ Rural wet-rice farming and smallholding
- ➤ Inland lake, coastal, and deep-sea fishing

➤ Long-distance interregional trading

➤ The full range of traditional and modern enterprises

For any such mode to be viably self-regenerating, it must attract a sufficient body of people, suitably organized and prepared to lead the required kind of life. Moreover, the attractions of alternative ways of life must be downplayed, especially where the various populations share the same cultural pool. These desiderata are best met when an appropriate societal imagery is implanted as the unspoken taken-for-granted basis for everyday life. Sociologists of modern society sometimes refer to such disguised implantation as "hegemony." In egalitarian tribal societies, how-ever, the hegemons are far harder to recognize because there is usually no recognizable elite. But this does not mean that hegemony is absent. Their very egalitarianism means that we are probably dealing with a conspiracy of all against all, disguised as "culture," involving notions of the person, cosmological imagery, patterns of language use, and so on. Here I shall concentrate on kinship, once regarded by many ethnographers as the core of "culture."

In the Malay World, kinship-based hegemonic images have come to be encapsulated in a trio of mutually dissimilatory societal traditions (or cul-tural regimes [see below]) that I label Semang, Senoi, and Malayic (see tables 7.1 and 7.2 and map 7.2.) The Semang and Senoi societal traditions are found only in the Malay Peninsula. The Malayic tradition, on the other hand, is found both there and in parts of Sumatra and Borneo. The Semang and Senoi traditions are manifested in segmentary, egalitarian, state-rejecting tribal societies whose present-day representatives form part of the Orang Asli (Aboriginal) populations. The Malayic tradition exists in two forms: (1) segmentary, ranked, state-rejecting tribal societies (also regarded as Orang Asli); and (2) centralized, ranked, state-based forms. The latter constitute the various historically known Malay (Melayu) kingdoms, several of which survive as sultanates to the present day.

These societal traditions, I argue, relate to the constraints and strategies associated with choosing one mode of environmental appropriation rather than another.[3] None of these variants simply *happened*, for they were institutionalized and locked in place by the subtle but consequential kinship games discussed below. These take the form of seemingly arbitrary and trivial rules, organized around some hitherto rarely considered kinship

Map 7.1 *Peninsular societal traditions (approximate distribution)*

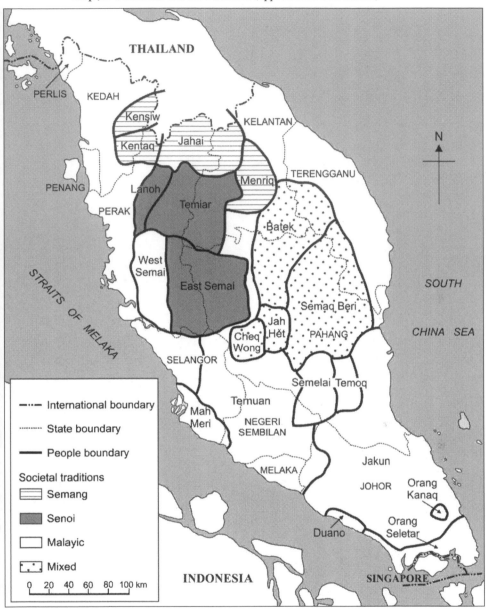

The historically known maximal distributions are indicated here. At the present time, most Orang Asli
occupy smaller and more discontinuous territories.

Malays (Orang Melayu) now live almost everywhere
in the peninsula and are therefore not indicated on
the map.

Table 7.1 *Peninsular societal patterns*

People	Population[a] (1999/2004)	Language	Mode of Societal Integration	Dominant Appropria-tive Mode	Kinship Reckoning	Social Unit of Productive Enterprise	Cousin Marriage	Ranking	Filiative Bias	Societal Tradition
Kensiw[b]	240	Northern Aslian	band	foraging	inclusive	conjugal family	forbidden	egalitarian	patri	Semang
Kentaq[b]	132	Northern Aslian	band	foraging	inclusive	conjugal family	forbidden	egalitarian	patri	Semang
Jahai[b]	2073	Northern Aslian	band	foraging	inclusive	conjugal family	forbidden	egalitarian	patri	Semang
Menriq	215	Northern Aslian	band	foraging	inclusive	conjugal family	forbidden	egalitarian	patri	Semang
Lanoh	349	Central Aslian	band	none dominant	inclusive	conjugal family	forbidden	egalitarian	cognatic	Senoi
Temiar	25,233	Central Aslian	tribal	farming	inclusive	descent group	forbidden	egalitarian	cognatic	Senoi
East Semai	43,505	Central Aslian	tribal	farming	inclusive	descent group	forbidden	egalitarian	cognatic	Senoi
West Semai		Central Aslian	peasant	farming	exclusive	conjugal family	permitted[c]	egalitarian	cognatic	Malayic
Temoq	681	Southern Aslian	tribal	collecting	exclusive	conjugal family	permitted	ranked	matri	Malayic
Semelai	6,584	Southern Aslian	tribal	collecting	exclusive?[c]	conjugal family	permitted?[d]	ranked	matri	Malayic
Besisi (Mah Meri)	2,858	Southern Aslian	tribal	collecting	exclusive	conjugal family	permitted	ranked	matri	Malayic
Jakun	21,484	Austro-nesian	tribal	collecting	exclusive	conjugal family	permitted	ranked	matri	Malayic
Orang Kanaq	72	Austro-nesian	tribal	collecting	exclusive	conjugal family	permitted	ranked	matri	Malayic

(continued)

Table 7.1 (continued)

People	Population[a] (1999/2004)	Language	Mode of Societal Integration	Dominant Appropriative Mode	Kinship Reckoning	Social Unit of Productive Enterprise	Cousin Marriage	Ranking	Filiative Bias	Societal Tradition
Melayu	13 million[e]	Austronesian	peasant	farming	exclusive	conjugal family	permitted	ranked	matri	Malayic
Minangkabau		Austronesian	peasant	farming	exclusive	descent group	permitted	ranked	matri	Malayic
Temuan	18,560	Austronesian	tribal	collecting	exclusive	variable	permitted	ranked	variable	Malayic
Duano[f]	3,221	Austronesian	tribal	collecting	?	?	permitted[g]	?	?	Malayic?
Orang Seletar[f]	1,037	Austronesian	tribal	collecting	?	conjugal family	?		?	Malayic?
Chewong	665	Northern Aslian	tribal	none	exclusive?	conjugal family	forbidden[h]	egalitarian	matri	Mixed
Jah Hět	5,082	Central Aslian	tribal	none	inclusive	variable	forbidden	ranked	matri	Mixed
Semaq Beri	3,629	Southern Aslian	band	none	inclusive	conjugal family	forbidden?	ranked	?	Mixed
Batek (Dè?)	1,842	Northern Aslian	band	none	becoming exclusive	conjugal family	permitted	egalitarian	becoming matri	Mixed

Source: updated from Benjamin 1985:251.

a Estimated figures based on Malaysian Census counts in 1999 and on unpublished materials supplied by Juli Edo.

b In Thailand there are additionally between 200 and 400 or more speakers of these and other Northern Aslian languages.

c First-cousin marriage is prohibited; second-cousin marriage and beyond is permitted.

d Semelai social organization appears to be changing in several respects, and reports differ. In some cases, for example, cousin marriages are tolerated (rather than preferred) on payment of fines.

e This approximate figure does not include the Orang Melayu of Thailand, Sumatra and Borneo, who together probably number about the same again as those of Peninsular Malaysia and Singapore.

f Relevant information on these two coast-dwelling populations is difficult to locate, but they probably follow the Malayic societal tradition.

g Cross-cousins only; parallel-cousins are forbidden.

h Patrilateral-parallel cousin-marriage is forbidden; other varieties of cousin-marriage occur, but receive varying evaluations.

features and established as taken-for-granted aspects of everyday life. The imposition of rules, of course, requires political action.

To talk of "*a* culture," "*a* tradition," or "*a* way of life" is to refer to a way of acting and thinking that has been actively *cultivated* and *instituted*. We are then dealing with a deliberately shaped limitation on access to knowledge, aimed at controlling the ease with which alternative views may be communicated to others. Consequently, people will be constrained to see just one particular way of living as more commonsensical than the alternatives. It is therefore more appropriate to talk of "(cultural) regimes" and "polities" rather than "cultures" and "societies" (Benjamin 1993:349–50, 2005:262). A regime is a cultural framework actively systematized by sanction-backed restrictions, so that only one of the possible ways of approaching the world remains capable of easy, overt, "matter-of-fact" expression. (It is here that structuralism best appears to work.) A polity is any social network institutionalized or thought of as a power-dominated domain: these may be families, clans, or corporations, as well as states both ancient and modern. (It is here that the various kinds of functionalism work best.)[4] The societal traditions discussed here therefore constitute cultural regimes, and the populations who follow those traditions constitute polities.

Table 7.2 *Semang, Senoi, and Malayic Traditions*		
Semang	Senoi	Malayic
Foraging	Swidden farming	Collecting for trade + farming
Inclusive kinship reckoning	Inclusive kinship reckoning	Exclusive kinship reckoning
Conjugal family as productive unit	Descent group as productive unit	Conjugal family as productive unit
Cousin marriage forbidden	Cousin marriage forbidden	Cousin marriage permitted
Egalitarian	Egalitarian	Ranked
Patrifocal bias	Cognatic	Matrifocal bias
Long postpartum taboo	Shorter postpartum taboo	Short postpartum taboo

The Semang, Senoi, and Malayic Traditions

Studies have shown that until the later Neolithic period Peninsular populations were switching facultatively between different ways of life, each of which involved varying periods of sedentism and nomadism.[5] A degree of sedentism had probably been established at least as early as 3000 BCE by gatherers who may also have been incipient farmers. Until around 500 BCE foragers could plant crops from time to time, farmers could go hunting and fishing, and both foragers and farmers could go trading seasonally in forest products without placing their livelihoods in any apparent jeopardy and without significantly modifying their demographic and social-organizational patterns.[6]

By two thousand years ago, however, the northern foragers would have had to come to terms with their neighbors. The latter by then would have been preoccupied with raising root crops, and possibly such grain crops as rice and millet, generating an increasingly dense and sedentary population. The foragers, now pressed into smaller territories in the foothills, would nevertheless have utilized the ecotonal areas emerging on the edges of the farming tracts. This would have allowed them to become *more* committed to nomadism by reducing their sedentary periods of desultory swidden tending. The opening-up of trans-Isthmian portage trade routes from around two thousand years ago would have granted the further opportunity of profiting from civilization's leftovers as well as from direct employment as porters. To maximize these benefits the attraction of sedentism had to be blocked out of the nomads' consciousness as far as possible by declaring the neighboring farmers an example *not* to follow. I suggest that, by mutual dissimilation, this eventually led to the establishment of both the Semang and Senoi societal regimes, based primarily on the imposition of formal kinship rules.

The Semang Tradition

The Semang tradition, followed today by several different ethnolinguistic populations (table 7.1), arose as a means of locking people into a nomadic foraging way of life. Because foraging brings in relatively constant amounts of protein—since it is gathered, not produced—the followers of the Semang tradition have placed high value on egalitarianism and a low-density, nonexpanding population. The low density is further aided by their long postpartum taboo on sexual relations. So as not to overwhelm the environment, they have maintained small local groups dispersed through the environment. In order to make the greatest use of resources, they have maintained a conjugal-family level of productive enterprise that nevertheless allows them to come together in larger groups when necessary in temporary camps. To obviate the drastic effects of random demographic fluctuations and to ensure the persistence of a large enough breeding base of like-minded people for the population to sustain itself through time, they have maintained intergroup links across wide distances. Above all, to resist the blandishments of more settled ways of life (such as those of the Temiars and Malays, discussed below), they have committed themselves to nomadism and an opportunistic outlook (Benjamin 1973:viii). Consequently, the Semang populations have had to see the wider Peninsular society as something they should turn their backs on, except when they had the chance to "forage" off it as casual laborers or suppliers of forest products.

The inventors of the Semang tradition did this through instituting a set of distinctive kinship observances (see table 7.3). First, although (like their neighbors the Temiars) they reckon kin relations inclusively and forbid marriage with traceable consanguines, they differ from the Temiars in forbidding marriage with traceable affines.[7] Thus, followers of the Semang tradition must avoid marrying where their own consanguines have already married. Instead, they marry at relatively great social and geographical distances, thereby maintaining a very wide-ranging spatial network of social relations.

Second, although Semang kinship terminologies make no distinction between links through males or females, greater emphasis is placed in practice on links through males. This patri-bias shows up in the skewed shape of individuals' personal genealogical memories, as well as in the relative patrilocality of domestic groupings.[8] In general, patri-biased groups tend to be more thinly spread on the ground because they keep all the related men of the local group together and therefore more able and likely to cooperate with each other if there is squabbling with other local groups. Other things being equal, a patri-biased regime will therefore be egalitarian within the local community, and it will generate a low overall population density (Murphy 1957:1033–34). Moreover, unless formal patrilineality is instituted (which was not the case in the Malay Peninsula), such a regime

Table 7.3 *Peninsular Patterns of Cross-Sex Relations*

People	Parent-in-Law WiMo/♀DaHu HuFa/♂SoWi	Sibling-in-Law Wi$_e$Si/♀$_y$SiHu Hu$_e$Br/♂$_y$BrWi	Sibling-in-Law Wi$_y$Si/♀$_e$SiHu Hu$_y$Br/♂$_e$BrWi	Sibling Adult Br/Si	Inter-actional Pattern	Societal Tradi-tion
Kensiw	avoidance	avoidance	neutral	avoidance		
Kintaq	avoidance	avoidance	neutral	avoidance	+avoidance, −joking	Semang
Jahai	avoidance	avoidance	avoidance	avoidance		
Menriq	avoidance	avoidance	avoidance	avoidance		
Lanoh	avoidance	restraint	joking	neutral		
Temiar	avoidance	joking	joking	neutral	+avoidance, +joking	Senoi
East Semai	avoidance	avoidance	joking	neutral		
Jah Hĕt	avoidance	restraint	restraint	neutral	+avoidance, −joking[a]	
Semaq Beri	restraint	restraint	restraint	restraint		Mixed
Batek (Dè')	restraint	restraint	restraint	neutral		
Chewong	restraint	restraint	restraint	neutral		
West Semai	restraint	restraint	restraint	neutral		
Temoq	restraint	?	?	neutral	−avoidance, −joking	
Semelai	restraint	neutral	neutral	neutral		Malayic
Jakun	restraint	restraint	restraint	neutral		
All others (including Melayu)	neutral	neutral	neutral	neutral		

Source: Modified from Benjamin 1985:252.

[a]The Jah Hĕt are listed as "mixed" because they follow "Semang-like" rules of cross-sex relations while also practicing "Malayic" matrifocality and ranking (Couillard 1980:88–102).

makes it difficult to maintain a supralocal level of organization. The Semang societal tradition, therefore, is best described as minimalist.[9]

Third, this minimalism is locked into place by a set of taboos that impose avoidance relations between precisely those opposite-sex adults whose relationships sit astride the boundary between the conjugal family and the rest of the kin network. These are (1) brother/sister, (2) brother-in-law/sister-in-law, and (3) mother-in-law/son-in-law and father-in-law/

daughter-in-law (as indicated in table 7.3: Kensiw, Kintaq, Jahai, Menriq). The three avoidance rules—especially that between brother-in-law and sister-in-law—serve to picture the most desirable form of society as one constituted of easily detachable conjugal-family groups linked together through the marriage of men and women who were not previously related either by traceable consanguinity or affinity. This would militate against sedentism, since it implies that the conjugal family can take off autonomously at a moment's notice without putting the wider social network at risk. Coupled with the Semang groups' low population densities, this would imply, in turn, a readiness to wander far and wide in search not only of food but of social relations.

The Senoi Tradition

For the neighboring hill farmers, on the other hand, Semang nomadism would have been an attractive but increasingly inappropriate model to follow. The farmers' longer-term commitment to sedentary village life would have reduced their access to the more exciting Semang-type nomadic hunting and gathering. Accordingly, to lock their sedentism in place, they established a kinship regime based on rules that contrasted directly with the Semang pattern. In place of the Semang taboo on cross-sex sibling-in-law relations, they switched the signs and imposed sexually laden joking relationships (see Lanoh, Temiar, and East Semai in table 7.3), thereby instilling the idea that it was a good thing to have sex with and/or to marry someone from the same group that one's siblings or cousins had already married into. This feature characterizes the distinctively Senoi societal tradition.

The Senoi populations, today represented mainly by the Temiars and East (upland) Semais, would have been aware of the increasing social complexification in the Malay (Melayu) areas (as discussed below), but they could hardly have wanted to follow that path themselves. In their upland fastnesses, beyond the reach of canoes, they would have felt secure against any peasantization of social relations and consciousness. Although they were exchanging forest products for knives, salt, or pots, they would have preferred to do so without entering into close social relations with the wider community from which those goods came. Committed to their sedentary swidden farming and forest product trading, the Senoi populations had to prevent these activities from leading them in the direction taken by the Malays or they would lose their autonomy. Slave raiding was such an endemic condition of life in the Peninsula until the early twentieth century that the Temiars and Semais developed an institutionalized "shyness," leading them to avoid, rather than confront, strangers (see Endicott 1983; and Dentan 1992).[10] This is similar to Gibson's argument (in this volume) that Southeast Asian tribal egalitarianism was a response to the "predatory ranking" of their lowland neighbors.

On the other hand, the Temiars and Semais would also have found much to attract them in Semang nomadism, for they still greatly enjoy hunting in the forest. But this activity has had to remain a spare-time one, or it would have compromised the localized sedentism necessary to their farming. The Temiars, in particular, would have been aware of the details of Semang social organization, for the two populations have long intermarried and shared religious revelations. This knowledge would have aided the Temiars in steering a course between the patri-biased dispersal of the Semang and the matri-biased local concentration of the Malays discussed below. This, I suggest, is why they instituted a joking relation between opposite-sex siblings-in-law (see table 7.3)—the exact reverse of the avoidance that the Semang enjoin between the same relatives. While the Semang avoidance is aimed at generating a network of social relations extending over great distances by placing an embargo on marrying those to whom one is already related by marriage, the Temiar joking relation implies the opposite: that one should positively reinforce one's local attachments by marrying where one's close relatives have already married. By increasing the sheer availability of sexual partners, and coupled with a shorter postpartum sex taboo, this would have led to a rise in Senoi population density—a further reason to reject the nomadic way and lock one's own people firmly into sedentism. (See Benjamin 1985 for further discussion.)

The Malayic Tradition

The Malayic tradition (see tables 7.1–7.3) developed mostly downstream and to the south of the Semang and Senoi traditions and resulted from the struggle to combine farming and the collecting for trade of forest products into a unitary way of life. The collecting component would have intensified around two thousand years ago, when Chinese, Indian, and West Asian interests had led to the exploitation by tribal "fetchers" of Peninsular and Sumatran products (Wang 1958; Wheatley 1961). In the Malay World, however, farming and intensified forest collecting impose contrary organizational demands: farming involves the joint cooperation of the men and women within the village sphere, while collecting for trade requires the dispersal of the men away from the village for considerable periods. The ethnographic evidence shows that within-village (and hence farming-related) core-group relations have tended to be thought of as matrifilial relations, while the dispersed extravillage relations generated in trading with foreigners have been thought of as patrifilial.[11]

Yet, if acted on too rigorously, this matrifilial/patrifilial imagery would generate an organizational pattern incompatible with the requirements of the males' collecting for trade. Sedentary farming carried out by a matrifiliated core of villagers would eventually lead to a network of matrifocal local groups whose male members move in from elsewhere on marriage. Closely related males would therefore tend to disperse and lose effective cooperation with each other, while the males within each local community would tend to be patrifilially unrelated to each other and less inclined to cooperate (Murphy 1957:1033).[12] There was a simple solution, however, and eventually it was taken up. Where previously, as in the Semang and Senoi traditions, the people had preferred not to marry traceable consanguineal kin (thereby generating a more inclusive kinship regime), they now solved their problems by modifying their "incest" fears and instituting preferential consanguineal endogamy—that is, cousin marriage. (This need not have been literally so; it could mean merely that husband and wife should think of each other as "cousins" [terminologically, "elder sibling" and "younger sibling," respectively], whether or not this was genealogically the case.) The males of each village could now think of themselves as consanguineally related after all, so that they could continue without hindrance to treat their cooperative trading as patrifiliatively organized. At the same time, their links with males in other villages could now be thought of as falling outside the sphere of kinship, preparing them ideologically for the competition that would have emerged between villages for the goodwill of the traders downstream.

As already remarked, the Malayic tradition is instantiated in both tribal and centralized varieties. In the rest of this essay I examine this claim in more detail by exploring the relevant information on the southern Orang Asli and the Malays. This will reinforce my argument that egalitarianism and ranking in the Malay World were shaped schizmogenetically from within the same general matrix through the application of a few simple switches in their kinship arrangements.

As just noted, the Malayic local communities came to combine a sexual division of labor with a preference for closed consanguineal settlements. They were linked through their male members with relatively wealthy outsider trading partners but displayed a matrifiliative bias with regard to village residence. As we shall see shortly, such social formations tend to become ranked. The Malays and many of the southern Orang Asli (such as the Temuans, Jakuns, Semelais, Temoqs and Besisis) do in fact display a formal political hierarchy that probably predates the development of centralized states in the Peninsula and is not simply the result of outsiders' appointments. This may also be true of some of the Malay-speaking tribal populations of Sumatra (see, e.g., Weintré 2003:55–58).

I propose that it was against this backdrop that the early Sumatran and Peninsular states arose in the millennium between 400 and 1400 CE. Little need be said about this here, except to make a few remarks as to the connection between court and rural populations in the formative period. The early rulers would have emerged from a societal tradition characterized, even before centralization and Indianization, by the possession of several Malayic features that prefigured the features typical of the later states. The most salient of these were:

> ➤ Patrifiliation as the idiom of organizing the "political" male-to-male links

> ➤ A propensity to see in local consanguineal endogamy the potential for political incorporation of subservient communities by means of marital alliance

> ➤ A degree of local-level ranking, compounded (as argued in more detail later) of (1) the rule that husband and wife should be related as *abang*, "elder sibling/cousin," to *adik*, "younger sibling/cousin"; and (2) the bringing together of unrelated males within a matrifocal domain

The emerging would-be "royals" could thus declare their kingship to be inherent in a patrilineal descent group (on the Indian model), allied by marriage with a series of progressively lesser-ranking communities upstream.

The latter, in turn, were predisposed to orient themselves according to what was going on downstream. In this way, petty chiefdoms could come to be progressively nested within each other to form states (and even "empires"), in the "mandala" formation discussed by Wolters (1999) and others.

Malay (Melayu) Kinship

As shown in tables 7.2 and 7.3, there is a complementary relation in the Peninsula between the mother-in-law taboo and the permissibility of marrying genealogically traceable kin. However, the connection between the two features is indirect, since it involves several other issues as well. The complementarity cannot be understood without first examining the character of the Malayic kinship systems of the Malays proper (the Orang Melayu) and of the southern Malayic Orang Asli. I start with the former, basing my account on ethnographic materials gathered some decades ago, mostly in rural communities.

The state-linked Malays were until recently mostly typical peasants operating within a largely monetized economy. Like the Semang, Malay peasants organize their productive activities on a conjugal-family basis. Unlike the Semang, however, they have no tabooed kinship relationships, since maintenance of the conjugal-family ideal poses no problems for them. Malay kinship reckoning is "exclusive" in character, so that only a few individuals are regarded as kin anyway, and the family is in little danger of being merged into a wider kin network. As we shall see, the same also applies, with some variation, to the Malayic Orang Asli, whose long-established adaptation to trading in natural products in the south of the Peninsula has led to a close similarity between them and the Malays.

Malays often show a reluctance to enter into close personal relations, but when they do so it is usually in the idiom of close consanguineal kinship modeled on the conjugal family (Djamour 1965:24). The ordinary words for "relatives" are *saudara* or *adik beradik*, the core meaning of both of which is "sibling." The various more corporate senses of "family" are expressed in the phrases *sanak saudara*, "(one's) children and siblings," or *saudara mara*, "(multiplicity of) siblings" (Maeda 1978:217). None of these terms makes any reference to affinal relations, and they are all weighted toward siblingship. Even husbands and wives come to call each other "elder brother" and "younger sibling" respectively. As Maeda points out (1978:232), this "sibling" usage implies that they are equally the "children" of either set of parents, so that all the in-law relationships become idealized as falling within a single consanguineal domain. As for the relative-age component of this usage, the husband is in fact usually a few years older than the wife. Until recently, Malay families tried to marry off their daughters before they entered their twenties, perhaps because of the strict rules of premarital chastity. Men, on the other hand, had to be able to support a wife in an independent household before they might marry. Marriage was (and still is) unstable, even after the birth of children, and is regarded as a contract, not a sacrament.

All the Malay kinship terms for one's own or proximate generations (except for *bisan* "child's spouse's parent," and *biras,* "wife's sister's husband") contain one of the nuclear terms followed if necessary by words meaning "collateral," "step-," "adopted," or "-in-law." Uncles and aunts are given terms combining "father" or "mother" with birth-order names, which are really fratronyms defining siblings in relation to each other (Benjamin 1968b:106; Wilder 1976:303–4). Malays frequently express a preference for marrying cousins rather than non-kin (although the different varieties of cousin are not equally preferred). The correct appellation for a cousin when the extended sibling terminology is being used is based on the relative ages of *ego* and *alter* and not (as in several originally immigrant and Orang Asli groups) on the relative ages of their connecting parents—an important point I will return to shortly.

The picture presented by these rules and preferences is one in which affinity is structurally downplayed in favor of consanguinity, which is expressed in a conjugal-family idiom. A person's closest relationships are couched in terms of a highly solidary, conjunctive siblingship. The psychological core of this system resides in the image of a band of siblings turned in warmly toward each other, away from the rest of the social world, which is constituted of non-kin who must be dealt with courteously and with much etiquette, for they cannot really be trusted. Such a picture will be familiar to students of peasant life: many of the usual concomitant features, such as an "image of limited good" and a tendency to accuse one's neighbors (and especially affines) of sorcery, are typical of both rural and urban Malay communities, even today (Karim 1990).

There is little room in the logic of such a kinship system for rules of prescribed avoidance or joking: in any society it would be disruptive to require such behavior within the conjugal family. Since the Malays picture the whole of their kinship domain—their only domain of affectively close relations[13]—as a conjugal family, it is not surprising that there are no kinship-based avoidance or joking relationships in Malay culture. On the other hand, joking and deference (an attenuated form of avoidance) form the very substance of Malay social interactional style in the village and wider community, which, as we have seen, are culturally defined as the spheres where kinship does *not* operate. It is now possible to see some sense in the association between exclusive kinship reckoning, the absence of a mother-in-law (or any other) taboo, and the permissibility of cousin marriage. But more is involved.

A striking difference between the Malayic tradition and the Semang and Senoi traditions lies in its hierarchical character. This relates to the sexual division of interests that began when collecting for trade started millennia ago: while the women retained their interest in farming and the internal organization of the village, the men were primarily interested in developing the forest activities and external relations necessary for trade. The long-term result of this has been that women in the Malayic tradition (both Melayu and Orang Asli) retain the egalitarian and solidary social manner that is still typical of both men and women in the Semang and Senoi traditions, while their menfolk lead a more hierarchical and disjunctive life. It was men from such trade-adapted groups on the coasts and islands who set up the first Malay states when a suitable (Indian) model presented itself in the first millennium CE, and who thereby first brought Malay (Melayu) culture and society properly so called into existence.

Tribal (Orang Asli) Malayic Kinship

A study of the southern Orang Asli societal traditions throws much light on the evolution of this pattern, for they display an interesting range of variation within their formally cognatic structure. Although there is insufficient published data on which to base a definitive statement, enough has appeared on Temoq, Semelai, Besisi, and Jakun social organization for me to venture some suggestions. Of these, the most detailed analysis of the relevant issues is Laird's account of Temoq kinship (1978:120f., 1979:60–64), which displays the highest degree of unilateral bias in the Peninsula (with the exception of the corporate matrilineal descent groups of the Negeri Sembilan Malays).

The Temoqs, who number probably fewer than seven hundred people, have ranked serially matrifiliative groupings known as *keturunan*, which relate not to economic undertakings or landowning (for which the conjugal family serves) but to marriage (see fig. 7.1).[14] Husband and wife must be respectively each other's categorial "elder" and "younger sibling/cousin": the cousin terminology is based on the relative age of their respective parents. But this relates to the ranking also, for one should preferably find one's "younger sister/wife" in another, and junior, *keturunan*. Laird reports that marital alliances tend to arise between different *keturunan*, especially coresidential ones. Marital residence is uxorilocal by rule, so brothers leave the uterine group on marriage. Relations between brothers are not close,

Figure 7.1 *Temoq "keturunan" (reworked from data in Laird 1978)*

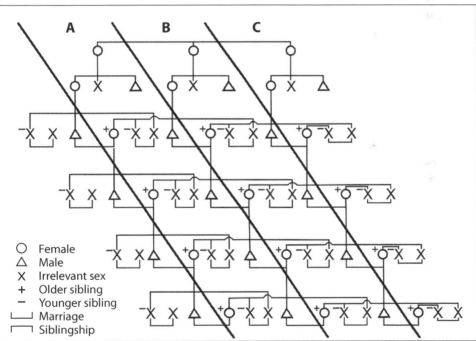

Figure 7.1 Temoq *keturunan* (reworked from data in Laird 1978). The diagram shows three *keturunan* (A, B, C). A man marries his "sibling's spouse's elder sister," while a woman marries her "younger sibling's spouse's brother." Therefore all relative-age reckonings are *through females only* ("elder sister," "woman's younger sibling"), not through males.

but relations between brothers and sisters are so close that Temoqs expressly say that the incest prohibition exists in order to ensure that they go out and find spouses elsewhere. The relation between father and child is rather remote, while mother and child are much closer: there is an avunculate respect relationship between mother's brother and sister's child. Inheritance is by female ultimogeniture. Thus, at the core of Temoq ideas, sex and relative age are inextricably collapsed together and cannot be disentangled. It is siblingship/cousinship (rather than descent or filiation) that lies at the core, but this siblingship/cousinship can only be realized by having *aunts*.

How closely do the other southern Orang Asli populations fit the Malayic pattern? The remaining populations characterized as Malayic in table 7.1 display tendencies that bear a family resemblance to the Temoq pattern but not to the same degree or so clearly. Among them, the village is usually autonomous, and intravillage marriage is preferred. On the other hand, up to six ranked inherited political offices have been reported from within single settlements. This suggests that, although the original push toward ranking was derived from the communally and sexually divisive effects of engaging in external trade, the more proximate causes relate more to kinship than to economics, as just suggested in relation to the Temoq case.

The Semelais were reported by Carey (1976:258–60) as following "unilineal" descent "through the maternal line," although it is doubtful whether this represents anything more than a matrilateral bias in residence and marriage preferences. (There is no evidence of corporate descent groups in that area.) But Carey's report nevertheless implies that the Semelais follow a Malayic kinship pattern. This is supported by their conjugal-family-based productive units (Hoe 2001:37–42) and by their permitting, even favoring, cousin marriage (51–53). Gianno's account (1990:39–44) shows that, while these features still characterized Semelai kinship to some extent, there was also much change occurring during the period of her fieldwork. Nevertheless, the Semelais do display several other Malayic features. They reckon the relative ages of cousins through the parental generation and allow first-cousin marriage on the payment of fines (Hood 1974:111; Gianno 1990:40, 43). They also forbid marriage with outsiders (suggesting an exclusive kinship pattern), with a preference for marrying generalized kin. Since these kin must by rule (often broken in practice) be of the same generation, this suggests an unexpressed preference for generalized cousin marriage, as long as it is not too close.

The Besisis (also known as the Betisék and Mah Meri), judging by Ayampillay's report (1976), display some interesting unifiliative tendencies. Their residence patterns seem statistically very matrifocal. Indeed, although Ayampillay does not remark on the fact, *all* of the stem-extended households in her table 2 (30) display a matrilateral bias, while her village genealogy (34) shows that the core sibling group was constituted by four sisters and that four and a half out of the six households were matrilaterally connected to the remaining households.

Besisi kinship terminology shows some unique features when compared to the other Malayan terminologies. No relative-age distinctions are made within the generations, but cousins are distinguished from siblings, with separate terms for "brother," "sister," "parent's brothers' child," and "parent's sister's child." This emphasis on a lineal/collateral distinction in the three core generations reflects the socioeconomic salience of the conjugal family, but this is combined with a most unusual concern to distinguish matri-filiation from patrifiliation in the cousin terms.[15] As we have seen, in the Malayic tradition matrifiliation is concerned with the continuity of village organization. Patrifiliation, on the other hand, is concerned with the negative regulation of marriage, which may not be contracted by those sharing the same "male seed."[16] Cross-cousins may marry, but patrilateral parallel cousins may not. The patrilineal principle is employed to organize succession to political office, which, as among the other Malayic Orang Asli, seems to be more elaborate than the generally low level of social complexity would appear to warrant.

The Jakuns, also known as the Orang Hulu (Tachimoto 2001), do not show these matrilateral tendencies to the same degree, but the following features are worthy of note. They prefer cousin marriage (usually with third or fourth cousins), with the proviso that the husband should be the wife's categorial "elder sibling/cousin," even if he is actually younger than his wife. As with the Temoqs and Semelais, the proper relative-age appellation is reckoned in terms of their *parents'* relative age.[17] Newlyweds spend the first weeks under taboo in the wife's parents' house. The married couple form a highly independent economic unit, although the sibling group as a whole displays great solidarity, even between brothers and sisters. Relations between affines, however, are marked by reserve and respect. Jakun villages display a marked insider–outsider distinction, with "insiders" constituted by a core sibling group, and there is a preference for kin not to move away from the village on marriage. Kinship reckoning appears to be more "inclusive" than among the Temoqs or Malays but not so inclusive as among the Senoi and Semang. A man's property (presumably goods related to collecting and trading) goes to his son, while a woman's (presumably household objects—the houses themselves probably not being very long-lasting) is inherited by her daughters. The slight matrilateral bias was explained to Maeda as resulting from the fact that "women find it harder to look after themselves," which presumably refers to the same complementarity between men's and women's tasks that I have taken as a criterial feature of Malayic social organization.

According to Hill (n.d., 3–4), ranking is present in Jakun society, in relation both to kinship-based distinctions of relative age and to political office. There is a tendency for transmitted relative-age distinctions between seniors and juniors to accumulate in contradistinction to real differences of chronological age, so that two individuals of the same age might call each other "grandparent" and "grandchild." The population is divided into two ranks, those of the headmen's level (*orang bangsa*; cf. Malay *orang bangsawan*, "nobility") and those of commoner level (*orang ratus*, "people of the commonalty"). Marriage should occur only between those of the same rank.

The Emergence of Malayic Ranking

The Malayic pattern of social organization exhibited by all the southern groups appears to have arisen as the vector result of certain preferences generated by engaging in trade. We have seen how matrifiliation became the principle of kin-incorporation and how, consequently, patrifiliation came to lead to kin-attenuation. At the same time, members of the local community redirected their attention toward the outside world. This led to an increasing and competitive autonomy between local communities and to the breakdown within the community of any (cognatic) descent structures that might previously have emerged (as among the Temiars and Semai Senoi) to organize farming and residence. Productive enterprise became increasingly a conjugal-family concern, and the autonomous tendencies led to a shying-away from "inclusive" kinship-based relations with other villages. Marriages, therefore, came to be contracted with one's "own" people, who were seen variously as fellow villagers, consanguines, or cousin/siblings. These three categories tended to become metaphors for each other, so that the reluctance to marry outside the village came to be expressed both as a preference for marrying cousins and as a lack of ease in relations between affines. But some cousins came to be preferable to others, for matrifiliation is closer than patrifiliation: mother's sister's child became the most favored spouse, father's brother's child became the least favored, and mother's brother's (= father's sister's) child fell somewhere in between.

Intra-generation relative age, previously concerned only with interpersonal relations, now became important as a principle of social organization. A young man would normally have taken longer to achieve the social maturity necessary for setting up an independent household since he had two worlds to become familiar with first, while a young woman only had one. Grooms were therefore normally some years older than their brides. This age difference then became a moral imperative to ensure that the household, now too independent to rely on help from other villagers, would be economically viable, since it depended for its well-being on complementarity between the wife's farming and the husband's trading. Given the preference for consanguineal marriage, this imperative converted easily into a kinship rule: husband should be to wife as elder sibling/cousin to younger sibling/cousin. To marry otherwise would be to "swim against the current."

Now, although the above outline is only a series of hypotheses, it corresponds so closely to the array of features I have just reported for the Temoqs, Semelais, Besisis, Jakuns, and Malays that we may be reasonably confident of its basic correctness. Many of the features, though not all, are also found in some of the Orang Asli societies farther north—the Temuans, Chewong (also known as Cheq Wong), Jah Hĕt, Semaq Beri, and Bateks— but there is no room to discuss them here. Instead, let me pursue the logic a little further to account for the ideology of ranking that is such a characteristic Malayic feature. By doing so, I wish to reemphasize my initial claim that the egalitarianism discussed earlier for the other Peninsular populations cannot be fully understood except in relation to the parallel emergence of ranking within the same broader social context.

Southerners who had not finally made up their minds whether to become traders or remain foragers or farmers could have imposed a decision on themselves by erecting a cultural boundary mechanism somewhat like those we have already encountered between the Senoi and Semang traditions. But now the boundary would have to fall not between themselves and their neighbors but between their own past and future. This they could do by making the marriage rules self-perpetuating, thereby transmitting the trader-adapted social organization automatically from one generation to the next. Instead of just marrying cousins chronologically younger than themselves, the men could inherit the requirement by marrying a *parent's* younger sibling's daughter. They could then alter the terminology to fit by making the choice between the "elder" or "younger" cousin terms depend on their parents' relative age rather than their own. Instead of taking the psychological risk of negotiating with strangers, the men could decide to marry where their fathers had married before by setting up some sort of marital alliance relationship between themselves and other kin groups. To ensure against the attenuation of kin relationships, they could decide to marry matrifiliated rather than patrifiliated cousins.

These requirements if collapsed together, and after operating for several generations, would mean that a man should preferentially marry a cousin who was (again, taking only the first-cousin instance) simultaneously his mother's younger sibling's daughter, his father's mother's younger sibling's child's daughter, his father's father's mother's younger sibling's child's child's daughter, and so on. Or, to put it more succinctly, he should marry into the same matrifiliated category of people whose relevant ancestor was originally related as "younger sibling/cousin" to the ancestress of his own matrifiliated category. This would produce within any village or intermarrying cluster of villages a set of ranked matrifiliative marital-alliance descent categories (not corporate groups), the senior such category being the collective "elder sibling" of the junior ones.

The system I have just outlined is not simply a hypothetical reconstruction, for it corresponds in almost every detail to the system of kinship and social organization followed by the Temoqs into the late twentieth century (fig. 7.1). It also has much in common with the somewhat different Besisi system. I suggest, therefore, that the southern groups did indeed evolve in the direction I have outlined, the Temoqs most completely, the Jakuns least so. The pre-Malays, I suggest, started along the same course but later took a rather different tack, toward the development of centralized states—a development made all the easier because they would earlier have become more willing, as a result of these hierarchization processes, to give up control over their own lives than were the egalitarian Semang or Senoi. Kinship and consciousness are thus intimately connected.

A significant feature of this process is the extent to which a form of ranking could evolve with only a slight push from economic factors and without any necessary restriction of access to land or goods. In fact, I know of no Orang Asli group in which headmanship or other ranked positions were associated with regular economic redistribution, trading monopoly, or sumptuary restrictions—even though these are all features of traditional chiefship and kingship among the Malays.[18]

Such a system of ranking, concerned in the first instance with marriage, not property, would become a characteristic way of thinking and talking about social relations rather than of imbuing those relations with political or economic substance. Yet the habit of thinking hierarchically is in such marked contrast to the egalitarian habits of the Semang and Senoi traditions that it is safe to assume that the response of the latter to contact with the outside world was very different from the Malayic response. And so it proved historically: it was groups following the Malayic regime only who responded by forming centralized states. The Semang and Senoi response, as we have seen, was to undertake an involutionary reinforcement of their egalitarian ways of life by becoming *more* tribal, not less.

It is a short step from thinking hierarchically to setting up ranked political offices in a society. The over-full headmanship systems of the southern Orang Asli spell out a division of societal tasks in greater detail than seems necessary. (See, e.g., Baharon 1983 on the Temuans; and Tachimoto 2001 on the Jakuns.) The degree of societal complexity is too low for the various officers to have any distinctive functions to perform—and indeed there is no evidence that they have functioned politically except as go-betweens with outside authorities. Yet, unlike what happened farther north (Benjamin 1968a), the southerners' various ranked political offices seem not to be simply the result of outsiders' administrative interference but of a genuinely indigenous response to the model of political organization brought by traders from the more complex societies with which they were coming into contact. I suggest that the same processes were in principle later responsible for the rise of Malay kingly groups among the coastal communities. There, a fortuitous set of circumstances allowed individuals to give substance to their rank for the first time by exercising a monopoly over the trade passing through the estuaries under their control. They needed only to endow their economic control with a Hindu-derived ritual propriety for them to become kings. Later, with the sanction of Islam, they extended their control into the hinterlands, too, creating a Malay peasantry as they went (Benjamin 2002:50–54). The Malay states (like all the coastal trade-based states of Southeast Asia) developed from the top down, but this was possible, I suggest, only because societal consciousness in the surrounding populations had already shifted in a direction that allowed them to see the state as a meaningful social form.[19] The incorporation of Hindu and Muslim ideas into the Malay political system ensured that the existing bias toward patrifiliative connections in trading and intercommunity relations gave way to the patrilineal mode of kingly and chiefly succession that still operates today.

Notes

1 Note the adjectival usage. I am referring to "*tribal* populations" considered as a particular kind of social circumstance, not "tribes" considered as purported social units. For justifications of this approach, see Benjamin 2002:7–9, 12–17; and Wawrinec 2010.

2 Leach's Kachin study (1964) is the best known of these, but even among the Kachins, the presence of state formations in the broader environment was a key factor. A more general survey is Fried's (1960), for whom "the ranked society is characterized by having fewer positions of valued status than they have individuals capable of handling them" (717). Ranking can take a variety of forms, all of which are found in the Malay World: (1) ranked hereditary leadership positions; (2) mutually ranked societal segments, not necessarily amounting to an overall "objective" ranking; and (3) "objective" society-wide stratification by rank. Except where it is obvious from the details of the discussion, I have not elaborated further on these differences in this essay.

3 Several other social formations fit less well into this typology but are not discussed in this essay; see the "mixed" traditions listed in table 7.1. There are also some gaps in the data, as well as occasional uncertainties stemming from differences between the reports I consulted. For earlier discussions of the Semang/Senoi/Malayic approach to Malay-World ethnology, see Benjamin 1985 (where the term Malay-type was used instead of Malayic); and Benjamin 2002. For relevant commentaries, see Bellwood 1993; Fix 1995; and Bulbeck 2004.

4 The reason we so often confuse "a culture" with regime, or "a society" with polity, I believe, is that we have employed the nation-state, with its political boundedness and ideological homogeneity, as our model for culture and society generally. We then naturalize this image by imposing it on tribal societies, hoping thereby to demonstrate its universality. But, as several writers have

shown, tribal populations do not fit this pattern (see, e.g., Wallerstein 1979; and Godelier 1977).

5 Discussion of the Peninsula's early culture history can be found in the following sources. For archaeology, see Wheatley 1961; Christie 1990; and Bellwood 1997. For social organization, see Benjamin 1985. For religion, see Benjamin 1979. For genetics and human biology, see Fix 2002; Bulbeck and Lauer 2006. For linguistics, see Diffloth 1979; and Burenhult, Kruspe, and Dunn, in press. It is still unusual for researchers to bring the tribal populations and the Malays together as a single field of study, as I have done here. This separation will be harder to maintain in future, however. Leonard Andaya's major study (2008) shows in detail that over the last few millennia the tribal populations of the Malay World have played as important a part as the Malays "proper" in the constantly emerging social character of the region.

6 On archaeological grounds, Barker (2008) has argued that this pattern of facultative switching between a diverse range of subsistence sources has been followed in parts of Southeast Asia for some fifty thousand years—tens of millennia before the development of farming proper.

7 Inclusive kinship reckoning means that everyone within the social formation (and sometimes beyond) is regarded as a kinsperson. Kinship then provides a means of talking about the social formation as a whole, and the kin terms are largely "classificatory" in application. With exclusive kinship reckoning (as in the Malayic tradition), only some people are regarded as kin. Kinship then provides a means of organizing voluntary and relatively intimate association only and of talking only about a subdomain (usually the family) within the total social framework.

8 These characterizations are based on my own field inquiries among the Kensiws, Kintaqs, Jahais, and Menriqs in the late 1960s and early 1970s. The patri-bias under discussion here is patri*filiative*, concerned only with sequential father-child relations, not with lineal ancestor-descendent relations.

9 Note that the "Semang" societal tradition was not followed by the Batek Dè' population later studied by Kirk and Karen Endicott. I suspect that this is because in the past the Bateks did not have direct contact with the Temiars and hence not with the Senoi tradition.

10 Etymologically, "Senoi" (from Temiar sɛn²ɔɔy and Semai səŋ²ɔɔy, "person, human") derives from a Mon-Khmer root meaning "shy" (Benjamin 2002:29–30, following Gérard Diffloth).

11 If this sounds difficult to grasp, think how easy it is to regard your own brother or sister as (1) your mother's child (matrifilial), (2) your father's child (patrifilial), or (3) your parents' child (cognatic) without necessarily implying any shift in the genealogical facts. Note that this need involve neither corporateness nor a concern for descent from an ancestor. At base, these patterns of filiative bias would have referred primarily—as they still do—to face-to-face relations, thought of in terms of the sex of the immediately connecting kinspersons.

12 This corresponds exactly to the Jah Hĕt situation as described by Couillard (1980:102).

There is therefore a tension in Jah Hut communities, between the uxorilocal pattern of residence and the handing down of titles in a patrilineal fashion, as opposed to the expressed bilaterality of descent. It is clearly manifested when a man accedes to his father's title and has to move back to his own village after having lived most of his life in his wife's village. He then has to establish himself in a position of authority almost as a stranger would.

The Jah Hĕt also have a rule of avoidance between adult brothers, which increases as they grow older (97). Perhaps this is an institutionalization of what for the Temoqs and Jakuns (discussed below) is merely a tendency. However, the Jah Hĕt have (not yet?) taken the next step in my proposed scheme, for they forbid cousin marriage—which is why I have categorized them as "mixed" rather than "Malayic."

13 As Djamour (1965: 31) reports, Malays tend to redefine close friends as kin, and they redefine kinspeople with whom they have little to do as nonkin (*orang lain*, "other people").

14 The Temoq *keturunan* (a Malay word meaning "of common descent") is neither corporate nor matrilineal. The analysis presented in figure 7.1 is the author's, but Peter Laird has affirmed to me that it is a fair representation of his findings.

15 Note that this is not a bifurcation of ego's relatives into matrilateral and patrilateral kin.

16 The Malays express this prohibition in the same way. The Malay prohibition is especially interesting because, while patrilateral-parallel-cousin marriage is much favored among Muslims elsewhere, the Malays here follow Peninsular patterns. (Under the influence of Islamic orthodoxy, this is now under pressure to change.)

17 Reckoning cousins' relative age through the parental generation converts "age" into "category"—just as in a European aristocratic family the eldest son of an eldest son may actually be younger than his cousin, the youngest son of a youngest son, without losing his category-based seniority. Needham (1966) argues that the overriding of real chronological age distinctions by category distinctions is typical of unilineal systems and that the reverse is true of cognatic systems. Those Malayan societies that have been reported to follow the "parental" (category-based) mode of reckoning cousin terminology—Temoqs, Semelais, Jakuns, Batek Dè', and Malays of Javanese origin—are (with the exception of the Batek Dè') neither rigorously cognatic nor rigorously unilineal but somewhere in between. The Semaq Beri have variously been reported to follow both modes of cousin terminology. The situation among the Jah Hĕt and Orang Kanaq is unclear. Dentan (1970), discussing the Semais, and Jensen (1977–78), on the Semaq Beri, present yet further permutations of relative-age issues. They show explicitly that (like the Temiars) the people allow age to override category. The Besisis seem to have substituted mode of filiation for relative age, which is quite logical given the equation *husband : wife :: elder sibling : younger sibling*. Their cousin-terminology usage is nevertheless still "parental."

18 This accords with Rousseau's more general finding (based largely on Southeast Asian data) that economic redistribution is less frequently a cause of ranking in

tribal "societies of the middle-range" than is commonly claimed (Rousseau 2001, further elaborated in Rousseau 2006:188–223).

19 I have discussed the religious dimensions of these changes elsewhere (Benjamin 1979, 2005). Malay states did not arise solely within the Peninsula, for the same processes were occurring simultaneously in Borneo, on the Sumatran mainland, and in the Riau-Lingga archipelago. (See Wee 1988 for an account of the remnants of this process as it can still be observed in the latter area.) Their marine interconnections have been such that the consciousness of a Malay world (*Alam Melayu*) has been shared by them all for several hundred years.

References

Andaya, Leonard Y. 2008. *Leaves of the Same Tree: Trade and Ethnicity in the Straits of Melaka*. Honolulu and Singapore: University of Hawai'i Press and NUS Press.

Ayampillay, S.D. 1976. "Kampung Tanjung Sepat: A Besese (Mah Meri) community of coastal Selangor." Provisional research report, School of Comparative Social Sciences, Universiti Sains Malaysia.

Baharon Azhar bin Rafie'i. 1983. "The Temuans of Melaka." In Kernial Singh Sandhu and Paul Wheatley, eds., *Melaka: The Transformation of a Malay Capital c. 1400–1980*, vol. 2, 3–29. Kuala Lumpur: Oxford University Press.

Barker, Graeme. 2008. "Footsteps and marks: Transitions to farming in the rainforests of Island Southeast Asia." Yale University Agrarian Studies Colloquium Series, no. 3. http://www.yale.edu/agrarianstudies/colloqpapers/03barker.pdf.

Bellwood, Peter. 1993. "Cultural and biological differentiation in Peninsular Malaysia: The last 10,000 years." *Asian Perspectives* 32:37–60.

———. 1997. *Prehistory of the Indo-Malaysian Archipelago*. 2nd ed. Honolulu: University of Hawai'i Press.

Benjamin, Geoffrey. 1968a. "Headmanship and leadership in Temiar society." *Federation Museums Journal* (new series) 13:1–43.

———. 1968b. "Temiar personal names." *Bijdragen tot de Taal-, Land- en Volkenkunde* 124:99–134.

———. 1973. "Introduction." In P. Schebesta, *Among the Forest Dwarfs of Malaya*, v–xii. 2nd impression. Kuala Lumpur: Oxford University Press.

———. 1979. "Indigenous religious systems of the Malay Peninsula." In A. Yengoyan and A.L. Becker, eds., *The Imagination of Reality: Essays in Southeast Asian Coherence Systems*, 9–27. Norwood, NJ: Ablex Publishing.

———. 1985. "In the long term: Three themes in Malayan cultural ecology." In K.L. Hutterer, A.T. Rambo, and G. Lovelace, eds., *Cultural Values and Human Ecology in Southeast Asia*, 219–78. Ann Arbor: Center for South and Southeast Asian Studies, University of Michigan.

———. 1993. "Grammar and polity: The cultural and political background to standard Malay." In W.A. Foley, ed., *The Role of Theory in Language Description*, 341–92. Berlin: Mouton DeGruyter.

———. 2002. "On being tribal in the Malay World." In G. Benjamin and C. Chou, eds., *Tribal Communities in the Malay World: Historical, Social, and Cultural Perspectives*, 7–76. Leiden and Singapore: International Institute for Asian Studies and Institute of Southeast Asian Studies.

———. 2005. "Consciousness and polity in Southeast Asia: The long view." In Riaz Hassan, ed., *Local and Global: Social Transformation in Southeast Asia—Essays in Honour of Professor Syed Hussein Alatas*, 261–89. Leiden: Brill.

Bulbeck, F. David. 2004. "Indigenous traditions and exogenous influences in the early history of Peninsular Malaysia." In I. Glover and P. Bellwood, eds., *Southeast Asia: From Prehistory to History*, 314–36. London: RoutledgeCurzon.

Bulbeck, F. David, and Adam Lauer. 2006. "Human variation and evolution in Holocene Peninsular Malaysia." In M. Oxenham and N. Tayles, eds., *Bioarchaeology of Southeast Asia*, 133–71. Cambridge: Cambridge University Press.

Burenhult, Niclas, Nicole Kruspe, and Michael Dunn. In press. "Language history and culture groups among Austroasiatic-speaking foragers of the Malay Peninsula." In N.J. Enfield and J. White, eds., *Dynamics of Human Diversity in Mainland Southeast Asia*. Canberra: Pacific Linguistics.

Carey, Iskandar. 1976. *Orang Asli: The Aboriginal tribes of Peninsular Malaysia*. Kuala Lumpur: Oxford University Press.

Christie, Jan Wisseman. 1990. "Trade and state formation in the Malay Peninsula and Sumatra, 300 B.C.–A.D. 700." In J. Kathirithamby-Wells and J. Villiers, eds., *The Southeast Asian Port and Polity: Rise and Demise*, 39–60. Singapore: Singapore University Press.

Couillard, Marie-Andrée. 1980. *Tradition in Tension: Carving in a Jah Hut Community*. Penang: Penerbit Universiti Sains Malaysia.

Dentan, Robert K. 1970. "Hocus pocus and extensionism in central Malaya: Notes on Semai kinship terminology." *American Anthropologist,* new series, 72:358–62.

———. 1992. "The rise, maintenance, and destruction of peaceable polity: A preliminary essay in political ecology." In J. Silverberg and J.P. Gray, eds.,

Aggression and Peaceableness in Humans and Other Primates, 214–70. New York: Oxford University Press.

Diffloth, Gérard. 1979. "Aslian languages and Southeast Asian prehistory." *Federation Museums Journal,* new series, 24:2–16.

Djamour, Judith. 1965. *Malay Kinship and Marriage in Singapore*. London: Athlone.

Endicott, Kirk M. 1983. "Slavery and the Orang Asli." In A. Reid and J. Brewster, eds., *Slavery, Bondage, and Dependence in Southeast Asia*, 216–45. Brisbane: Queensland University Press.

Fix, Alan. 1995. "Malayan paleosociology: Implications for patterns of genetic variation among the Orang Asli." *American Anthropologist,* new series, 97 (2):313–23.

———. 2002. "Foragers, farmers, and traders in the Malayan Peninsula: Origins of cultural and biological diversity." In K.D. Morrison and L.J. Junker, eds., *Forager-Traders in South and Southeast Asia: Long-Term Histories*, 185–202. Cambridge: Cambridge University Press.

Fried, Morton H. 1960. "On the evolution of social stratification and the state." In S. Diamond, ed., *Culture in History*, 713–31. New York: Columbia University Press.

Gianno, Rosemary. 1990. *Semelai Culture and Resin Technology*. Memoirs of the Connecticut Academy of Arts and Sciences, no. 22. New Haven: The Connecticut Academy of Arts and Social Sciences.

Godelier, Maurice. 1977. "The concept of the 'Tribe.'" In Maurice Godelier, *Perspectives in Marxist Anthropology*, 70–96. London. Cambridge University Press.

Hill, Andrew. N.d. Unpublished research report on Orang Hulu.

Hoe Ban Seng. 2001. *Semelai Communities at Tasek Bera: A Study of the Structure of an Orang Asli Society*. Ed. A.S. Baer and R. Gianno. Subang Jaya: Centre for Orang Asli Concerns.

Hood Mohd Salleh. 1974. "An Ethnographical account of the Semelai of Malaysia." BLitt thesis, University of Oxford.

Jensen, Knud-Erik. 1977–78. "Relative age and category: The Semaq Beri case." *Folk* 19–20:171–81.

Karim, Wazir Jahan. 1990. "Prelude to madness: The language of emotion in courtship and early marriage." In W.J. Karim, ed., *Emotions of Culture: A Malay Perspective*, 21–63. Singapore: Oxford University Press.

Laird, Peter. 1978. "Temoq shamanism and affliction." PhD thesis, Monash University.

———. 1979. "Ritual, territory, and region: The Temoq of Pahang, West Malaysia." *Social Analysis* 1:54–80.

Leach, Edmund R. 1964. *Political Systems of Highland Burma: A Study of Kachin Social Structure.* 2nd ed. London: Bell. Originally published in 1958.

Maeda, Narifumi. 1978. "The Malay family as a social circle." In L.J. Fredericks, ed., *Proceedings of the Seminar on the Problems of Rice-Growing Villages in Malaysia. Southeast Asian Studies* 16 (2):40–69.

Murphy, Robert F. 1957. "Intergroup hostility and social cohesion." *American Anthropologist,* new series, 59:1018–35.

Needham, Rodney. 1966. "Age, category, and descent." *Bijdragen tot de Taal-, Land- en Volkenkunde* 122:1–35.

Rousseau, Jérôme. 2001. "Hereditary stratification in middle-range societies." *Journal of the Royal Anthropological Institute,* new series, 7:117–31.

———. 2006. *Rethinking Social Evolution: The Perspective from Middle-Range Societies.* Montreal: McGill-Queen's University Press.

Scott, James C. 2009. *The Art of Not Being Governed: An Anarchist History of Upland Southeast Asia.* New Haven: Yale University Press.

Tachimoto, Narifumi Maeda. 2001. *The Orang Hulu: A Report on Malaysian Orang Asli in the 1960s.* Subang Jaya: Centre for Orang Asli Concerns.

Wallerstein, Immanuel. 1979. "A world-system perspective on the social sciences." In Immanuel Wallerstein, *The Capitalist World-Economy,* 152–64. Cambridge: Cambridge University Press.

Wang Gungwu. 1958. "The Nanhai trade." *Journal of the Malayan Branch, Royal Asiatic Society* 31:1–135.

Wawrinec, Christian. 2010. "Tribality and indigeneity in Malaysia and Indonesia." *Stanford Journal of East Asian Affairs,* 10 (winter):96–107.

Wee, Vivienne. 1988. "Material dependence and symbolic independence: The construction of Melayu ethnicity in Island Riau, Indonesia." In K.L. Hutterer, A.T. Rambo, and G. Lovelace, eds., *Ethnic Diversity and the Control of Natural Resources in Southeast Asia,* 197–226. Ann Arbor: Center for South and Southeast Asian Studies, University of Michigan.

Weintré, Johan. 2003. "Organisasi sosial dan kebudayaan kelompok minoritas Indonesia: Studi Kasus Masyarakat Orang Rimba di Sumatra." Unpublished thesis, Universitas Gadjah Mada, Pusat Studi Kebudayaan, Yogyakarta.

Wheatley, Paul. 1961. *The Golden Khersonese: Studies in the Historical Geography of the Malay Peninsula before A.D. 1500.* Kuala Lumpur: University of Malaya Press.

Wilder, W. 1976. "Problems in comparison of kinship systems in island Southeast Asia." In D.J. Banks, ed., *Changing Identities in Modern Southeast Asia*, 291–310. The Hague: Mouton.

Wolters, O.W. 1999. *History, Culture, and Region in Southeast Asian Perspective*. Rev. ed. Ithaca and Singapore: Cornell University Southeast Asia Program Publications and Institute of Southeast Asian Studies.

8

Encapsulation and Solidarity in Northeast Borneo: Punan of the Malinau Area

LARS KASKIJA

JAMES WOODBURN (1980, 1988) HAS SUGGESTED that a preference for immediate return and a number of interrelated cultural features—such as egalitarianism, individual autonomy, and the importance of sharing—are particularly associated with groups of hunter-gatherers that are "encapsulated," that is, surrounded by groups of non-hunter-gatherers that, in most cases, are much larger and more powerful (cf. Gardner 1966, 1991:545–46). "Encapsulation" therefore seems to entail some form of political dominance and "pressure from outsiders" (Woodburn 1988:34). In central Borneo, for example, "The nomads must always have felt surrounded: wherever they go, there are swiddeners, and even if they can flee one oppressive group, they have to come to terms with another" (Rousseau 1990:241).

This essay will take encapsulation as a point of departure.[1] It explores a number of conspicuous features of Punan culture—such as immediate return, sharing, egalitarianism, and sources of social solidarity—and how these features reflect the nature of the interface between the Punan of the Malinau area and the various others by whom they are surrounded.[2] In the first part of the essay I will discuss these features in terms of local variation among communities with different histories of contact. This will be exemplified by two contrastive cases of interaction between local groups of Punan and their immediate neighbors. The first is interaction of Punan of the upper Malinau River with stratified swidden cultivators to whom they have acknowledged their political subordination and whose orders they usually have obeyed without demur. These Punan are generally more silent and timid in their interaction with outsiders. The second is interaction of Punan of the middle and lower Tubu' River with competitive egalitarian swidden cultivators with whom they have intermarried and even become partially assimilated. These Punan are generally more outspoken and self-assured in their interaction with outsiders.

These contrastive cases of interaction will provide the base for a more general discussion of variation and interaction. The various facets of contact with capitalist consumer society, in which the most salient form of Punan self-identity is a sense of shared deprivation, are also of importance. As the various "surfaces" or "zones" of contact provide contrast between self and others, these zones create a sense of sharing a common fate and thereby become a source of social solidarity. This is particularly obvious in moments of communal commiseration, known as *pelulup urip*, which will be the focus of the second part of the essay. It is suggested that this sense of shared deprivation is part of a set of core values, including individualism and immediate return, that are—more or less—shared by all Punan in the Malinau area. Despite local variation and a marked difference in the external "face" that individual Punan present to the outside, it is still possible to discern something among these various local groups that could be labeled a common "mode of thought" (Barnard 2002) or "cultural core" (Sellato 1993).

Where "Encapsulators" Are Minorities

Everywhere in central Borneo, nomads "were surrounded by the more numerous agriculturalists" (Rousseau 1990:244). One example is the Apau Kayan—the very heartland of central Borneo—where 500 Punan were surrounded by 12,000 agriculturalists in 1970 (Whittier and Whittier 1974:7). Three decades earlier, in 1938, the same area had a total population of 16,656—99 percent agriculturalists, 1 percent nomads (Rousseau 1988:9).

In relation to these figures, it is interesting to note that the Punan of the Malinau area—a group of former nomads in the northern part of East Kalimantan in Indonesian Borneo—are the largest ethnic group in this area, which consists of two river basins, the Tubu' and the Malinau. These rivers join forces downstream in the major Sesayap River, where the regional center, the town of Malinau, is situated.[3]

Out of a total population of 18,000 souls, almost 3,000 are Punan, which means that these foragers constitute more than 16 percent of the total population.[4] The majority live in, or close to, the town of Malinau, but approximately 6,500 live upstream from the regional center, along the Malinau or Tubu' Rivers. This upriver population, also known collectively as "Dayaks"—that is, indigenous, non-Muslim people—can be divided into five major ethnic groups: the Merap (1,100), Putuk (1,400), Kenyah (1,700), Abai or Tebilun (400), and Punan (1,900).[5] Based on these figures, we can conclude that in the early 1990s the Punan constituted 40 percent of the population living upstream from the town of Malinau. The proportion of Punan in the upstream population may have been even greater in the past, as one of the largest groups of agriculturalists in the Malinau area today, the Kenyah, arrived in the area as recently as the late 1960s. In addition, one-third of the Punan in the area currently live downstream, close to the regional center of Malinau.

These Punan have thus been not a minority encapsulated by a majority, but a minority encapsulated by minorities. The situation in the Malinau area is therefore quite remarkable and has some important implications. For instance, the other ethnic groups of the area—various groups of swidden agriculturalists—have been dependent on having a good relationship with the local Punan. One reason is economic, as the Punan have been the prime suppliers of nontimber forest products. Another reason is political and strategic. Well into the twentieth century the Punan acted as armed guardians of the watershed, and they thereby protected their agricultural neighbors from attacks by enemy groups from other areas (cf. Rousseau 1990:243, 272–273). As a military force, the Punan played a crucial role in preventing their agricultural allies from being exterminated by their enemies, which is openly acknowledged by the agriculturalists themselves. This may be one important reason why the relationships between Punan and their immediate neighbors have been characterized by a certain degree of mutual respect and trust and even, in some cases, intimacy.

This means that the peacefulness ascribed to such groups as the Semai of Peninsular Malaysia (cf. Dentan 1979, 2008) does not seem to apply to the Punan. Not only did they engage in warfare on behalf of their agricultural neighbors, but they also occasionally raided distant villages in other river basins. They even, though rarely, brought back slaves and human heads—in much the same way as they brought back commercially valuable forest products—at the request of their patrons. It is important to point out that when Punan raided distant villages outside the Malinau/Tubu' area

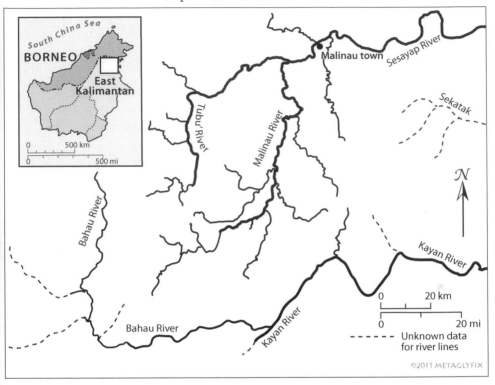

Map 8.1 *The Malinau area*

and engaged in headhunting they did this because they were ordered to do so by a leading agricultural chief. Despite occasional engagement in this kind of aggression, the various local groups of Punan in the Malinau area probably never opposed the demands of their agricultural patrons by any other means than withdrawal, that is, nonviolence. Especially the Merap chiefs at times exerted much pressure on the Punan. The Punan may have had many reasons to complain among themselves when they felt exploited, but they never seem to have opposed these agricultural chiefs with open resistance or violence. If the pressure could no longer be tolerated, the Punan would react in a way very similar to that of the peaceful Semai, that is, with avoidance of overt aggression and by leaving the area (cf. Rousseau 1990:242; and Sellato 1994:170–71).

Despite their numbers, the Punan of the Malinau area have been scattered and fragmentized, having no social or political organization above the level of the local group or band. When larger numbers of Punan were mobilized, such as when enemy groups from other areas were approaching, this was achieved because of the organization provided by their agricultural neighbors. Punan themselves did not have such organizational means. Traditional Punan forms of procuring a livelihood have not served to shape stable, overarching social, political, or religious institutions. Each band has been autonomous, and there are no forms of organization at the level of the ethnic group (cf. Sellato 1994:144). At the core of the Punan social universe is the loosely assembled band, but even this basic group will often segment into smaller units as individuals and households respond to divergent interests and perceived opportunities elsewhere. Therefore, even though most of them may very well share a common origin and they do have a common language, which is distinct and not similar to any other language spoken within this area, it would be misleading to classify the Punan of this area as a single group.

Local Variation and Contact

Despite sharing a common language, there are important differences between individual Punan and among Punan settlements in various parts of the Malinau area. This variation makes it difficult to present a clear-cut and co-herent portrayal of the Punan as an ethnic group. It is not surprising that an increasing number of researchers on hunters and gatherers are now empha-sizing the importance of variability (Biesbrouck, Elders, and Rossel 1999; Kelly 1995; Kent 1992; Lourandos 1997). It is well known that hunter-gatherers commonly utilize a wide range of economic possibilities besides hunting and gathering, what Sather (1995) has described as "economic polymor-phism"; the variability, however, is not only economic. In the Kalahari, for example, "Basarwa groups differ in language, kinship, religion, settlement pattern, economy and historical circumstances, but this is rarely recognized" (Kent 1992:48), and Motzafi-Haller paints a "picture of great variety and complexity of modes of livelihood and strategies of survival of groups, both within an area and throughout changing historical times" (1994:539).

In the case of the Punan of the Malinau area, one factor of importance when discussing local variation is the location of settlements—upstream or downstream—as this affects the availability of various resources and oppor-tunities, as well as the degree of contact, and thereby the degree of political subordination, and the degree of familiarity with the norms and practices of various others. Another factor behind the variation is political and historical, as each local group has its own history of contact with neighboring societies, as well as with other categories of outsiders, such as representatives of the colonial or national administration, missionaries, traders, companies, or nongovernmental organizations.

The details of encapsulation and the history of contact of specific local groups or individuals—which includes, of course, their present residential location—give important clues to the variation among different Punan communities and between individuals within the Malinau area. This is relevant not only when comparing attitudes toward the outside world, subsistence strategies, or the degree of immediate or delayed return in economic practices, but also when comparing sharing practices, religious beliefs, ritual observances, depth of genealogical memory, and so on. I am not suggesting that all these aspects are externally generated; that would be an oversimplification. Punan have faced many serious challenges from their "encapsulators," and heavy pressure has been exerted on them, but they also have an impressive toolbox for the examination and manipulation of any surface of contact.

In an earlier publication (Kaskija 2002:13–15), I divided the Punan of the Malinau and Tubu' Rivers into three "subgroups": (1) Punan of the Malinau River, (2) Punan of the upper Tubu'; and (3) Punan of the middle and lower Tubu' (cf. Sellato 2001:33–37). These subdivisions are not recognized by the Punan themselves, but they may serve as an analytical tool in terms of which local variation can be discussed. In the following I will focus on two of these subgroups, Punan of the Malinau River (subgroup 1) and Punan of middle and lower Tubu' (subgroup 3), as these provide the most contrast.

Stratified versus Competitive Egalitarian Swiddeners

The Punan of the Malinau River have been affiliated with the Merap, a group of strictly and formally stratified agriculturalists.[6] The social asymmetry between these Punan and their Merap allies has been apparent, and Punan have—at least until recently—fully accepted the Merap as the masters of the Malinau River area. In stratified groups, such as the Merap, social ascription has been very rigid. In "such a bounded society, an individual is either a full member of the community ... or a complete stranger" (Sellato 2007:74). The ethnic boundary between nomads and agriculturalists has

been reinforced by a rigid system of social stratification, and inter-
marriages across this ethnic boundary have therefore been uncommon or
nonexistent.

Generally speaking, Borneo nomads have intermarried and been
assimilated into nonstratified groups of rice farmers, whereas they have not
done so with strictly stratified groups. There are some cases of Borneo
nomads who have been assimilated by stratified farming groups, but they
are few (Sellato 2007:75). Lack of stratification makes assimilation easier
(Rousseau 1990:245; Sellato 1994:183–84, 212), which is exemplified by the
Punan of the middle and lower Tubu' River. These Punan have been
affiliated with less stratified groups of agriculturalists, such as the Abai (or
Tebilun), Saben, Merau, and Ngurik, all of them characterized by a more
"open" social organization. These societies do recognize rank and they are
indeed very competitive, but as vertical mobility is allowed the social
dynamics of these swidden societies can also be characterized as "competitive egalitarianism" (Woodburn 1982:446). The borderline between nomads
and agriculturalists has been less well marked in this case, and intermar-
riages across the ethnic border have occurred. Therefore, to some degree
Punan in this area are intermixed with their agricultural neighbors, some
of them less (or not at all), others to the point of being almost inseparable
from their agricultural neighbors. Despite varying degrees of assimilation,
all these Punan have retained their own language (Kaskija 2007:140; cf.
Sellato 2001:34–35).

The Punan of the lower and middle Tubu' have been involved in rice
agriculture for a longer time than the Punan of the upper Malinau, who
remained nomadic and "up to a short time ago, practiced no agriculture"
(Sellato 1994:177). Although a few Punan Tubu' individuals demonstrate
extensive genealogical memories, most Punan, including those of the upper
Malinau, can rarely recount more than a few generations. While Punan of
the lower and middle Tubu' demand a high, or very high, brideprice for
their daughters—as do their agricultural neighbors in the Tubu'—Punan of
the upper Malinau have not done so until recently. The practice of secondary
burials, common among most groups of agriculturalists in the Malinau
area until the 1960s, was also practiced by some groups of Punan in the
middle and lower Tubu'. The majority of Punan, however, including all
those in the upper Malinau, have buried their dead in one stage (Kaskija
2007:140–41).

Immediate-Return Systems

Brideprice and the practice of agriculture are associated with delayed-return systems rather than systems based on immediate return. Does this mean that the economy of the Punan of the lower and middle Tubu' is most correctly described as a delayed-return system? This is a sticky question, as it is difficult to characterize Punan economy as either-or. Despite variation in economic practices, most Punan in both the Malinau and Tubu' River basins display a clear preference for immediate-return activities and usually quickly consume whatever they have procured. This is the general picture, however, and there are also many elements of delayed return. Even in the past, Punan practiced some delayed-return activities, such as the "steward-ship" of sago palm groves or the plantation of fruit trees or cassava, a root crop that may be cultivated even by nomadic bands. Today, all local groups of Punan in the Malinau area practice agriculture to some extent, though with varying degrees of success. Although the cultivation of cassava is easily adapted to an immediate-return economy, this does not apply to the cultivation of hill rice, as this crop is harvested only once a year and therefore necessitates both long-term planning and storage. Even if all Punan families plant at least some rice each year, some will not attend their fields sufficiently and therefore will have nothing to harvest; other families may harvest enough rice for two or three months of consumption, while a few may harvest enough for six months or more. This variation among families can be observed in almost all the settlements within this area.

I would like to suggest that, even if people, like the Punan, regularly engage in delayed-return activities, they may still possess an immediate-return mentality or "mode of thought" (cf. Barnard 2002), that is, they may continue to prefer activities that give immediate returns and they may continue to consume immediately whatever they have procured. In some cases, we may talk about a delayed-return system that is chronically unsuccessful, mainly because it is constantly hampered by the immediate-return mentality of its practitioners. The accumulation of wealth seems to fail, partly or completely, and most long-term projects either proceed irregularly or fail altogether.

I therefore find it difficult to make a clear-cut separation between immediate- and delayed-return systems. A similar view has been expressed by Pedersen and Waehle (1988:76–77), who "do not believe that whole societies ... may be depicted as having the one or the other return system."

Instead, "the relations with agriculturalists provide the basis of *both* imme-
diate- and delayed-return tendencies" (88). In the case of the Punan of the
Malinau area, there seems to be just such a combination of return systems,
and the balance between them fluctuates constantly. The Punan are, without
doubt, fully capable of long-term planning, but it seems that the sudden
appearance of attractive (immediate-return) opportunities may tip the
balance of the whole system in favor of immediate return. What I have earlier termed a "feast and famine mentality" makes individuals quickly spend
whatever money they have earned in a kind of rush of happiness (Kaskija
2007:143). Afterward they are once again back at square one, and any
ongoing long-term project in need of investment may therefore remain
underdeveloped. Woodburn refers to this when he points out that an
efficient and fully functional delayed-return system is not viable without
"organization" and "binding commitments" (1988:33).

Assertive versus Timid

> It has been said that nomads have been exploited because they are timid.
> While this is true, it is not an explanation. The nomads are timid because
> they are surrounded by the more numerous agriculturalists. Differences in
> economic rationality also put them at a disadvantage. An egalitarian ideology
> and generalized reciprocity do not prepare nomads to resist an organized
> system of exploitation.
>
> —Jérôme Rousseau, *Central Borneo*, 1990

The general attitude of individual Punan toward the world around them
shows much variation. The Punan of the upper Malinau are generally more
subservient in their relations with farming groups, traders, or representatives
of the government or various companies, while many Punan in the middle
and lower Tubu' are much more self-assured. It should come as no surprise
that it is among these Punan of the Tubu' that we find the best-educated
and politically aware Punan in the Malinau area, and these features have
become even more pronounced. As residents of the regional center these
Punan often have acquired detailed knowledge about "modern" life, and
that makes them much less likely victims of deception and swindle. These
circumstances have probably made them even more outspoken and self-
assured than they were in the past. In their interactions with outsiders,
these Punan can indeed be very assertive and daring.

Tom Harrisson, who traveled through parts of the Tubu' area in the 1940s, described the Punan of the lower Tubu' as "rich and business-like" (1975:3), while other Punan in the Tubu' and neighboring rivers were portrayed as nomads who "roam in small bands over great distances, without cultivating anything" (1986:265–66). Approximately fifty years separate this portrayal by Harrisson and the variation described in this essay with reference to the Punan of lower and middle Tubu' and those of the upper Malinau.

Hoffman (1983:164), in his dissertation on the Punan, declares that some of the most "modernized" groups of Punan are to be found in the remote interior of East Kalimantan, while some of the most "materially impoverished and behaviorally simplified" are living in the coastal areas (158), close to urban centers and the oil companies' offshore installations. These coastal groups, such as the Basap, Punan Batu, and Punan Binai, "are considered locally by virtually all who know them to be the most 'primitive'" (154). Hoffman explains "why Punan groups appear increasingly more 'primitive' and culturally pristine the nearer one gets to the coast" (162) by reference to the importance of trade. These coastal Punan are "much more specialized in ... the collection and trade of forest products" (164), thus explaining their apparent primitiveness.

Contrary to Hoffman I would attach much more importance to the nature of encapsulation and the specific history of contact that characterize these small groups of Punan along the east coast of Borneo. These groups, besides being small minorities, have been the clients of coastal Malays and the petty kingdoms near the coast. The Punan Batu, one of these groups, were the direct subjects of the sultan of Berau in the past. Some of these coastal Punan were perhaps most accurately described as enslaved populations (cf. Rousseau 1990:242), "totally subordinate to a coastal ruler" (Sellato 2007:72). Many of these nomads may even "have been slaves imported through the inter-island trade networks" (72). The kind of strongly asymmetrical relationship, political dominance, and clear stigmatization that we can see here between the nomads and their neighbors or patrons is probably an important reason why these Punan appear so subservient in their interactions with the world around them and why they stand out as "primitive" and impoverished in comparison with the "rich and businesslike" Punan of lower Tubu' (72–73).

Implicit Egalitarianism, Explicit Stratification

The Punan of the Malinau area are most correctly described as egalitarian, even though all Punan within any single community are not necessarily equal in terms of authority or material possessions. There are, however, leveling mechanisms, such as sharing and immediate-return consumption, that effectively reduce differences in material wealth, just as the high degree of individual or family autonomy tends to neutralize or counteract the attempts of individuals to assert their role as leaders.

Punan egalitarianism is marked by contradictions. For example, most Punan admire eloquent speakers enormously, and they greatly delight in witnessing the actions of skillful cultural brokers, young or old, who cleverly defend and promote the interests of their community. Such skillful leaders are met with reverence, respect, and approval as long as they do so. The fact that Punan claim to possess a system of social stratification, similar to that of their agricultural neighbors, may also appear to be a contradiction. This is particularly common among Punan of the middle and lower Tubu', but such claims are also occasionally made by Punan of upper Malinau. It may be useful to make a distinction between the implicit practice of equality and the explicit expression of egalitarianism, or stratification, as an ideological choice in a situation of contrast with encapsulator societies. Among Borneo foragers, such explicit expressions of egalitarianism are quite unusual, with the exception of the Bukat, a group of former nomads, who explicitly express their rejection of stratification (Sellato 1994:69). Otherwise, although most Borneo foragers may have an implicit practice of equality, they still make explicit claims of having some degree of stratification.

Foraging for Ideas

When the explicit expression conforms to the norms of surrounding societies, as in the case referred to above, it is also known in hunter-gatherer studies as "code switching" (Kratz 1981) or "lip-service to the conventions of the others" (Bird-David 1988:29).[7] The adoption of ideas and values from surrounding societies is not only a defensive strategy to avoid ridicule and conflict; it is also a "cultural digging stick" (29), which foragers use to manipulate and cultivate their surrounding social environment for their own purposes. This exploration and adoption of cultural traits from surrounding societies can also be characterized as "foraging for ideas" (Endicott 1979:221; cf. Barnard 1993). In these conditions we find one important reason why there is such a lack of coherence in the external "face" that individual Punan present to the outside. The explicit expressions are often subject to considerable variation. One example is found in the religious and cosmological beliefs of the Punan, who have no single, formalized version of religion. Each individual is equipped with a collection of borrowed items, the contents of which very much depend on each individual's personal history of contact with other people. Brunton (1990) has argued that egalitarian and immediate-return societies are "culturally unstable," as they do not safeguard their own cultural integrity. Brunton quotes Woodburn when he states, "In immediate-return systems people often do not, at least explicitly, seem to value their own culture and institutions very highly and may, indeed, not be accustomed to formulating what their custom is or what it ought to be" (Woodburn 1980:106, cited in Brunton 1990:675).

According to Brunton, the available literature on hunting and gathering societies reveals some common themes, such as the "cultural fluidity of egalitarian societies, their susceptibility to acculturation and the rudimentary nature of their collective representations" (1990:677; cf. Dentan, this volume). Among the Punan, components of religious ideas are embraced or disposed of with surprising ease and, it seems, the same underlying pragmatism that characterizes their adoption or rejection of almost any item of material culture. This gives a sense of "cultural fluidity," but it still seems a bit far-fetched to characterize them as "culturally unstable," as Brunton does. Among foragers, we often find "a fluidity in cosmology comparable to the fluidity in social relations" (Barnard 1991:559), but this fluidity, or "instability," relates to what Sellato has described as "an outer, mainly borrowed, cultural layer" (1993:50). Opposed to this "outer" culture is a set of core values that Barnard has characterized as a "foraging ethos" (1993) or "foraging mode of thought" (2002) and Sellato has described as an "'internal' culture," "ideological core," or "habitus" (1994:210–11). The inner core referred to here is often of a rather implicit nature, and among the Punan it seldom finds open expression or is given a clear and coherent formulation. It concerns such core values as social and gender equality, the autonomy of individuals and nuclear families, the preference for immediate return, or the feast-or-famine mentality. Besides these implicit values, there are other core values, among them the ideology of sharing and mutual support, which probably is the most basic source of social solidarity, that are verbally codified and regularly communicated and made explicit.

When we look at these core values we find many close similarities between Punan from different parts of the Malinau area. It seems that we here find elements that, to some degree, transcend the local variation that we have discussed so far. It is some of these similarities and sources of unity that will be the topic of the next section.

Collective Commiseration and Solidarity

In this essay, it has not been my intention to explore solidarity within single communities, bands, or families but rather to focus on a larger, ethnic level. This may appear to be a futile undertaking in this case. As we have seen, there are no forms of organization at the level of the ethnic group, and individuals and families are autonomous units that decide for themselves where to reside, with whom to cooperate, and what goals to pursue. This individualism is a prevalent feature among the Punan, who clearly tend to pursue individual goals rather than common-good goals—a factor that regularly hampers the development of common projects. In addition to this, there is also considerable variation between individuals and communities, all of which points in the direction of diversity rather than unity. However, in the remainder of this chapter I will focus on a source of solidarity that has relevance at levels beyond the single community and possibly even at that of the ethnic group.

"Culture of Sharing"

Within single settlements there is often a strong sense of unity, or solidarity, generated by close personal relations (of kinship), as well as by the practice of mutual support and sharing. Although kinship is not central to Punan social organization, it is still important to remember that the core population of an individual band is, basically, an extended family. While sharing is still the norm among Punan living upstream, at least those living in smaller settlements or encampments, much has changed in larger settlements, especially those located downstream, close to the regional center (cf. Klimut and Puri 2007; and Howell, this volume). Nonetheless, sharing and mutual support is still considered to be one of the most central characteristics of the Punan. This is the way they perceive themselves to be, or to have been, or what ought to be. Klimut—a Punan Tubu' elder presently living in the town of Malinau—mentions sharing and mutual help among Punan as a source of solidarity when he maintains that it is a "proof of their unity (one-ness)" (Klimut and Puri 2007:120). He continues:

> The Punan people of today are very different from those of the past. If a Punan catches a pig or a fish, at best we will only see it, but one cannot ask for it anymore. If you ask, he will not give you anything, except if you pay for it. … This is the difference between the Punan people of the past and the Punan today. The difference is immense. Many Punan have rubbed shoulders with town people, who do not have a culture of sharing and mutual help. This [adopting the townsfolk's culture] is the mistake often made by Punan, whereas in fact it is they who have a culture of mutual help.
>
> (Klimut and Puri 2007:121)

There is no doubt that Punan attach great significance to the ethic of sharing, but this does not mean that people in smaller settlements far upstream always share their resources generously and voluntarily. Even in small settlements, most items are not shared freely but on demand (cf. Peterson 1993); *Em micop hok*, "don't forget me," is a commonly used re-minder. A Punan will thus ask for a share of whatever he or she desires, and such a request is not normally refused, as in the case referred to by Klimut. The only way to refuse a request without causing both parties embarrass-ment is to hide the coveted belonging or simply lie and say that one does not have the desired item (864). Concealment is an option only if it can be kept secret, which is not very easy in small communities where people can do hardly anything without others knowing about it. The disappointment, sadness, and anger caused by anyone who is selfish, and "eats alone," is in itself a strong incitement to share rather than cheat.

There may, or may not, be a strong sense of solidarity within single settlements. Between different communities or local groups, however, there is normally no real sense of affinity or solidarity in everyday life, and Punan rarely think of themselves as Punan. Instead, they identity themselves and other groups of local Punan by reference to locality, saying, for example, that they "are *a' Metut*," meaning that they are "the people from the Metut River" (cf. Dentan, this volume). Despite this, there are occasions when the various local groups of Punan of the Malinau area do express a sense of being Punan. This sense of a common identity is always expressed in relationship to others, or, more specifically, what these others have that they, Punan, do not have—opportunities, things, money, health care, and so on. It is only in opposition to the surrounding world—and especially in relation to the aspects of that world of which they feel deprived—that group sentiment and a sense of "Punanness" are expressed. A case in point is a kind of ritualized collective commiseration, known as *pelulup urip*, which becomes an "emotionalization" of group solidarity, not only at the level of the family or band but far beyond the small circle of coresidents.

Pelulup Urip: Unity in Destitution

In times of scarcity, or when families face difficulties and disappointments, Punan often sit together at the end of the day and perform melancholic monologues. Seconded by an audience of their companions, individuals take turns bemoaning their current hardships and reflecting on events of the past, both good and bad. This semipublic airing of their grievances and nostalgic memorializing of former deeds and occurrences take a very stereotypic form, in terms of both style and content. There is even a Punan term for this practice, *pelulup urip*, "thinking about life." Among close relatives and friends, these are moments for a kind of collective contemplation of their own shortcomings and the inequities of life.[8] Such communal commiseration and pondering of life's woes can sometimes continue from sunset until well after midnight (Kaskija 1997:348–51, 2007:154). One young man gave the following explanation.

> *Pelulup urip*, it is a feeling of sorrow inside the heart. *Pelulup urip*, it is not anything that occurs when there are a lot of people, but when you are alone, when you face difficulties, when your destiny is unfair, when sad thoughts are popping up inside you, when you are hungry, as well as when you are full.

During *pelulup urip*, Punan often make comparisons between themselves and others, such as when they compare themselves with downriver dealers in nontimber forest products.

> We walk very far. We are bitten by mosquitoes and leeches, and we are scratched by thorns. Our bodies are in pain. If we're lucky, we find some *gaharu* [incense wood], but we have to sell it cheap. Those who buy have a lot of money and a lot of things, but they never have to enter the forest, and their bodies have no wounds.

The problems and difficulties expressed on these occasions are not individualized, and the word *I* or *me* is never, or at least seldom, used. One man may have been cheated that very same day and returned home empty-handed, or another person may have injured himself while collecting nontimber forest products. Both these men may express their feelings among friends and family members, but during *pelulup urip* they will say, for example, "Pity *us,* who are seriously injured but have no health care." Every type of hardship is suffered by "us," as these are problems that they all have in common. And a special form of "we" is used, namely, *toh*, which includes those spoken to but also refers to everybody in the same settlement and may even include all other Punan, who share the same living conditions, the same hardships and inequities.

Another word that is frequently heard on these occasions is *mai'*, which means "compassion," "pity," or "sympathy." *Mai'* may also have the meaning of "love," as in "I love you," although the literal meaning would be "I feel sympathy for you" or "I feel sorry for you." During *pelulup urip* the feeling of compassion, *mai'*, is directed toward themselves. For example, one might say "Pity us, who are old and have difficulties walking, who have few teeth and difficulties chewing," or "Pity us, who work hard but receive tiny salaries." The statement "pity us," when used internally, among themselves, does not include any sense of inferiority; rather it expresses a sense of the inadequacy of their lives and their disadvantaged position within a regional system. It may be seen as an expression of powerlessness, something akin to the "learned helplessness" of the Semai of Peninsular Malaysia (Dentan 2000), but it does not imply that Punan talk about themselves in a derogatory way during *pelulup urip*. On the contrary, they rather repeatedly point out their own superior knowledge and special skills, mainly in order to highlight the deplorable discrepancy between their expertise and labor investments, on the one hand, and the tiny salaries they receive for their services on the other. They may be hired as experts, but they are always paid as servants. Whatever the Punan do, their services are always devalued.

As one Punan elder explained, when talking about the feeling of pity or compassion, "only human beings can be compassionate and feel sympathy for other human beings. Humans like to help other humans." The feeling of compassion is regarded as a basic human quality among the Punan, something that separates humans from nonhumans and good people from bad people. It is this quality that lies at the very heart of practices such as sharing and mutual support. In this way *pelulup urip* becomes an important way in which Punan of the Malinau area express their self-image, and it also becomes a deeply felt expression of being at one in destitution and hardship. They are, in a sense, united by the difficulties and adversities, the inequities, the pain and the sorrow that they all have in common. This comes very close to Rodney Needham's definition of *solidarity* as the "common recognition of a moral duty to help one another, and the consciousness of being at one in interests, sympathies and values" (1959:80).

The information we have on *pelulup urip* in a historical perspective is very meager. We know that this particular kind of brooding over life's hardships has occurred among the Punan for at least eighty to ninety years, as this is the time span covered by the memory of those who were living in the 1990s. While complaining about being disadvantaged is a recent phenomenon among the Chewong of Peninsular Malaysia (Howell, this volume), this is not the case among the Punan. However, the contents of their melancholic monologues are changing in response to changes in the world around them. The subject matter of *pelulup urip* reflects contemporary issues. Punan may have practiced *pelulup urip* for centuries and bemoaned their hunger, the lack of wild boar or fruit, and so on, but today they bemoan their lack of health care and other "things" only after having witnessed those things possessed by their neighbors. Recently increased globalization has introduced more things to become matters for *pelulup urip*. Klimut, the Punan Tubu' elder quoted earlier, has recently written an interesting and eloquent plaint about the contemporary problems facing the Punan. In this article he complains that

> not many [Punan] get the opportunity to become a civil servant or a big businessman. ... There is still favouritism based on ethnicity in Indonesian society .... After a Punan person has sent in his application, he is told that they already have enough and that he was too late to apply. That is the actual situation we have experienced all along.
>
> (Klimut and Puri 2007:117–18)

This is, of course, not an example of *pelulup urip*, but the full article can still be read as a short catalog of some urgent issues that may just as well find expression in sessions of *pelulup urip* among Punan Tubu' living in or very close to the town of Malinau. These Punan, some of whom are very well educated, may talk frequently about problems that have little or no relevance at all to Punan from far upriver. Despite differences in detail between Punan of the periphery and those at the center, the basic problems are still the same: everywhere Punan consider themselves to be the victims of discrimination and injustice. Assets and opportunities are unequally distributed. Some people have a lot, others have less, but always at the very bottom are the Punan.

Concluding Remarks

The Punan of the Malinau area can be described as a cluster of autonomous social units with a common language, and common principles for making a living, as well as a common identity, which is expressed and developed in relation to the surrounding world. As local bands, they have always been surrounded by other people, with whom they usually have established some kind of contact. What is particularly striking is that they have been surrounded not by a single, powerful ethnic group or society but by a number of smaller groups of agriculturalists, thereby making the surface of encapsulation remarkably diverse and variable. In the course of the twentieth century, their external relations have become increasingly complex, involving a growing number of outsiders.

Because of this external diversity, each Punan band or community has had its own particular constellation of contacts, and its own particular intensity of contact with specific others, whether neighboring agricultural groups or other categories of outsiders. This does not imply that all individuals within a single band or community have a similar history of interaction with others. Most community members have many similarities in this respect, but there are individuals who have had very extensive relations with outsiders, while others have spend most of their time in the forest and kept contacts with outsiders to a minimum.

The variation among local groups, or between individuals, has been the central topic of the first part of this essay. It concluded that, in order to better understand this local variation, we have to take a closer look at each local group's particular history of interaction and contact with the world around it. Local variation reflects the specifics of encapsulation and is likely to increase when foragers, such as the Punan, are dispersed among and encapsulated by a variety of small (or like-sized) ethnic groups. If they had been encapsulated by one single, powerful neighbor, there would probably have been much less variation among the different local groups of Punan in the Malinau area.

The particularities of the diverse and varied social landscape surrounding various local groups are often explored by the Punan with the same inquiring minds and curiosity that they employ when they explore the minute details of their forest surroundings. Both environments require intimate knowledge in order to facilitate efficient manipulation and resource acquisition, as well as to prevent people from getting into trouble or danger. It is well known that Punan make a living by utilizing the resources of the forest, but their foraging strategies extend beyond that point and include diverse surfaces of contact with other people. Expressed in the vocabulary of Alan Barnard, the Punan are "'foragers' in many ways," who not only engage in subsistence foraging but in "social 'foraging'," as well as "'foraging' for ideas" (Barnard 1993:33).

In their interactions with different outsiders, Punan thus take into consideration the expectations and perceptions of these others in order to be able to exploit any opportunity that arises or simply to avoid conflict or annoyance. When Punan conform to the norms of others in this way, or conceal anything that may be met with disapproval, they switch strategically between cultural codes (cf. Kratz 1981). This does not imply that they can give a clear and coherent formulation of what their own culture is all about. There is considerable variation among individuals, and it is an unfeasible task to try to figure out what is uniquely Punan in the body of religious ideas expressed by different individuals, or in the details of their (rudimentary) ritual practices, oral literature, or material culture, which all seem to be a mixture of items borrowed from neighboring agricultural groups or other outsiders. This highly variable cultural repertoire, also described as "an outer, mainly borrowed, cultural layer" (Sellato 1993:50), can be seen as a product of a long history of encapsulation.

In this essay, a general picture has been drawn of local variation, lack of overarching organization, lack of binding commitments, and individuals presenting a very diverse, mainly borrowed, cultural repertoire while pursuing their own individual goals and for much of the time doing whatever they feel like. In such a setting it is difficult to find any sources of solidarity, especially not at the level of the ethnic group; everything seems to point in the direction of dissociation and diversity, rather than unity. The only real counterforce in this context is the ideology of sharing and mutual support. Yet, even though Punan constantly remind each other about the vital importance of sharing and mutual support, these values still remain unreliable and fragile, as they are in the hands of clever individualists. This is probably the reason why, in contrast to the implicit nature of other inner core values, the ideology of sharing and compassion is emphasized in such an explicit and verbal way. Consequently, the procurement of resources as opportunities arise; the preference for immediate return; the value of individual autonomy, independence, and self-sufficiency; and the inclination for social equality, spatial mobility, and flexibility need no reminders, no reference to guiding principles, and no tutelage, but sharing obviously does.

Against this background, *pelulup urip,* as a possible source of social solidarity at the level of the ethnic group, becomes an intriguing practice. Needham depicted solidarity as "the consciousness of being at one in interests, sympathies and values" (1959:80), which comes very close to what *pelulup urip* is all about: a deeply felt expression of being united in destitution and hardship. This solidarity may be restricted to the hearts and minds of people and thus never be accomplished in practice at the level of the ethnic group. Still, by creating a sense of sharing a common fate, *pelulup urip* is a *source* of social solidarity, besides providing emotional comfort and representing a collective confirmation of their choice of a particular *way of life* (cf. Barnard 2002:5).

Notes

The research, on which this essay is based, was financed by the Swedish Agency for Research Cooperation with Developing Countries (SAREC). Additional support was provided by the Center for International Forestry Research (CIFOR), Bogor, Indonesia. I would also like to acknowledge valuable comments on earlier drafts generously offered by Charles Macdonald, Enid Nelson, Jan Ovesen, Titti Schmidt, Bernard Sellato, and the editors of this volume.

1 Although there are several alternative terms, such as *encystment* (Gardner 1991:545), *enclosure,* and *enclavement* (Woodburn 1988:36), with similar meanings, in this essay I will consistently use Woodburn's term *encapsulation.*

2 When referring to the Punan of the Malinau area I include those of the Malinau River basin (i.e., Punan Malinau), as well as those of the Tubu' River basin (i.e., Punan Tubu'). In 1990, at the time of my field research, both river basins were part of the same administrative area, the Malinau District.

3 The area referred to here is the Malinau District as it was defined before the administrative changes that took place in 1997. In the early 1990s the Malinau District was 9,000 square kilometers in size and encompassed both the Malinau and the Tubu' River basins. In 1997 the Tubu' River basin was instead incorporated into the neighboring district of Mentarang.

4 Population figures are based on Indonesian government statistics from 1990–91.

5 At the beginning of the 1990s approximately 1,200 Punan were living in resettlement villages close to the town of Malinau, whereas the remaining 1,800 to 1,900 were living farther upstream. It can further be noted that, out of a total

number of 3,000 Punan, approximately 2,000 were Punan Tubu' (i.e., Punan from the Tubu' River area), 1,200 of them living close to the town of Malinau, 300 still living in the middle or upper part of the Tubu' River, and an additional 500 living in the middle part of the Malinau River. This means that there were some 1,000 Punan Malinau (i.e., Punan from the Malinau River area), all of them living in the middle or upper reaches of the Malinau River.

6 During the 1970s several Punan communities from the middle Tubu' moved across the watershed to the middle part of the Malinau River basin. These Punan Tubu' communities, although they are located in the Malinau River area today, are not included in the Punan Malinau category in this discussion.

7 When Punan explicitly present themselves as Christians, they are paying lip-service to the norms of the wider society by indicating that they are a modern people who do have a "real" religion and at the same time making a clear contrast and distinction between themselves and the wider society by asserting that they are not Muslims.

8 *Pelulup urip* does not occur in the presence of outsiders. This is also the reason why I have only witnessed this kind of communal commiseration in households or small settlements where I have spent a relatively long period of time. This also means that the data on which this chapter is based were gathered from a limited number of families or bands from upper and middle Malinau, as well as middle and lower Tubu'. However, additional information has been gathered through conversations with various Punan Malinau/Tubu' on the topic of *pelulup urip*.

References

Barnard, Alan. 1991. "Comments on Gardner." *Current Anthropology* 32:558–59.

———. 1993. "Primitive communism and mutual aid: Kropotkin visits the Bushmen." In C.M. Hann, ed., *Socialism: Ideals, Ideologies, and Social Practice*. 27–42. Association of Social Anthropologists Monographs, no. 31. London and New York: Routledge.

———. 2002. "The foraging mode of thought." In H. Steward, A. Barnard, and K. Omura, eds., *Self- and Other-Images of Hunter-Gatherers*, 5–24. Senri Ethnological Studies, No. 60. Osaka: National Museum of Ethnology.

Biesbrouck, Karen, Stefan Elders, and Gerda Rossel, eds. 1999. *Challenging Elusiveness: Central African Hunter-Gatherers in a Multidisciplinary Perspective.* Leiden: Research School for Asian, African, and Amerindian Studies, Universiteit Leiden.

Bird-David, Nurit. 1988. "Hunter-gatherers and other people: A re-examination." In T. Ingold, D. Riches, and J. Woodburn, eds., *Hunters and Gatherers*. Vol. 1: *History, Evolution, and Social Change*, 17–31. Oxford: Berg.

Brunton, Ron. 1990. "The cultural instability of egalitarian societies." *Man,* new series, 24:673–81.

Dentan, Robert. K. 1979. *The Semai: A Nonviolent People of Malaysia.* New York: Holt, Rinehart and Winston.

———. 2000. "This is passion and where it goes: Despair and suicide among Semai, a non-violent people of West-Malaysia." *Moussons* 2:31–56.

———. 2008. *Overwhelming Terror: Love, Fear, Peace, and Violence among Semai of Malaysia.* Lanham, MD: Rowman and Littlefield.

Endicott, Kirk. 1979. *Batek Negrito Religion.* Oxford: Clarendon Press.

Gardner, Peter. M. 1966. "Symmetric respect and memorate knowledge: The structure and ecology of individualistic culture." *Southwestern Journal of Anthropology* 22:389–415.

———. 1991. "Foragers' pursuit of individual autonomy." *Current Anthropology* 32:543–72.

Harrisson, Tom. 1975. "Further notes on Sarawak and Kalimantan Punan (and Penan)." *Borneo Research Bulletin* 7:3–4.

———. 1986. *World Within: A Borneo Story.* Singapore and New York: Oxford University Press.

Hoffman, Carl L. 1983. "Punan." PhD diss., University of Pennsylvania.

Kaskija, Lars. 1997. "The Punan of Borneo: Cultural fluidity and persistency in a forest people." In A. Hornborg and M. Kurkiala, eds., *Voices of the Land: Identity and Ecology in the Margins,* No. 1:321–61 Lund Studies in Human Ecology. Lund: Lund University Press.

———. 2002. *Claiming the Forest: Punan Local Histories and Recent Developments in Bulungan, East Kalimantan.* Bogor, Indonesia: Center for International Forestry Research.

———. 2007. "Stuck at the bottom: Opportunity structures and Punan Malinau identity." In and P.G. Sercombe and B. Sellato, eds., *Beyond the Green Myth: Hunter-Gatherers of Borneo in the Twenty-first Century,* 135–59. Copenhagen: NIAS Press.

Kelly, Robert. L. 1995. *The Foraging Spectrum: Diversity in Hunter-Gatherer Lifeways.* Washington, DC: Smithsonian Books.

Kent, Susan. 1992. "The current forager controversy: Real versus ideal views of hunter-gatherers." *Man* new series 27:45–70.

Klimut, K.A., and Rajindra. K. Puri. 2007. "The Punan from the Tubu' River, East Kalimantan: A native voice on past, present, and future circumstances." In P.G. Sercombe and B. Sellato, eds., *Beyond the Green Myth:*

Hunter-Gatherers of Borneo in the Twenty-first Century, 110–34. Copenhagen: NIAS Press.

Kratz, Corinne. 1981. "Are the Okiek Really Maasai? Or Kipsigis? Or Kikuyu?" *Cahiers d'Études Africaines* 79:355–68.

Lourandos, Harry. 1997. *Continent of Hunter-Gatherers: New Perspectives in Australian Prehistory*. New York: Cambridge University Press.

Motzafi-Haller, Pnina. 1994. "Ethnicity, and differentiation in rural Botswana." *American Ethnologist* 21:539–63.

Needham, Rodney. 1959. "Mourning-terms." *Bijdragen tot de Taal-, Land- en Volkenkunde* 115:58–89.

Pedersen, Jon, and Espen Waehle. 1988. "The complexities of residential orga-nization among the Efe (Mbuti) and Bamgombi (Baka): A critical view of the notion of flux in hunter-gatherer societies." In T. Ingold, D. Riches, and J. Woodburn, eds., *Hunters and Gatherers*. Vol. 1: *History, Evolution, and Social Change*, 75–90. Oxford: Berg.

Peterson, Nicholas. 1993. "Demand sharing: Reciprocity and the pressure for generosity among foragers." *American Anthropologist* 95:860–74.

Rousseau, Jérôme. 1988. "Central Borneo: A bibliography." Special monographs, no. 5. *Sarawak Museum Journal* 33 (59).

———. 1990. *Central Borneo: Ethnic Identity and Social Life in a Stratified Society*. Oxford: Oxford University Press.

Sather, Clifford. 1995. "Sea nomads and rainforest hunter-gatherers: Foraging adaptations in the Indo-Malaysian archipelago." In P. Bellwood, J.J. Fox, and D. Tryon, eds., *The Austronesians*, 229–68. Canberra: Department of Anthropology, Research School of Pacific and Asian Studies, Australian National University.

Sellato, Bernard. 1993. "The Punan question and the reconstruction of Borneo's culture history." In V.H. Sutlive Jr., ed., *Change and Development in Borneo*, 47–81. Williamsburg, VA: Borneo Research Council. Selected papers from the first extraordinary conference of the Borneo Research Council, August 4–9, 1990.

———. 1994. *Nomads of the Borneo Rainforest: The Economics, Politics, and Ideology of Settling Down*. Honolulu: University of Hawai'i Press.

———. 2001. *Forest, Resources, and People in Bulungan: Elements for a History of Settlement, Trade, and Social Dynamics in Borneo, 1880–2000*. Bogor, Indonesia: Center for International Forestry Research.

———. 2007. "Resourceful children of the forest: The Kalimantan Punan through the twentieth century." In P.G. Sercombe and B. Sellato, eds.,

Beyond the Green Myth: Hunter-Gatherers of Borneo in the Twenty-first Century, 61–90. Copenhagen: NIAS Press.

Whittier, Herbert. L., and Patricia. R. Whittier. 1974. "The Apo Kayan area of East Kalimantan." *Sarawak Museum Journal* 22:5–15.

Woodburn, J. 1980. "Hunters and gatherers today and reconstruction of the past." In E. Gellner, ed., *Soviet and Western Anthropology*, 95–117. London: Duckworth.

———. 1982. "Egalitarian societies." *Man,* new series, 17:431–51.

———. 1988. "African hunter-gatherer social organization: Is it best understood as a product of encapsulation?" In T. Ingold, D. Riches, and J. Woodburn, eds., *Hunters and Gatherers*. Vol. 1: *History, Evolution, and Social Change*, 31–64. Oxford: Berg.

9

Mending Nets of Relatedness: Words and Gifts as Sources of Solidarity in a Sama Dilaut Fishing Community

CLIFFORD SATHER

MY PURPOSE IN THIS ESSAY is to explore the role of mobility, the performative use of speech, and the reciprocal sharing of food and other gifts in maintaining conditions favorable to a highly "gregarious" form of sociality among an "open-aggregated" (see Macdonald 2008; and in this volume) community of once-nomadic maritime fishing people. In this context, *sociality* refers to both a desire by persons to be present in the company of others (Geddes 1954:16) and the characteristic form taken by their collective interactions with one another. *Gregarious sociality* describes in this case a form of interaction characterized by informality, equality as opposed to hierarchy, harmony as opposed to order, and a preference for being fully present to one another in a spirit of face-to-face interaction.

The people who concern us here, the Sama Dilaut, are part of a larger congeries of Sama/Bajau-speaking peoples who live scattered over a vast area of maritime Southeast Asia, from northeastern Borneo and the Sulu Archipelago of the Philippines through coastal Sulawesi to the easternmost islands of Indonesia (cf. Nimmo 2001; Sather 1997, 2004b; Stacey 1999).[1] Here I focus on a single community of Sama Dilaut living in the Semporna district of Sabah (Malaysia). When I first began fieldwork in 1964–65 there were two Sama Dilaut settlements in Semporna with a combined population of 660 persons. Historically, until 1955, the Semporna Sama Dilaut lived entirely aboard boats, but by 1965 all but twenty families had erected wooden pile-houses over the sea at what had formerly served as two fixed anchorage sites.

Village life in 1965 was still conditioned, as it had been earlier when the Sama Dilaut were entirely boat living, by a pattern of constant family dispersal and aggregation. In going to sea, families, even those living in houses, returned to their boats, dispersing typically for from one or two days to several weeks at a time. Although voyages were often undertaken to visit kin in other settlements, the great majority focused on economic activities: net fishing or spearfishing, inshore collecting, and marketing. Outward voyages were rarely described in terms of precise destinations. Instead, families described their travels chiefly by reference to locales of activity. The most frequent, *anebba'* or *magtebba'*, referred to a zone of intertidal reefs and shallows (*tebba'*). For the Sama Dilaut, this, in the 1960s, was a "tactile" zone, constantly traversed and deeply invested with local knowledge. It was also a locale given over almost exclusively to fishing and so was a realm largely devoid of community rituals and the convivial sociability that the Sama Dilaut so highly valued. While at sea, families often complained of "loneliness" (*telingus-lingus*) due to the absence of friends and loved ones. Hence homeward voyages were keenly anticipated and typically ended in emotional reunions, the distribution of gifts of freshly caught fish, welcoming visits, and, at times, feasts of thanksgiving.

Village aggregation, by contrast, was characteristically described as *lamai*, meaning "bustling," "noisy," "active," and "intensely social." Here interpersonal relations were not only intense but also intimate and informal. Returning families were at once enmeshed in larger groups, but these, though tight-knit, were, as we shall see, weakly structured and impermanent. As a result, interpersonal relations favored, in Macdonald's terms, "open aggregation," "personal autonomy," and "a quest for harmony" over a prescribed order of corporate groups, formal roles, and statuses (2008). Within the village, the prevailing stress was on kinship, giving and sharing, freedom of action, amity, and dialogue, a propensity, in short, for "the informal and performative as against the formal and institutional" (cf. Overing and Passes 2000:xiii).

In returning to Semporna in the 1970s and, again, briefly, in 1995, I found that the food-sharing system I describe later in this essay was no longer practiced, as, by the 1990s, only a small number of local Sama Dilaut families continued to fish, their former role in the regional economy having been taken over largely by Sama Dilaut newcomers. During these years, the largest of the two former settlements had become almost wholly enveloped within Semporna town, so that today social life in this community, which is now far larger, more heterogeneous, and settled, no longer displays the features of mobility, food sharing, and gregarious sociality that had been its hallmarks in the 1960s. Consequently, the final sections of this essay discuss the demise of these distinctive features, which once sustained cohesion and conditions of amity within what was once a remarkably open and intensely sociable community.

A Brief History of Boats, Houses, and Settlements

Historically, the Sama Dilaut were distinguished from other Sama speakers by their "encapsulated" status (see Kaskija, this volume) and the highly specialized role they played in the wider economy of the region (Sather 2002). Before European penetration, the Semporna Sama Dilaut were part of an extensive procurement economy in which, as self-described "sea people" (*a'a dilaut*), they supplied maritime commodities of trade such as dried fish, pearl shell, turtles' eggs, and *trepang* (*Holothuria*) to political patrons ashore, non–Sama Dilaut (*a'a saddi*, "other people"), who acted as titleholders on behalf of the Sulu Archipelago–based Sulu sultanate (cf. Sather 1997; and Warren 1981). In return, the Sama Dilaut were provided with access to local sources of agricultural foodstuffs, fresh water, cloth, and craft goods, as well as some measure of physical security (Sather 1997:35–44, 2002). Within the Sulu sultanate, authority was defined territorially (Kiefer 1971), with the result that the Sama Dilaut, as a scattered, highly mobile people, were essentially excluded and without political status, except indirectly as the clients of local land-based patrons.

In the first years of the twentieth century, the British North Borneo Chartered Company imposed direct rule over the southeastern coast of Sabah and established an administrative center and market port at what is now Semporna town. For the local Sama Dilaut, the consequences were far-reaching. Freeing themselves from their local shore-based patrons, they redirected their trade through the Semporna town market. At the same time, they also relocated their principal moorage sites along the periphery of the town harbor, thereby placing themselves, in effect, directly under the company's protection.

These changes were a key to the construction of the first pile-houses. Prior to their construction, families lived exclusively aboard boats (*lepa*).

Between voyages, related families moored at fixed anchorage sites, where they typically tied their boats together in groups usually composed of matrifocally related families, typically organized around a core of married sisters, their husbands, and children. With house construction, a similar pattern of residential aggregation prevailed. Thus, in the 1960s, houses were generally built by family heads who gathered under their roofs their married daughters and husbands. Through the first years of marriage, couples thus lived, as a rule, in the house of the wife's parents and contributed to a common household budget. Later, as they bore children, gained economic independence, and acquired a circle of regular fishing partners, they typically built houses of their own, generally erecting them in a dense cluster around the original parental house. Theses clusters were called *ba'anan*, and today they, together with the individual households (*luma'*) that comprise them, constitute the primary social units that make up a village community.

None of these groups was, or is today, in any way "transcendent" (Macdonald, n.d.) in the sense of outliving its individual members. The boats and houses that in the 1960s constituted the principal material objectification of these groups had only a limited temporal existence. Even with frequent repairs, both required replacement at least once in an average life span. In the case of households and *ba'anan*, members were free to come and go at will. For households, each successive generation was expected to depart and eventually found new households of their own. *Ba'anan*, as a rule, tended to be even more ephemeral. The term *ba'anan* means simply a "collection (of things)," or, in the case of fish, a "school," and so carries with it no implication of permanence, fixed boundaries, or exclusiveness. Membership in all of these groups was therefore impermanent, with the only long-term constants being the processes by means of which they came into being, reproduced themselves, and ultimately dissolved (cf. Sather 1976, 1997).

In the long run, settlements, too, were fluid in makeup. To borrow an analogy from Deleuze and Guattari's *A Thousand Plateaus* (1987:1–25), Sama Dilaut communities, as well as the constituent groups that comprised them, had a decidedly "rhizomelike" nature. Consisting, like rhizomorphic plants, of momentary nodes of aggregation plus outward-spreading filaments, each capable of generating a new node of radiation, "rhizomorphic societies" are characterized in Deleuze and Guattari's terms not by their boundaries or dimensions, like more settled societies, but, rather, by their "masses and flows," "aggregates of intensity," and "directions of motion" (16). Thus, in the past, moorage sites were frequently relocated, often in response to shifts in trade or changing political relations ashore. Boats not only made Sama Dilaut mobility possible but were also, to a large degree, emblematic of their relative autonomy as a self-perceived society of "sea people" (*a'a dilaut*).[2] Though dependent on trade, by preserving their mobility communities were able to move between rival patrons and so fashion for themselves a notably egalitarian way of life, which, in contrast to that of the "onshore people" (*a'a déa*) who lived around them, was largely free of outside surveillance and direct state control.

Mending Relations within a Meshwork of Kin

For the Sama Dilaut, moving within this mobile setting, kinship in the 1960s was the primary idiom of interpersonal relations, both at sea and within the village.[3] In general terms, webs of relatedness were seen as centered on the family, as their defining point of reference, and from there extending outward. In describing these webs, a single married pair, plus their children, was referred to as a *damataan*, meaning, literally, "those of one (*da-*) eye (*mata*)" (Sather 1997:134–35). The "eye" referred to in this case was not an ordinary eye but the individual opening (*mata*) of a fishnet. The term *mataan* thus referred to the totality of this meshwork visualized, like a net, as comprising a multitude of interconnected "eyes" or openings. The term was both family- and sociocentric and, in this sense, counterbalanced the pervasive element of individual autonomy otherwise inherent in Sama Dilaut social relations. Married couples existed not separately but embedded in a relational meshwork. The strands of relationship that defined them as a single eye also connected them, directly or indirectly, to other eyes in an indefinitely expanding meshwork of relationships. Upon marriage, a husband and wife were said to initiate a new *mataan*, centered on themselves. The birth of children added strands to this meshwork, while death, enmity, or divorce severed these strands. Thus, each couple's *mataan* continually changed as new strands of relationship were added and as old ones were severed or allowed to lapse. For most families these strands of relationship tended, at any given time, to be heavily concentrated within the particular house group (*luma'*) and *ba'anan* to which they belonged. However, reflecting the open, rhizomorphic nature of these groups, *mataan* relations were by no means confined to, nor did they define, these groups in any exclusive sense. Moreover, as existing house groups dissolved and new ones were founded, a family's *mataan* relations underwent a corresponding rearrangement, as ideals of relatedness were brought into accord with practical experience, with the actualities of sharing and with the ways in which families chose to aggregate themselves with others.

Ideally, *mataan* relations should be "close" (*asékot*) in the sense of being intimate, supportive, and socially binding. Families typically worked in various ways to preserve this closeness. One way was through marriage. Thus, the Sama Dilaut strongly favored marriages between cognatic kin, including the consecutive marriages of a son and daughter between a pair of closely related families (a practice called *magtumbuh sengkol*) (Sather 1997:263–68).[4] Other, more commonly occurring ways were, as we shall see, by sharing food and other gifts, labor and material support, and exchange of visits. Fittingly, this work of maintaining and renewing relationships was likened to the work of mending and repairing a family's stock of fishnets. In the 1960s, the idiom was highly appropriate, as the task of mending nets was, for adult males, virtually never-ending.

In addition to renewing ties and mending possible ruptures, Sama Dilaut families also, through their voyaging, continually explored and extended the limits of these networks of relatedness. Kinship itself was often a social imperative for travel. Thus, families often journeyed to other villages, some of them across the Philippine border, to attend sick relatives, grieve the dead, or participate with kinsmen in the arrangement of marriages and other rituals. In the process, forgotten relatives might be discovered, new marriages forged, or opportunities found for possible future relocations.

Maintaining Amity through a Flow of Words

Despite its fluid, rhizomorphic structure, village life was intensely social. In returning from voyages, family members lived a highly gregarious existence surrounded by housemates, kin, and neighbors. Among other ways, this intense sociality was expressed through a steady flow of words. Verbal courtesies helped foster feelings of closeness, while people gathered together with obvious pleasure to exchange news, gossip, joke, and tell stories. But the villagers expressed not only their relations of amity through their use of words, but also their disagreements and conflicts.

In distinguishing themselves from surrounding land-based people, the Sama Dilaut often said, "We [Sama Dilaut] fight only with our mouths" (Sather 1997:62; 2004a). While others might interpret this as an insult, the Sama Dilaut saw fighting with words as a virtue. The phrase not only expressed a collective aversion to physical violence but also a recognition of the ever-present reality of conflict as a threat to the social harmony they so valued, and the possibility that speech allowed for both expressing and resolving conflict. Very early, within the first few weeks of my fieldwork, I came to realize that the Sama Dilaut were not a people who silently repressed their disagreements. Instead, verbal harangues, exchanged almost always between married women, each standing at the edge of a house platform or at the top of a boat-landing ladder, shouting complaints at the other for the entire village to hear, were a frequent and highly public village occurrence. The complaints cataloged often included verbal insults or accusations of disrespectful speech. These public harangues resembled, in some respects, a similar form of speechmaking described by Langub (2004) for the Western Penan. In the Penan case, however, after a serious dispute or breakdown in relationships, it is the headman who, in the early hours of the morning, delivers a loud monologue addressed to no one in particular but meant to be heard by the entire camp. By contrast, it was Sama Dilaut women who, through these accusatory dialogues, were empowered to act as social critics, exposing conflicts and possible wrongdoing, and so, by the forcefulness of their speech, bringing these things to the notice of an extended audience, including, at times, the entire village. These dialogues were intended, like their Penan counterparts, to have an effect on the behavior of others. Not only were persons chastised in public, men as well as women, but, because they were made public, household and ba'anan elders were compelled to initiate negotiations meant to redress the conflicts revealed in the course of these dialogues. While Langub (205) describes the monologues of Penan headmen as consisting in part of "moral exhortations," for the Sama Dilaut it was not on the occasion of these dialogues but during the negotiations that followed that the elders engaged in such exhortations or what Sillander (2004:282–286) fittingly calls "authoritative speech," that is, in this case, speech evoking the values of relatedness and amity.

If others failed to intervene or negotiations proved ineffective, conflicts might escalate, particularly if others became involved, into an exchange of curses (*magsapa*). As a performative speech act, such an exchange transformed the relationship between the two persons involved, and so some-times ended, as we shall see, with a public declaration of enmity (*magbanta*). As a hallmark of their transformed status, the two persons terminated all further communication and so ceased to speak to one another. Thus, at one extreme, words were used to repudiate ties of relatedness and so foreclose the possibility of continuing sociality.

But, in addition, the villagers also used words to repair strained relations, particularly by talking out their differences through the give-and-take of verbal mediation. As long as words continued to flow, relationships remained intact and open to possible mending. It was only when speech was cut off, and with it the accompanying flow of gifts and support, that disagreements hardened into formal enmities. Once this occurred, a relationship could only be reestablished through a formal act of public reconciliation.

Leadership and Village Mediation

The primary task of household heads and other village leaders was to create the conditions that made it possible for their followers to live together in a state of relative amity. For this, a gift with words was essential, as leaders lacked the power to coerce unwilling followers. Leaders of temporary work groups—such as fish-netting parties—family heads, and house group and *ba'anan* leaders were referred to as *nakura*. Most were also described as "elders" or *matto'a*. Although egalitarian, the Sama Dilaut had, and still have, a deep respect for age and generational seniority. However, they also valued generosity in those they acknowledged as their leaders. Hence, house group and *ba'anan* leaders, because of the pivotal role they played in food sharing and in other forms of reciprocal support, were generally men in their economically productive years and so not necessarily the eldest or most senior members of these groups. By contrast, the truly elderly generally withdrew from the everyday management of household affairs and pre-dominated, instead, as village prayer leaders (*imam*), seers (*ta'u nganda'*), and spirit mediums (*jin*).

Because of the intensity of interaction between household and *ba'anan* members, any discord or friction in their relations tended to generate equally intense feelings of grievance, feelings that deeply threatened the integrity of these groups. As a consequence, a major task of village leaders and other elders was to intervene in disputes and try to resolve them, often through the use of joking and humor or by means of rhetorical appeals to the social ideal of "acting in accord (with others)" (*magsulut*). For the Sama Dilaut, disagreements were an expected part of living together. In contrast to the formality-inclined Bentian described by Sillander in this volume, the Sama Dilaut valued intimacy and openness, the ideal person being one who was "open hearted" (*pabuka'na atai*), that is, who not only showed his or her own true feelings but was open and responsive to the feelings of others (Sather 1997:295).[5] Thus, social harmony, however valued, could not be taken for granted, nor feigned, but was something that could only be achieved through hard work. The villagers said that most "quarrels" (*magsaghau*) arose between women. Certainly, these were the most visible, as women were, in a sense, socially licensed to expose conflict. On the one hand, the frequency of quarrels between women might be explained, at least in part, by the fact that related women, due to the preference for uxorilocal residence, tended to comprise the core members of most household and *ba'anan* groups. Hence, on behalf of their husbands or fathers, women generally managed most aspects of food sharing and other types of kin support, areas in which grievances were most likely to arise. On the other hand, the public nature of their quarrels tended to ensure that others would intervene, hence they were generally said to be more readily amenable to reconciliation. Quarrels between men, by contrast, though less frequent and often initially put into words by their women, were thought to be more disruptive, as they were more likely to lead to the breakup of households or even entire *ba'anan* groups. In the case of serious quarrels, *ba'anan* leaders and other elders were expected to help talk out an informal settlement by calling together those involved and encouraging them to negotiate their grievances. Failing this, a quarrel might develop into a "verbal challenge" (*magsasa'*) and so, finally, into an exchange of curses. This, as noted, represented a serious escalation, only one step removed from physical fighting (*magbono'*). Before this stage was reached, the dispute was likely to be referred by the elders to the village headman for formal mediation.

Unlike other elders, the headman had authority to convene an open village hearing. This authority was almost certainly a recent one, deriving from the colonial period when the first community headman was appointed.[6] As a first step, the headman usually invited the parties involved to his house for an informal face-to-face meeting. In this, the headman acted chiefly as a mediator. If the two sides were unable to find an informal settlement, he then called for a public hearing. These hearings took two forms. One, called *magsalassai*, dealt chiefly with marital or personal disputes and aimed at reconciliation.[7] The second, *maghukum*, generally involved an accusation of wrongdoing (*sa'*) and often resulted in a fine or payment of compensation (Sather 2004a:136–38).[8]

Village mediation was frequent. In 1964–65, the headman called, on average, at least one open hearing and two or three informal meetings each month.[9] In the case of village hearings, anyone was free to attend and express an opinion, but the headman generally guided the course of discussions. He typically began by outlining the nature of the dispute and, throughout, reminded those present that their purpose was to reach a settlement that restored conditions of *magsulut* or mutual accord. The root *sulut* means, literally, "to go along with" or "to go parallel with." In the context of mediation, *magsulut* was said to be best achieved if both sides emerged as more or less "equal" (*tabla'*), thereby reaffirming the basic ideal of interpersonal equality.

Given the important role of speech in maintaining convivial relations among housemates and kin, it is not surprising that accusations of verbal discourtesy, broken vows, slander, and false accusations were frequently mentioned sources of disagreement. Here a settlement often involved, again, a performative use of speech—for example, a public retraction of an insult or accusation of wrongdoing—an exchange of apologies, or a mutual pledge to put aside differences. In the case of hearsay slander, or a charge that one person had secretly "cursed" (*anukna'*) another, the accused might clear himself or herself by swearing a public oath of innocence. While the headman and other elders might intervene and require the disputing parties to discuss their differences, they could not compel them to accept a settlement. For this, the headman had to rely on the influence of house and *ba'anan* elders and the notion that those who refused to negotiate, swore falsely, or rejected the advice of their elders invited spiritual retribution (*busung*) (Sather 1997:298–99).

Enmity and Reconciliation

Not all dissension was successfully resolved. In the course of the everyday flow of speech, food, and other gifts, a breakdown in relations might occur, almost always the result not of a single incident but of a long history of accumulated grievances that was so irreconcilable that it resulted in a complete rupture of relations. Those who severed a relationship in this way were almost always kin, often, in fact, *damataan*, "those of one eye," that is to say, siblings, or parents and children. Hence, even the closest of kin ties was open to verbal repudiation. A person had, as a rule, a right to expect support from a close kinsman, especially a housemate or cluster ally. Nonkin, on the other hand, if they had disagreements, could simply ignore one another or pursue their differences through formal village mediation. Neither option was available to close kinsmen. The only way they could openly repudiate claims to their support was by declaring themselves parties to a relationship of formal enmity (*magbanta*). Those who stood in such a relationship described one another as *banta*, "enemies." The relationship was thus a dyadic one, and, as already noted, those who became *banta* severed all contact with each other, including speech and obligations of support.

A verbal declaration of enmity normally marked the final repudiation of a relationship that had become so strained that maintaining it had become a burden to both parties. Entering a *magbanta* relationship was typically formalized by pronouncing a "curse" (*sapa*). To make this curse more binding, it often made reference to the Qur'an or to the ancestors (*embo'*), both significant sources of ritual authority. For example,

> *Sapahanku tellumpu' jud Kura'an bo' aku pabalik ni luma' iti.*
>
> "I swear on thirty surah of the Qur'an that I will never come back to this house."

or

> *Allum sajja embo'ku boho' aku amolé' ni luma' iti.*
>
> "Only if my deceased grandparents come back to life will I return to this house."

Once spoken, these words became a *suvali*, a sworn vow (*janji'*) that could not be broken.[10]

While this declaration created a dyadic relation of enmity between a single pair of *banta*, it often had, in fact, far-reaching ramifications. If the persons involved either lived in the same house or belonged to the same *ba'anan*, as was often the case, their withdrawal was likely to have a chain-reaction effect, causing, in many cases, an entire *ba'anan* to fragment. As a result, houses were dismantled, connecting catwalks pulled up, and new houses rebuilt among more congenial kin in other parts of the village. Oftentimes, enmity brought to the surface fissures that had already begun to develop as one generation of household leaders succeeded another. As a result, the withdrawal of families and the breakup of house group clusters often had the effect of removing from the makeup of these groups particularly contentious relations. Consequently, once these relations were repudiated, through the sanctioning of person-to-person enmities, the new groups that emerged were usually more harmonious than those that they replaced. With the dissolution and realignment of household and *ba'anan* groups, networks of *mataan* relations, as I have noted, also underwent realignment, with the result that kinship in its more extended sense came to more closely reflect the experienced realities of sharing and cooperation.

In the long run, however, enmity was said to be a source of *busung*. Those who, as the years passed, continued to harbor grievances were thought to invite misfortune on both themselves and their enemies. Moreover, enmity, as the obverse of amity, conflicted with Sama Dilaut notions of social well-being, which required that one live in the company of others, with no one left out or, even worse, left alone. Hence, friends and relatives generally tried to persuade *banta* to undergo a formal ritual of public reconciliation called *magkiparat* (or *magtiparat*). This was particularly so if one or the other of the two fell ill or appeared to be close to death. Above all, the villagers said, no one should go to his or her grave still a *banta*. As *banta* were almost always kin, there were usually a number of persons related to both who shared a common interest in organizing a *magkiparat* ritual to bring about their reconciliation.

Magkiparat took place at sunrise, with the two *banta* sitting side by side, facing westward (*kasaddopan*). The presence of other families beside those of the two *banta* was required, including those that had initiated and organized the ritual. The latter were also required to provide all of the necessary materials. The ritual itself consisted essentially of splitting a coconut above the two *banta* and allowing the water inside to flow over their heads (Sather 1997:212–13, 2004a:143–45). The two were then bathed and joined their families and other guests in public prayers (*doa salamat*), followed by a community feast of thanksgiving (*majamu/kenduri*). Only after this were the two former *banta* permitted to speak. This final act of "resuming speech" (*mahilling pabalik*) marked a resumption of their former relationship.

What made *magkiparat* so effective as a ritual of reconciliation was that it was organized and carried out not by the *banta* directly but by others, many of whom were related to one another as mutual kin or friends. Thus, all of the preparations were made by others, including the initial planning of the ritual, and these persons also supplied the rice, fish, and other necessities for the *magkiparat* feast. The two *banta* and their families were thus made the recipients of gifts of food and labor provided by others, with the result that they were drawn back again, as a consequence of these gifts, into the larger meshwork of relationships that had formerly connected them to one another.

In addition to the flow of words and their use in managing conflict, mobility, too, served as an important means of containing discord. While the villagers said that they often missed the intense conviviality of village life while at sea, they also said that voyaging sometimes came as a relief from the equally intense quarrels and verbal contestation that, by the same token, often accompanied village aggregation. Dispersal, in this sense, allowed families to regulate, or adjust, as it were, the intensity of kin and house group relations by creating temporary distance between them and their housemates and other village kin. In addition, freedom of movement allowed families to relocate, moving to other parts of the village or even to other settlements as a way of escaping irreconcilable differences.

The Performative Use of Vows to Solemnize Relations of Gift Giving

Closely related to the sharing of gifts, an important way in which the Sama Dilaut expressed their preference for personal autonomy and the performative over institutionalized aspects of social life was through their use of verbal pledges or vows. Vows (*janji*) were centrally important to how the Sama Dilaut actively constructed and maintained their social relationships with one another (Sather 1997:287–89). Vow taking also linked the flow of words to acts of reciprocal sharing and lent to both an aura of spiritual or religious significance.

Interpersonal relations between village kin and neighbors took the characteristic form of linked transactions, which, through what the Sama Dilaut described as the rendering and returning of "help" (*tabang* or *tabang-manabang*), had the cumulative effect of creating and discharging "debts" (*utang*). The obligations of reciprocity involved in these transactions were frequently backed by a pledge or verbal promise. But, more than this, the pronouncement of a pledge was thought to solemnize and impart a religious significance to any form of promissory agreement (*magjanji*) that one person chose to enter into with another.

Besides the forms of *magjanji* associated with kinship and directly related to the exchange of social favors and support between kin and housemates, there were also other forms of vow taking that had an even more overtly religious nature. As one pious elder, Lamarani, once explained to me, promises have sanctity because (Sather 1997:287):

> We, as human beings (*mundusia*), enjoy the gift of life from God (*Tuhan*). … For this gift, we, as … recipients, must repay God by living in accordance with His wishes. These wishes are revealed to us through the Prophet's teachings. Otherwise, if we refuse to live as God wishes, we will suffer misfortune in this life and eternal damnation in the next.

Hence, God Himself is the final source of all vows. As the ultimate bestower of gifts, most notably the gift of life, God is also ultimately responsible for vouchsafing the terms of all promises. Violation of these terms is therefore an act of impiety punishable by ill-fortune (*busung*) and the loss of God's favor. Thus, in addition to kin, a person might also make a vow to himself or herself (*magjanji ni kandi*) or directly to God (*magjanji ni Tuhan*). In the latter case, in return for a special favor, such as the birth of a child or an escape from danger, the vow taker was expected to dedicate himself to an act of piety as a sign of thanksgiving (*magsukul*). The most common form this act took was the sponsorship of public prayers and a community feast, like that which accompanied, for example, the ritual reconciliation of former *banta*.

Gifts, Commodities, and Social Boundaries

In the past, of all the various gifts shared between families, none was more important than gifts of fish, or, in the 1960s, fish plus purchased goods, including even cash, obtained through the sale of fish. At the time, transactions of fish and income derived from fishing constituted the principal material medium by means of which village kinship and community sociality were maintained.

Sama Dilaut fishing, even in precolonial times, was geared in part to outside markets. Down to the end of the nineteenth century, the Sama

Dilaut were engaged, as I have noted, in a procurement economy, supplying maritime commodities of trade to land-based patrons ashore (see Sather 1997; and 2002). In Semporna, these maritime commodities consisted chiefly of *trepang* (sea slugs, *Holothuria*) and dried fish. Both were produced by Sama Dilaut families as commodities, that is, as goods intended exclusively for exchange. Indeed, *trepang* functioned only as a commodity, as sea slugs (*bat*) have never been consumed by the Sama Dilaut themselves. The situation with regard to fish was much more complex. Fish were transacted in the past in two sharply differentiated circuits. In the first, they were exchanged as gifts of fresh fish, or as cooked food, within a social circuit defined largely by village kin and household relations. In the second, they were transacted as dried fish across ethnic boundaries in formalized commodity relations that, in large measure, defined the Sama Dilaut as "sea people" in relation to those living around them, including, in the Semporna district, other Sama/Bajau speakers.

At sea, families were largely autonomous in terms of subsistence, with each family preparing its meals independently on a portable earthenware hearth (*lapoan*), which the family carried aboard its boat. However, in returning to the village, families were absorbed into a wider network of relationships that focused in particular on house groups and *ba'anan*. Within these groups, families acknowledged food-sharing obligations (*binuanan*). Each household shared a common kitchen (*kusina*), where, when all were present, housemates prepared and consumed common meals. Thus, families, in returning from fishing, contributed to a joint household larder. Beyond the household, gifts of freshly caught fish, described by the Sama Dilaut as "cooking fish" (*amilla' daing*), were distributed to other families. These typically included immediate kin and related families living in the same *ba'anan*. While all food items were potentially shareable, the principal item shared was thus "cooking fish." Families, as a result, not only set aside fish for their own consumption and that of their housemates but also reserved a portion of their catch as gifts to village kin and their immediate *ba'anan* neighbors. In addition, families sometimes went to sea in order to obtain fish specifically for a household-sponsored feast. Whatever remained after these distributions were made was available to the family head and his wife for outside sale. In the 1960s, any income derived from the sale of fish belonged to the family for its own use. In this regard, there existed a clear division in these transactions, reflecting, on the one hand, kinship and household interests and, on the other, the individual interests of each separate family. The sharing of cooking fish was managed not by the male head of the family but by his wife, daughters, or daughters-in-law. Women, in other words, had charge of that portion of the family's catch that was reserved for fulfilling food-sharing obligations. In this respect, the Sama Dilaut situation clearly resembled that described by Janet Carsten (1989:137–38) for the Langkawi Malays, in which women, she argues, "socialize" or "de-individualize" the economic contributions of their husbands. However, in the Sama Dilaut case, these contributions were not those of their husbands alone, for, unlike the Langkawi Malays, Sama Dilaut women also took an active part in fishing.[11] Nevertheless, in both cases women transformed the social status of fish, a transformation that, for the Sama Dilaut, was similarly symbolized by a cultural idiom of "cooking." However, to describe this sharing of cooked food, or food earmarked for cooking, as creating the "substance of kinship" (Carsten 1995) would be, in the Sama Dilaut case, an overgeneralization. Such sharing did, however, generate feelings of relatedness that, in the case of household-sponsored feasts of thanksgiving, extended at times to the whole village.

Whatever fish remained after the sharing of gifts of cooking fish was available to the family for outside trade or, in the 1960s, cash sale. The money that a family received from the sale of its fish might be transacted later on within the community as a gift if the family head or his wife were asked by housemates or other close village kin for monetary help, for example, to finance a marriage. In the case of fish, its transformation from gift status to commodity use was typically signified by its conversion from fresh fish, suitable for cooking, to a less perishable form as dried fish. Similarly, sea slugs, too, were dried before being sold. Drying therefore acted, in the case of fish, as a reverse process that "desocialized" part of the family's catch, thereby removing it from the food-sharing and feasting circuit. *Trepang*, on the other hand, never entered this circuit to begin with, being gathered solely for outside exchange.

While anthropological discussions have tended at times to downplay the distinction between gifts and commodities (see Appadurai 1986; and Thomas 1991), the distinction remains an analytically useful one (see, e.g., Sather 2002:32–33). As Godelier (1999:101–7) has argued, what is significant in this regard is how different kinds of things circulate in different ways depending on how they are socially framed and culturally represented. In these terms, I find particularly useful Paul James's distinction between what he calls "reciprocal exchange," in which "the exchange of goods occurs within a network of exchange relations that carries the 'spirit' of face-to-face integration between the persons involved," and "commodity exchange," which, by contrast, occurs between "abstracted strangers, based on their mutual, usually taken-for-granted confidence in an abstract system of exchange value" (2001:5). Reciprocal exchange thus occurs within "an integrative frame of embodied relations," while, in the case of commodity exchange, the social frame is, instead, "the abstract market which acts to disembody, objectify and rationalise the particularities of the persons" involved (5). As James argues, these contrastive forms of exchange are not mutually exclusive but frequently co-occur, each within its own culturally demarcated circuit. Hence, in the case of the Sama Dilaut, within the community itself reciprocal gift giving was the dominant mode of integration, with gifts of fish and other foodstuffs circulating within a social setting of embodied, face-to-face relations. However, a circuit of commodity exchange also existed, on which the Sama Dilaut were heavily dependent, but this typically involved impersonal relations with outsiders, land-based strangers whose way of life and political and economic status were very different from their own. Hence, while gift exchange embodied the "spirit" of village kinship, and helped to sustain it, commodity exchange was, in effect, boundary defining and, to a large degree, set the terms by which the Sama Dilaut interacted with outsiders.

These distinctions help, I think, to illuminate the alternative ways in which the Sama Dilaut transacted fish and other sea products historically. Kopytoff (1986:69), stressing these same qualities of embodiment versus abstraction, describes a "commodity" as a good that is exchanged in "a discrete transaction for a counterpart," whereas a "gift" is characteristically "given in order to evoke an obligation to give back a gift, which in turn will evoke a similar obligation—[producing] a never-ending chain of gifts and obligations." This nondiscrete, chainlike aspect of gift giving highlights what was most distinctive about Sama Dilaut food-sharing relations. While Macdonald (2008) has argued that sharing among "open-aggregated communities" is characteristically nonreciprocal, this chainlike principle of reciprocity was, by contrast, at the very heart of Sama Dilaut food sharing (see also Sillander 2008). Here the repeated sharing of gifts of fresh fish and other foodstuffs not only took the form of repeated material transactions but was also expressed in words, in verbal acknowledgment of gifts given and other forms of support received, and in promissory vows of return, all of which were couched in an explicit language of debts, repayments, and counterdebts (cf. Sather 1997:238–42, 287–89). As long as sharing partners remained on amiable terms, these relations continued to be, in Kopytoff's words, "never-ending," with repayments setting the stage for new debts and further gifts. Fishing was notably unpredictable, and food sharing in the past lessened the risks of short-term failure faced by individual families, particularly those of younger, less experienced fishermen. It also allowed those who were economically successful, and so able to express their generosity by generally giving more than they received, to attract and hold together larger circles of kin and housemates as gift-sharing partners. Through the use of gifts, ambitious men were thus able to increase their influence as house group and *ba'anan* leaders and to create among their followers, through the sharing of food, both the obligations and something of the material substance of kinship sociality (Sather 1997:182–83). At the same time, food-sharing obligations, by "deindividualizing" part of each family's catch, checked the outward flow of fish into the wider commodity market.

Since the 1960s, this system of food sharing has very largely broken down, except among immediate kin and family members, as the role of monetized market trade has grown enormously. During the 1970s, as a consequence of rapid population growth, the principal Sama Dilaut village in Semporna became increasingly enveloped and has now largely merged with Semporna town. Consequently, almost all younger men have now abandoned fishing for wage work or, by utilizing their village connections, have entered the local Semporna market as intermediating fish traders (Sather 1997:129–32). As families have withdrawn from fishing, the reciprocal basis of sharing has been lost. At the same time, for those who continue to fish, fishing has come to be seen primarily as a source of cash income. Consequently, by the 1990s fish were no longer being shared between households, as the villagers' involvement in a money economy had by now collapsed the cultural barriers that had once insulated transactions of fish as gifts from their circulation as commodities. Today, fish, even among kin, are no longer a medium of embodied sociality but are regularly bought and sold even within the village (Sather 2002:38–39).

Conclusion

Throughout this essay, I have sought to explore the role that words and gift giving once played in creating and maintaining conditions of gregarious sociality among a community of maritime fishing people. In particular, I have focused on the ways in which the Sama Dilaut sought to manage conflicts that otherwise threatened relations of relative amity. Historically lacking corporate groups and the coercive constraints of hierarchical authority, Sama Dilaut society was, in many ways, anarchic, yet it was also intensely social, its members bound together, ideally at least, by a never-ending flow of words and gifts.

Exemplifying the intensity of village sociality, the Sama Dilaut were not, as we have seen, a people who repressed their feelings, whether of goodwill or enmity, but, rather, they continually chose to put their feelings into words or committed them to acts of generosity. Hence, a flow of words and gifts was the principal way in which sociality was expressed and maintained, including even, at times, its temporary repudiation.

Goodwill was expressed, as we have seen, through verbal courtesies and an exchange of acknowledgments, pledges of support, and promissory vows that were a constant accompaniment to acts of food sharing and other forms of reciprocal support. Quarrels were most often "brought to an end" (*sinalassai*) by talking them out. In the process, rhetorical appeals were constantly made to re-create conditions of *magsulut*, "mutual accord," or, literally, in the idiom of a highly mobile people, of "moving together in the same direction." Respect for the elders reinforced the pressure on those involved in quarrels to restore relations of cooperation and mutual support. As community leaders, the elders were expected to educate their followers on the importance of relatedness and to intervene and constrain younger followers in order to preserve long-term networks of village and house-group relationships. On the other hand, married women were given license to expose conflict, thus prompting the intervention of the elders and the active negotiation of disputes. Even children could appeal against harsh treatment by their parents by taking refuge with their grandparents or other elders, in this way checking physical expressions of anger, even within the family. This strong aversion to physical violence, as well as respect for the elders, was reinforced by the notion of *busung*, in terms of which discourtesy, false swearing, or a refusal to put aside differences were all said to invite spiritual retribution. The same notion also gave spiritual sanctity to vow taking and pledges of mutual help.

In short, the Sama Dilaut managed, by and large, to maintain convivial relations among themselves and to confine their fighting almost entirely to words. What made this possible was the importance that the Sama Dilaut attributed to words generally and, above all, the powerful binding force they assigned to words, strongly committing those who uttered them to some particular line of action.

Finally, this intensely verbal way of coping with discord was effective, in part at least, because the Sama Dilaut had available to them, in the past, avenues of escape. One of these was an escape into person-to-person enmity. Declarations of enmity allowed individuals to repudiate ties of relatedness. This, as we have seen, often had a cascading effect, bringing about a more general reordering of kinship and house-group relations, which allowed families to disengage from ties that had become a source of friction and refocus them, instead, around kin and neighbors to whom they felt a greater degree of affinity. At the same time, by defining enmity dyadically, this repudiation was not generalized, setting group against group, but, rather, confined to specific individuals, thus making easier their eventual reconciliation through the intervention of others. Finally, the most common way of escaping discord was, in the past, by going to sea. In this way, voyaging allowed families to modulate the intensity of their inter-actions with others, interposing distance in times of discord.

Today, as they lose their former mobility, and as monetization effaces the distinctive social and cultural significance that once attached to food sharing, particularly the sharing of fish, the Sama Dilaut appear to be losing those features of sociality that once characterized them as a gregarious, open-aggregated community, when they were still, a half century ago, truly a sea people.

Notes

1 Sama Dilaut is an autonym; in the ethnographic literature, these people are more commonly known as Bajaw, Bajo, or Bajau Laut (cf. Nimmo 2001; and Sather 1997, 2004b). The fieldwork on which this essay is based was carried out initially in 1964–65, with the support of a predoctoral fellowship and grant from the U.S. National Institute of Mental Health, and for much briefer periods in 1974, 1979, 1995, and 2010. Today much of what is described in the earlier

sections of this essay no longer exists. Beginning in the 1970s, due primarily to sectarian warfare in the southern Philippines, large numbers of Sama Dilaut crossed the Malaysian border into the Semporna district. By 1979, the Sama Dilaut population in Semporna had grown to over two thousand. By 1997 it had increased to nearly six thousand and consisted of five settlements, two of which were comprised entirely of Sama Dilaut "refugees" (Sather 1997:69–79). Since then, the legal status of these newcomers, redefined as "stateless," has become even more problematic and, with a continuing exodus from southern Sulu, the number of new settlements has more than doubled. For a detailed ethnographic account of the Semporna Sama Dilaut, see Sather 1997.

2 Here *society* is used in the sense discussed by Endicott in this volume.

3 Here I use *kinship* in the same manner as Sillander in this volume to refer to "relatedness in a broad sense" that is not exclusively genealogical but is couched in what Sillander calls a "genealogical idiom." As with the Bentian, kinship, as expressed primarily through shared values and activities, is similarly a principal source of self-identity and community cohesion.

4 *Sengkol* refers to the wooden cross-timbers within a boat that reinforce the two sides of the hull (Sather 1997:266–68).

5 By contrast, to have a "bad heart" (*ala'at ataina*) is to be deceiving, to maintain an outward facade of goodwill while secretly harboring feelings of hatred or envy (cf. Sather 1997:295).

6 The first Sama Dilaut headman in Semporna, Panglima Atani, who had served during the post–World War II era, died shortly before I began fieldwork. He and his son-in-law, the headman at the time of my fieldwork, had built the first two pile-houses in the district. Hence, in addition to serving as headmen, both men played a major part in the settling down of the Sama Dilaut community in Semporna.

7 The root, *sinalassai*, means "to conclude," "end," or "dispose of (something)," such as, for example, a debt; its meaning is therefore similar to the Malay *berselesai*.

8 The term *maghukum* is also used to refer to state-administered court hearings conducted by the Native or District Court (Mahkamah Session) or the Islamic Religious Court (Mahkamah Syariah) (Sather 2004a:136). Until the construction of pile-houses, the Sama Dilaut in Semporna were generally regarded by others as "a people without religion" (*a'a halam magugama*) (see Sather 1997:43–44). Today, however, they regard themselves, and are generally accepted by others, at least in Semporna, as Muslims.

9 During this time, I lived as a guest of the village headman and his wife, as part of their household, and so was present during the majority of these hearings.

10 The Sama Dilaut observed a number of vows; for an extended discussion of their significance, and the occasions and purposes for which they were sworn, see Sather 1997:240–42, 287–90.

11 Sama Dilaut women in the 1960s and 1970s not only accompanied their husbands on fishing voyages but were also the principal collectors of *trepang*,

which they processed and dried for sale. At the time, *trepang* collection was a particularly important source of cash income for elderly women, as sea slugs can be easily gathered by hand, often in areas close to the village.

References

Appadurai, Arjun. 1986. "Introduction: Commodities and the politics of value." In A. Appadurai, ed., *The Social Life of Things*, 3–63. Cambridge: Cambridge University Press.

Carsten, Janet. 1989. "Cooking money: Gender and the symbolic transformation of means of exchange in a Malay fishing community." In J. Parry and M. Bloch, eds., *Money and the Morality of Exchange*, 117–41. Cambridge: Cambridge University Press.

———. 1995. "The substance of kinship and the heat of the hearth: Feeding, personhood, and relatedness among Malays of Pulau Langkawi." *American Ethnologist* 22 (2):223–41.

Deleuze, Gilles, and Félix Guattari. 1987. *A Thousand Plateaus: Capitalism and Schizophrenia*. Trans. Brian Massumi. Minneapolis: University of Minnesota Press.

Geddes, W.R. 1954. *The Land Dayaks of Sarawak: A Report on a Social Economic Survey of the Land Dayaks of Sarawak presented to the Colonial Social Science Research Council*. London: Her Majesty's Stationery Office.

Godelier, M. 1999. *The Enigma of the Gift*. Chicago: University of Chicago Press.

James, Paul. 2001. "Abstracting modes of exchange: Gifts, commodities, and money." *Suomen Antropologi: Journal of the Finnish Anthropological Society* 26 (2):4–22.

Kiefer, Thomas M. 1971. The Tausug polity and the Sultanate of Sulu: A segmentary state in the southern Philippines. *Sulu Studies* 1:19–64.

Kopytoff, I. 1986. "The cultural biography of things." In A. Appadurai, ed., *The Social Life of Things*, 64–91. Cambridge: Cambridge University Press.

Langub, Jayl. 2004. "Leadership among the Penan of Belaga District in Sarawak, Malaysian Borneo." *Contributions to Southeast Asian Ethnography* 12:187–217.

Macdonald, Charles. 2008. "Order against harmony: Are humans always social?" *Suomen Antropologi: Journal of the Finnish Anthropological Society* 33 (2):5–21.

———. N.d. "*Personne morale* and fellowship." Unpublished manuscript.

Nimmo, H. Arlo. 1986. "Recent population movements in the Sulu Archipelago: Implications to Sama cultural history." *Archipel* 32:25–38.

———. 2001. *Magosaha: An Ethnography of the Tawi-Tawi Sama Dilaut.* Quezon City: Ateneo de Manila University Press.

Overing, Joanna, and Alan Passes. 2000. "Preface." In J. Overing and A. Passes, eds., *The Anthropology of Love and Anger: The Aesthetics of Conviviality in Native Amazonia,* xi–xiv. New York: Routledge.

Sather, Clifford. 1976. "Kinship and contiguity: Variation in social alignments among the Semporna Bajau Laut." In G.N. Appell, ed., *The Societies of Borneo,* 40–65. Special Publications, no. 6. Washington, DC: American Anthropological Association.

———. 1997. *The Bajau Laut: Adaptation, History, and Fate in a Maritime Fishing Society of South-Eastern Sabah.* Kuala Lumpur: Oxford University Press.

———. 2002. "Commodity trade, gift exchange, and the history of maritime nomadism in southeastern Sabah." *Nomadic Peoples* 6 (1):23–47.

———. 2004a. "Keeping the peace in an island world of violence: The Sama Dilaut." In G. Kemp and D.P. Fry, eds., *Keeping the Peace: Conflict resolution and Peaceful Societies around the World,* 123–47. New York: Routledge.

———. 2004b. "Bajau." In Ooi Keat Gin, ed., *Encyclopedia of Southeast Asian History,* vol. 1, 200–202. Santa Barbara: ABC-Clio.

Sillander, Kenneth. 2004. *Acting Authoritatively: How Authority Is Expressed through Social Action among the Bentian of Indonesian Borneo.* Swedish School of Social Science Publications, no. 17. Helsinki: University of Helsinki Press.

———. 2008. "Comments on Charles Macdonald's 'Order against harmony.'" *Suomen Antropologi: Journal of the Finnish Anthropological Society* 33 (2):22–26.

Stacey, Natasha. 1999. "Boats to burn: Bajo fishing activity in the Australian fishing zone." PhD diss., Northern Territory University, Darwin.

Thomas, Nicholas. 1991. *Entangled Objects: Exchange, Material Culture, and Colonialism in the Pacific.* Cambridge: Cambridge University Press.

Warren, James Francis. 1981. *The Sulu Zone, 1768–1898.* Singapore: Singapore University Press.

10

Nicknames at Work and at Play: Sociality and Social Cohesion among the Cuyonon of the Philippines

JAMES F. EDER

THIS ESSAY EXAMINES MODES OF SOCIALITY among the Cuyonon of the Philippines through the lens of their nicknaming practices. The Cuyonon are an ethnolinguistic group of the Palawan region originating from the Cuyo group of islands that lies in the Sulu Sea between Panay Island and Palawan Island. Cuyonon experienced long and intense contact with the Spanish colonial regime, and they fall on the lowland side of the "lowland Filipino/indigenous Filipino" cultural and political divide. But they are also shifting cultivators who share cultural and linguistic affinities with the indigenous peoples of Palawan Island, especially the Tagbanua. As with the other peoples discussed in this volume, Cuyonon also lacked any corporate group structure beyond the household or any other enduring groups based on preexisting social relationships. Instead, traditional economic and social life played out largely through various temporary social aggregations and open-ended and ego-centered networks whose members coalesced and dispersed according to need and desire, under conditions of considerable personal autonomy. While Cuyonon are today thoroughly integrated into the Philippine state and are otherwise "peasantlike" in many of their social and political forms, persisting among them are some of the same solidarity-generating cultural practices typical of the more isolated open-aggregated societies discussed in this volume. This circumstance makes Cuyonon sociality particularly worthy of study.

Nicknaming has now fallen into disuse among the Cuyonon, but until recent decades nicknames and associated practices were a vibrant part of

Cuyonon culture, and they are still nostalgically remembered by an older generation of Cuyonon, many of whom recall with fondness the nicknames of their contemporaries (if not their own). I will show how nicknames themselves and the manner in which they were deployed in social interaction exemplified the joking, teasing, and self-effacement characteristic of everyday social life in the societies considered in this volume and thereby helped to promote the values of egalitarianism and easygoing familiarity—and indeed, intimacy—on which this social life rested.

In the first part of my essay, I introduce the Cuyonon and the principal social groupings within which most work and leisure-time activities unfolded. Work groups were based on reciprocal labor exchanges between households and for the most part were associated with the annual cycle of shifting cultivation. Leisure-time groups were aggregations of individuals formed for various social purposes, often, in the case of women, to play dominos, and in the case of men, to drink alcoholic beverages. Nicknames and nicknaming practices were an important aspect of all of these groupings, and after explaining what I mean by "nicknames" and giving some examples, I show how the playfulness that surrounded nicknaming "worked" to promote intense, familylike sociality in all of these groups and particularly in male drinking groups.[1] Cuyonon, however, no longer engage in nicknaming, and in the next section of the essay I consider the reasons why. In closing, I summarize my findings about nicknaming practices and briefly relate them to other studies that similarly emphasize the importance of attending to the idioms and processes of intimate, everyday social relationships to the theoretical understanding of social life generally. I then reflect on how the demise of nicknaming practices may be related to the emergence of newer and more cosmopolitan modes of Cuyonon sociality.

Cuyonon and the Palawan Region

The Cuyonon are a people of the Palawan region who trace to the small island of Cuyo lying between Palawan Island and Panay Island in the Sulu Sea. They speak a language classified in the Western Visayan group of Philippine languages (Zorc 1977) and are for the most part Catholic. Indeed, Cuyo figures prominently in a local history that revolves around the Catholicization of its populace by the Spanish in 1640 and subsequent centuries of indecisive military conflict in the Sulu Sea between the Spanish (long garrisoned at Cuyo) and the feared "Moros" (Muslim seafarers emanating from the Sulu zone) for political control over the Palawan region. In part a product of this regional colonial history, Cuyonon evolved their own distinctive version of Hispanized or "lowland" Filipino life. This life centered economically on short-fallow cultivation of upland rice, corn, sweet potatoes, yams, and plantains and socially on churchgoing, annual village fiestas, and other events of the Catholic religious calendar (Eder 2004:630–32).

Until well into the twentieth century, most Cuyonon lived in Cuyo. But beginning in the 1930s and particularly after World War II, pressed by land scarcity in Cuyo and lured by agricultural opportunity on Palawan, growing numbers of Cuyonon traveled by boat to plant upland rice in the island's fertile, virgin forest soils and, later, to settle there. On Palawan, Cuyonon intermingled with the island's indigenous inhabitants (the Tagbanua, Palawan, and Batak) as well as with Visayans, Ilocanos, and numerous other migrant peoples from within and beyond the Palawan region. The Philippine census does not classify persons according to ethnolinguistic group membership, but based on municipality-by-municipality key informant interviewing, I estimate the total Cuyonon population to be on the order of 150,000 persons. Subtracting the approximately 30,000 persons who today live in Cuyo (a population that remains overwhelmingly Cuyonon and due to out-migration has changed little since World War II) and another 10,000 or so persons of Cuyonon ancestry who live on various other outer islands, about 100,000 to 120,000 Cuyonon today live on Palawan Island and account for 15 to 20 percent of its total population (Eder 2004:634).

At first glance, the Cuyonon may appear an unlikely people among who to explore the issues considered in this volume. While Cuyo itself may be an isolated place, Cuyonon are scarcely an isolated people. They are thoroughly integrated into the fabric of the Philippine state, and they dominate governance and political life throughout the Palawan region. Cuyonon also pride themselves on their Catholicism and modernity, and many have gone abroad to work or reside in the United States or elsewhere. On the other hand, Cuyonon were long shifting cultivators and many remain so, and they share significant linguistic and cultural affinities with the Tagbanua (Fox 1982), however they may attempt to distance themselves from these and other "natives" of the Palawan region (Eder 2004). Further, and as I will show in this essay, the rich social life that evolved over centuries in small and isolated communities on Cuyo resembled, in its open-aggregated forms of sociality and its solidarity-generating cultural practices, the social life of other peoples discussed in this volume. Aspects of this social life importantly persist today, despite the peasantlike absorption of Cuyonon into wider Philippine society. Like Sather (this volume), I thus hope to "expand the comparative possibilities" for the ideas discussed here by considering sociality among a people who also *differ* in important ways—in the case of the Cuyonon, a people who are more robust demographically and more visible politically and culturally in the Philippines than most of the other peoples considered here are in their respective nation-states.

In any case, the notion that in Cuyo "it was the social aspect of life that mattered" remains deeply embedded in an adult Cuyonon's own sense of Cuyononness regardless of whether he or she today lives in Cuyo, Palawan, San Diego, or Toronto. Indeed, older Cuyonon today even remember work for its sociality and affective satisfactions, as enjoyed in the reciprocal swidden-labor parties in Cuyo or frontier Palawan or in the groups of men and women going down to the sea to collect mollusks during low tide. But once the day's work was done or the annual harvest was in, that is when the real pleasures of life began; as Cuyonon also sometimes say, "Our parents and grandparents worked nine months of the year to live the remaining three." Dances, where young people could pursue friendships and courtships begun during the agricultural season and where older persons were called on to perform traditional Spanish and indigenous dance forms; *komedia*, plays or parodies in which elaborately costumed players reenacted various accounts of the violent seventeenth-century confrontations between Christians and Muslims at Cuyo; and *erekay*, humorous ballads involving riddlelike and sexual-innuendo-laden exchanges between old men and women—these were the things that made life worth living in Cuyo and frontier Palawan.

This is also the social life whose more general properties I shall explore in this essay. While I have benefited from numerous conversations about this topic with Cuyonon throughout the Palawan region, my analysis here draws primarily on data obtained during visits to Cuyo Island in 1977 and 2009 and during long-term fieldwork conducted between 1970 and 1995 in San Jose, a farming community near Puerto Princesa City on Palawan Island first settled by pioneer Cuyonon farmers during the 1930s (Eder 1982, 1999).

Traditional Cuyonon Social Groupings for Work and Leisure

The social groupings that Cuyonon traditionally formed beyond the level of the household for their various work and leisure-time activities were loose, ego- or household-centered aggregations of neighbors and kin recruited from wider social fields that coalesced and dispersed over time. In a word, these were highly flexible groups, always subject to change in composition and connections depending on opportunity and personal predilection.

The most visible such aggregations were the reciprocal labor groups Cuyonon organized to expedite the completion of various tasks associated with the annual round of shifting cultivation, particularly clearing, planting, and harvesting. In an institution termed *iriloan* of a general form familiar throughout Southeast Asia, households that had agreed to work together to complete a particular task on their respective fields set a schedule of dates and then, working as group, rotated daily from one field to the next until the task was completed on each field. For purposes of labor exchange within these groups, the quasi-corporate nature of households and relatively egalitarian gender roles in insular Southeast Asia came into play; any adult member of a household, male or female, could reciprocate a day of swidden labor thus given.

While households were morally obligated to reciprocate for any labor "debts" they incurred in the course of completing a particular swidden task, the composition of exchange labor groups changed from year to year and even from task to task over the course of a single agricultural cycle. As with the composition of camp groups among the Batek described by Endicott or the local residential groups among the Palawan described by Macdonald (this volume), Cuyonon farmers might associate with one set of neighbors and kin to plant their fields and a different set to harvest them, depending on opportunity, happenstance, and individual desire for a change in work-mates or scenery. As well organized as they may appear to be, traditional Cuyonon exchange labor groups hence nicely illustrate what Macdonald has termed "the general looseness of everything" in the societies considered here.

A second kind of work group, *tarabangan*, was not reciprocal in nature or at least not immediately so. *Tarabangan* groups organized on occasions when many additional hands were needed to complete a onetime task such as a house moving or preparing for a wedding or funeral. These aggregations were even more ad hoc than *iriloan* aggregations but were similarly part of the rhythm of Cuyonon social life. But personal autonomy and flexible group composition in both kinds of labor groups were matched by an intense, familylike gregariousness, the more so in the case of exchange labor groups as swidden workmates were sometimes also voyage mates. As Cuyo's soils were exhausted and the island's man-land ratio declined in the late nineteenth and early twentieth centuries, Cuyonon turned to various stratagems to increase agricultural productivity, but beginning around 1920 they came to rely on sailboat (and later, motorboat) voyages to make their annual upland rice fields in the fertile, virgin forest soils of Palawan Island, voyages that in later decades led to permanent Cuyonon settlements on the island (Eder 1982:40–41). While the details are beyond the scope of this essay, older Cuyonon still warmly remember both the hardship and the fellowship of these annual journeys.

Turning to leisure-time pursuits, informal, off-hours socializing with friends and neighbors provided Cuyonon with some of the most important affective satisfactions they realized outside their own families. Not all such socializing can easily be mapped onto one or another kind of "group." The most pervasive kind of everyday socializing, interhousehold visiting, mostly by women, is an example. Nonetheless, much socializing did occur within more visible social aggregations. Examples include the groups of women who gathered for the *pabasa* (the singing of a Cuyonon translation of the Passion) and to celebrate other events of the Catholic religious calendar and the groups of men who gathered at sundown to drink coconut wine and other alcoholic beverages.

These latter gatherings, of multilateral male friendship groups, are a focal point of nicknaming-related activity and hence of particular interest in this essay. I originally thought of these groups as "cliques," and this is how I first described them in San Jose, a frontier Cuyonon farming community on Palawan Island.

> Cliques primarily involve drinking but may also involve domino or card playing. They form freely and without external constraints among men who enjoy interacting with one another. Clique-mates are above all friends, who may overcome great residential distances to meet together. Some cliques meet every afternoon or evening; most meet at least once a week. The meeting place is often one of San Jose's three stores. One clique meets at Maria's store every afternoon at dusk to drink coconut wine. Another clique, whose members all work at the (mercury) mine, meets there several nights a

week for the same reason. Other cliques meet at houses, particularly if games are played. One card-playing clique meets every Sunday afternoon at the house of a member. Some of these men drink at this time, but others do not. Several men are accompanied by their wives.

(Eder 1982:131)

I then went on to explain my use of the term *clique* in the following fashion.

A clique, according to M.G. Smith, is a "stable, bounded group of close friends, most of whom are not kin" (1965:58). Members of San Jose cliques are often related as kin, and even when they are not they may use the idiom of kinship to regulate their interactions. But a high degree of interrelatedness among clique members does not violate the spirit of Smith's definition, for personal choice is decisive in cases where kinsmen share a common clique. According to Smith (1965:58), "kin who belong to the same clique are selectively recruited from a wider range of equally close relatives."

(131)

And finally:

There is not word in Cuyonon that readily translates as "clique," but cliques are given indirect recognition by a variety of linguistic forms. *Say* Dado, "Dado's group," refers to Dado and his friends. The question, "Where is Dado?" may elicit a vague response, *sa anang mga kaibaan da*, "with his (usual) companions," suggesting that Dado's usual companions are so well known as not to require enumeration.

(131)

I am still comfortable with these descriptions, but I have come to regard the term *clique* as problematic, as these aggregations lack the elements of elitism and exclusivity or boundedness popularly associated with the term. In this regard, the term *coterie* might better capture the unpretentious nature of these relaxed groups of equal and independent-minded close associates. Also, regarding boundedness, over time I came to see greater flexibility in the compositions of these groups than I had first attributed to them, a flexibility that follows inexorably from their voluntary nature. Indeed, even to my earlier characterization and in the course of acknowledging the partially subjective nature of my effort to enumerate clique memberships in the community (an effort then aimed at uncovering the influence of then-emerging socioeconomic differences between households on informal social interactions), I added the caveat that San Jose residents did not themselves divide their neighbors into "those who clique and those who do not" (Eder 1982:131).

Besides the flexible manner in which the members of these male friend-ship groups associate or disassociate as groups and initiate or terminate interpersonal relationships within them (see Sillander, this volume), the other point to highlight is the camaraderie that group members enjoy, no doubt enhanced by drink that keeps bringing most participants back for more. While I recognize the semantic difference between the two terms, both *companionship* (Gibson 1985) and *fellowship* (Macdonald, this volume) seem to me equally suited to characterize the warm sociality and what Macdonald has termed the "conditions of felicity" of these groups.

In social aggregations of all kinds, then, and whether for work or leisure, men and women enjoyed considerable personal autonomy to come and go, or to participate or not, as they saw fit. The autonomy of Cuyonon shifting cultivators hence resembled in important ways the personal auton-omy of hunter-gatherers as characterized by Ingold (1999), and I find the term that Karen and Kirk Endicott (2008) have coined to describe Batek autonomy, *cooperative autonomy*, particularly apt to describe Cuyonon autonomy as well.

While I have not chosen to focus on them in this essay, significant eco-nomic benefits attended participation in one or another of these social aggregations. Besides the economic benefits of participation in the exchange labor groups associated with the annual round of swidden making, whereby the work of upland rice farming was shared and (hopefully) expedited, there was the ubiquitous sharing of foodstuffs in everyday life, whereby women in particular would ask of their neighbors (and rarely be refused) small amounts of sweet potatoes or plantains, a couple of coconuts, a few vines of swamp spinach leaves or some ginger, all for immediate household use. Writing of hunting-gathering peoples in the Philippines and elsewhere, Peterson (1993) has characterized such sharing as "demand sharing," a kind of generosity when asked, but both he and Ingold (1999:408) have empha-sized that this kind of sharing should not be seen as denoting stinginess, for "the morality of demand sharing is as positive as that of (unsolicited) generosity" (Peterson 1993:870).

The sharing that interests me in this essay, however, is less the sharing of agricultural produce and other material resources and more the sharing of time and how time was spent when it was shared—what Gibson (1985) has termed the "sharing of activity," a sharing he suggests generates solidarity through the relations of companionship that emerge from the experience of living and doing things together. For in addition to whatever economic benefits may have rewarded participation in the various social aggregations considered here, for most Cuyonon participation brought intense affective satisfactions as well, a topic to which I now turn.

Nicknaming Practices and Other Cultural Intimacies in Cuyonon Sociality

Promoting social solidarity within and across these various work and after-hours social groupings were a variety of intimate cultural behaviors such as the sharing of a single glass by a group of drinking clique mates or the frank joking between women about the vagaries and predilections of their husbands. These intimacies reflected the fact that the members of these groups were typically neighbors or kin who had often long lived together and had come to know the intimate details of each other's lives. These details regularly figured in the highly personal joking and teasing (often involving sexual innuendo) that marked the easygoing sociality of everyday Cuyonon life, a sociality also marked by egalitarianism, self-deprecation, indirection, and deference.

Rather than attempting to cover all of these cultural values and themes in their own right, I will show how they came together and were manifested in a particular cultural institution, nicknaming, now in abeyance but until a generation ago a ubiquitous feature of everyday life. How nicknames came into being and were subsequently deployed in everyday social inter-actions provides a useful window, I believe, on the nature of Cuyonon sociality and on what I sometimes think of as the "social glue" that in Southeast Asia holds together work and leisure-time groupings of the sort discussed in this volume.

What I have here termed "nicknames" are known to Cuyonon as *aran-aran*, a diminutive of *ngaran*, the Cuyonon word for "name." At some point in their lives most men came to have nicknames, and a few women did as well. Other women came to be associated with the nicknames of their husbands, but most did not participate in this particular cultural practice. Nicknames were given by others either to recognize some distinctive aspect of a person's physical appearance or personality or to commemorate some revealing or embarrassing life experience. Nicknames were used in a variety of everyday social interactions, but not for address, and nickname bearers did not want to hear their nicknames spoken, or at least that was the pretense. Nicknames were used especially among groups of men who regularly drank or socialized together, and they were only used and for the most part only known within local communities and social networks. In Cuyo virtually all men were said to have nicknames; in frontier Cuyonon communities on Palawan, half or more did.

Nicknames vary considerably, but representative examples include Mareges, meaning "insistent"; Comang, "hermit crab"; and Parimukos, "wrapped in a blanket." It should be clear from these few examples that these are not the commonly heard nicknames that in the Philippines and elsewhere are based on a contraction of or otherwise reflect a person's first name (e.g., "Berting" for Roberto and so on). Although I will continue to use it as convenient shorthand, the term *nickname* does not quite capture what these names are about. The slang term *moniker* is in some ways closer, and likewise the term *pet name*, because why someone has the nickname that he does is usually not obvious and reflects the detailed knowledge that a circle of intimates has of his life. Cuyonon themselves will sometimes use the English term *alias* for what I here term their nicknames. Cuyonon nicknames resemble a class of nicknames among the Palawan indigenous to southern Palawan Island that similarly reference life experiences or are otherwise descriptive in nature, although Palawan nicknames may be used more broadly within communities than Cuyonon nicknames are (Macdonald 2004:64). The *aran-aran* of Cuyonon finally resemble a class of teknonymlike nicknames among the Bentian that Sillander (2010) has termed "pseudoteknonyms," in that both designate qualities, habits, or life experiences of the name bearer. Bentian pseudoteknonyms, however, also include a teknonymlike kinship term element lacking in Cuyonon nicknames.

For reasons discussed below, nicknaming has disappeared with the present generation of Cuyonon, and few young men today have nicknames. Hence it was often not possible to discover why people had the nicknames that they did, the reasons having been "lost to history." But often it was possible, and for those names that could be traced to particular reasons, there appear to have been two main types. Some names were given in recognition of an aspect of a person's physical or psychological persona. A tall and lanky man was known as Indong, the name of a long and thin fish. Another man, similarly named for a fish, was called Balanak; the distinctive angular shape of the back of his cranium resembled the similarly squared-off head of his namesake. A woman with slightly protruding eyes was called Pale', the name of yet another fish whose eyes are similarly distinctive. A small and compactly built man was known as Binled, the term for a particularly small-grained variety of rice. And so on.

More common and interesting were those names Cuyonon acquired that referenced some humorous or revealing life experience. A man who while still single was once caught in a sexual encounter with a young woman under a tree was thereafter known as Inyiam, the name of the tree. Another man was known as Rosas, or "roses," for his allegedly heavy use of cologne when he was courting women in his youth. Some nicknames forever commemorate life experiences that their owners would surely prefer to forget. How had a certain man earned the nickname Bolawan, the term for gold? I was told that once he had sat carelessly in loose-fitting short pants, such that his genitals could easily be seen by others, "glinting in the sun." Why was another man called Hermit Crab? It seems that in his unmarried youth he was so smitten by a particular girl that he could be seen crawling after her everywhere she went. Again, another man, with a reputation for heavy drinking, wandered out onto the public pier in town one night and accidentally fell into the ocean. He was thereafter called Talogpo', a verb that means "to jump down" and is most commonly used to talk about chickens descending from their roosts at dawn.

How were nicknames deployed in everyday social contexts and conversations? This is how I previously discussed one of the rounds of nicknaming I was once party to.

> Nicknames are not used for address but are dropped into a conversation in which the owner of the nickname is present, particularly if he has just arrived, thus easing his entry into the group already gathered. Upon hearing his nickname, the owner responds in mock anger, often utilizing, in turn, the nickname of someone already present. Thus, should "Dove" arrive, "Fiddler Crab" may suddenly mention that doves have been eating his rice. "Dove" retaliates by saying that he'd seen a dead fiddler crab on the beach yesterday but it was "Rotting," thus dragging someone already present into the exchange. Premiums are placed on ingenuity. Should the man nicknamed "Cooking Oil" approach, someone might ask, "How do you cook doves, anyway?" and wait for the inevitable response, "You fry them." Teasing is hence inextricably part of nickname use but is always good-natured and indicates social approval and inclusion. Nickname-dropping may occur in any setting where people are gathered informally but reaches its fullest expression among members of the same clique. Particularly in the middle (socioeconomic) group, nicknames

and clique participation are mutually reinforcing, and we can readily appreciate the sense of social acceptance a gregarious person must feel when he hears his nickname bantered about by his peers.

(Eder 1982:134–35)

Modest statistical support for the direct association of nicknaming practices with the more intense modes of male Cuyonon companionship is found in my earlier-noted effort to classify all the men in a Cuyonon settler community on Palawan according to whether they belonged to what I then called cliques or not and whether they had nicknames or not. Among the community's then 112 male household heads, 46 men belonged to identifiable cliques and 32 had nicknames, while of the 68 men not belonging to identifiable cliques, only 11 had nicknames (Eder 1982:135). At the same time, whether or not a man is bestowed with a nickname also depends, as in the case of Bentian pseudoteknonyms, on the creative wit of his consociates (Sillander 2010), and a man who never acquired a nickname should not be presumed on that basis alone to be less sociable than his nickname-bearing peers.

The emphasis on ingenuity in nickname use means that the deft player should not simply mention the nickname of another but cleverly slip it into a conversation or allude to or pantomime the name without actually speaking it. Employing a nickname in a sexual innuendo is an especially popular gambit. In addition, some names are more fun to speak or play with verbally than others, and some people are more fun to tease. Whenever the man known as Goat approached a social gathering at the corner store or attempted to speak at a community meeting, he risked being greeted by a chorus of goatlike bleats from the community's more mischievous residents. ("Doesn't he get angry"? I once asked. "Of course not," came the reply; "we're his friends.") The Cuyonon word borikat is fun to speak, both for the way it sounds and for the humorous imagery it conjures up of everything from smiling faces to pants accidentally split at the crotch; likewise for the term seng-seng, which characterizes the act of corking a bottle but, at least among the inebriated, can readily be extended to quite different activities. The men who had these terms as nicknames probably found themselves, more than others, the butt of merrymaking. So, too, with the man known as Mantika, or "Cooking Oil," my good friend, informant, and eventual compadre, who is still indelibly associated in my mind with endless silly allegations of oiliness and slipperiness.

A revealing, below-the-surface pointedness accompanies at least some of the silliness associated with nickname invention and use. The man who fell off the town pier one night could have been called by a variety of nicknames that would equally have commemorated his misfortune. But Talogpo' seemed especially fitting for him, for just as there is an inevitability about chickens descending from their roosts at dawn, so, too, with drunks on the town pier at night, for they will surely descend into the ocean. Similarly, some men appeared to derive particular pleasure from teasing the man whose bananas had spoiled during an ill-timed trip to Manila and was thereafter known as Ronot. He was reportedly a prideful person, and he had boasted before the trip about the financial killing he expected to make, and so in some views the fact that his plan went awry was a well-deserved comeuppance. (The term for the descriptive Palawan nicknames noted earlier comes from a word that means "to quarrel or to tease," and it is certainly in this spirit that nicknames are employed by Cuyonon [see Macdonald 2004:64]).

Not being very agile verbally, I only occasionally attempted to contribute to nickname merriment. Once, however, running into the man known as Borikat late one night, I spontaneously sang out "What's new, Borikat?" to the tune of the then locally popular Tom Jones song "What's New, Pussycat?" That nicknames could be somehow worked into song became a bit of a fad after that, and my own contribution was regarded as particularly clever—and for a spell widely emulated—because the man known by that term was not simply loquacious but had a gossipy manner of being "first with the news" that some people thought excessive.

If I have belabored some of my points about nicknaming here, perhaps it will help make the additional point that for an outsider much nicknaming in practice was repetitious and even tedious or at most only mildly amusing. Indeed, for a long time what most struck me about nicknaming was the amount of time people invested in it for what to me seemed like so little effect. But traditional social life was itself time consuming—recall the earlier observation that in Cuyo it was the "social side" of life that mattered—and it was in this highly social setting, where people spent long hours together at work and play, that nicknaming practices and associated cultural intimacies flourished. Returning again to Sillander's (2010) analysis of Bentian naming practices, Cuyonon nicknames served, as Bentian pseudoteknonyms did, to help reconcile autonomy and individuality with attempts to establish solidarity between people living under egalitarian and open-aggregated social conditions. When nicknaming fell out of favor, and for the entire role that the penetration of market relations and other aspects and consequences of state-sponsored development and modernity played in their demise, there was also an important sense in which people simply no longer had time for them.

The Demise of Nicknaming Practices

Once a vibrant part of Cuyonon social and cultural life and still fondly remembered by an older generation of rural Cuyonon, nicknaming is today largely a thing of the past. I doubt that but a few Cuyonon less than thirty-five years old have nicknames or engage in the nicknaming practices discussed here. What happened? The short answer is that nicknaming practices disappeared because the kind of sociality that they supported and promoted has also disappeared and new forms of sociality—only subtly different on the surface, but profoundly different beneath—are taking their place. Before I consider the nature of these new social forms, I will address more precisely why nicknames and associated merrymaking fell into disuse.

I will first pause to recall that even in the past not everyone had a nickname and, more broadly, not everyone was equally sociable. There were always some nonjoiners. Some households went their own ways economically; they did not join exchange labor parties but instead accomplished their swidden chores on their own. They would not share agricultural produce even when asked, nor would they ask others to share. In the same fashion, some people went their own private ways socially and for the most part eschewed participation in the various leisure-time groups and activities discussed above. Those who did not share food when asked were spoken of harshly by drawing on a rich vocabulary of Cuyonon words that refer to various forms of selfishness and stinginess. Those who merely went their own ways socially were not so much criticized as they were commented on or wondered about.

In any case, that there were always people who did not exchange labor or share resources, or who kept to themselves and seemingly had no time to visit others or join in the social merrymaking, is consistent with the simultaneous emphasis on personal autonomy. No one was or could be obligated to join any of the social aggregations associated with these practices.

Granted, there were strong pressures to join them, and most people did not need to be pressured because they found them enjoyable or beneficial, but just as one was expected to help a neighbor in distress but not required to, so, too, were people expected to join these groups but not required to. But even if there were always some people who were in a sense "social free-loaders" who left the good work of social glue making to others, the traditional social order could withstand such social outliers.

What traditional forms of sociality could not withstand were a series of more systemic changes in Cuyonon economy and society with enduring structural implications. I have written about these changes in detail elsewhere (Eder 1982, 1999), and here I will only suggest their broad outlines. First, population growth and development on Palawan Island brought expanded market opportunities for agricultural produce that saw the penetration of market relations into the subsistence sector of rural communities. Over a period of decades, and over different time periods in different locations, Cuyonon farmers reoriented production away from subsistence and toward the market, and eventually market relations penetrated most aspects of local economies. Labor was increasingly commoditized, and reciprocal labor arrangements gradually disappeared in favor of wage labor; the incidence of food sharing between households diminished as all agricultural products came to have monetary value; and time itself became a more valuable commodity, with the intensification of agriculture and the growing importance of supplementary income-earning activities to household economic well-being.

Second was the emergence of significant socioeconomic differences and, eventually, class differences between Cuyonon who long differed little in these regards. While sociality can and does occur across class and status lines, the particular kind of sociality associated with nicknaming emphasized egalitarianism, autonomy, and intimacy—values that were difficult to reconcile with social differentiation. Rural Cuyonon who once worked and played easily together came to have different social circles and reference groups, different wherewithal, and in the end different values, and the presumptions of equality and intimacy associated with nicknaming became increasingly untenable.

Third was a host of changes all associated with modernity. When electrification came to rural Cuyonon communities, so did television. Much social life quickly moved indoors and became less visible publicly, undermining the spontaneity and easygoing familiarity of traditional modes of sociality. On Palawan, population growth saw the emergence of ethnically mixed communities where many residents no longer knew their neighbors, and men became more cautious about displaying behaviors in public, like drinking and nicknaming, on which they might be judged unfavorably by others who knew nothing else about them. And with modernity, finally, came a heightened sense of tradition and with that the notion of rusticity. For younger Cuyonon today, the nicknaming practices of their parents are not simply a cultural tradition but hopelessly old-fashioned. This is simply not how people, especially young and educated people, behave in wider and more cosmopolitan social circles.

Summary and Conclusion

To summarize, nicknaming practices were one element in a skein of traditional Cuyonon cultural forms and understandings that acknowledged the voluntarism and personal autonomy of everyday life while simultaneously promoting the solidarity on which that social life in part depended. My emphasis on nicknaming practices being "one element" of the wider business of social glue making is deliberate, as I would here like to briefly highlight the broader theoretical importance of attending to all kinds of idioms and processes of everyday social relationships among kin, neighbors, and friends. In Southeast Asia, for example, Carsten (1995, 1997) has shown how the commensalities and intimacies of daily social life do not simply reaffirm kinship but also help to create it, and Cannell (1999) has similarly shown the importance of these same aspects of everyday social life to an understanding of power. Beyond the region and in the course of discussing male friendship relationships in Aegean Greece that are remarkably reminiscent, in their subjective aspects, of male Cuyonon drinking groups, Papataxiarchis (1991) shows how coffee shops can be understood as male enclaves of relaxation and intimacy where egalitarianism and camaraderie are promoted and masculine identity is formed. What all of these studies have in common is an emphasis on social relationships that have, in effect, lives of their own that transcend particular social structures or economic or political ties. Properly understood, however, these same social relationships hold the key to the better understanding not just of social solidarity but also of related domains, including kinship (Carsten), power (Cannell), or masculinity (Papataxiarchis).

Returning now to the social import of nicknaming practices in particular, I will close by asking, with the recent demise of these practices, what modes of sociality today hold Cuyonon society together? What are its present sources of social cohesion? Surely nicknaming practices were not its only social glue, but other forms of traditional sociality have seemingly fallen by the wayside as well. Exchange labor groups have given way almost everywhere to the hiring of labor. Few Cuyonon today dare ask their neighbors for or expect to be freely given bananas, coconuts, and the like. Social activities of all kinds, once so spontaneous and consuming of time, are now more carefully calculated and scheduled. More is at stake, in short, than the simple disappearance of nicknaming practices from the Cuyonon cultural inventory, a transition that, by itself, could be simply be explained away as the rustic giving way to the modern.

But there is more to consider here. Cuyonon men still get together at sundown to drink alcoholic beverages, and Cuyonon women still visit their neighbors or meet to play dominos. In a word, Cuyonon are still "social" and markedly so. How, then, are we to characterize Cuyonon sociality today in a way that neither understates nor overstates differences with Cuyonon sociality in the past? This task poses a significant challenge, I believe, and it has both representational and theoretical dimensions. Put differently, I worry about making too much of certain specific changes in cultural practice. Are men less close to one another because they do not banter around with nicknames anymore or because (to conform with modern practice) many no longer share a single glass when drinking together? How much difference to the quality of their social life together do these (and other) changes really make? Is it basically the same thing, in a changed form, or is it now a different thing?

I do not have firm answers to these questions. I am uncomfortable with the value judgments that answers appear to require (although I will shortly make some anyway), and I believe that evidence can be mounted for either position. At this point, however, it is helpful to recall the wider social and political context of what I have here presented as "traditional" Cuyonon society. For centuries, Cuyo and Cuyonon fell well within the orbit of the Catholic Church and the Spanish colonial administration and, later, the American colonial administration. For generations, then, Cuyonon also had the "ascribed statuses" that attended membership in parishes, local political units, and school districts, and more structured and more scripted modes of sociality were hence long present. While it may be simplistic, I think we can usefully imagine a long-term social evolutionary process, one that continues today, whereby Cuyonon have been increasingly drawn into the social structures and accompanying modes of sociality of the state and wider Philippine society, with all its differences between people in religion, cultural background, educational attainment, occupation, and social class. Again with the understanding that this is an ongoing process, unfolding on different time horizons in different places, these state-related social structures and modes of gathering are edging aside, attenuating the importance, or rendering obsolete the more primordial forms, of, traditional sociality discussed in this essay.

Nonetheless, we still have to deal with the continued presence in Cuyonon society of the more traditional modes of sociality, and I see two choices for thinking about them. First, some primordial modes of sociality and associated cultural forms may survive only as two-dimensional shadows of their former selves, similar in form but not in function. One example is seen in the resurgence of Cuyonon nicknaming on, of all places, the Internet. If modernity rendered nicknames old-fashioned, postmodernity has made them popular again, at least among members of the Cuyonon diaspora living in Canada who maintain a Web site (www.cuyopress.com) dedicated to keeping in touch over a lighthearted look at Cuyonon language and culture. Regular contributors to the Web site have all adopted such pseudonyms for themselves as Centipede, Shrimp, and Sea Urchin, pseudonyms that evoke life in a nostalgically remembered Cuyo and are intended to resemble the *aran-aran* of their parents and grandparents. But (and now I am making a value judgment) the similarity is only superficial, for the name bearers selected their own nicknames, their nicknames do not reference any defining life experiences shared with a circle of intimates, and they are otherwise just that—pseudonyms.

A second "form but not function" example may be found in the ubiquitous children's birthday parties popular with both urban and rural Cuyonon. In the past, the attendees at a child's birthday party would be an ad hoc gathering of playmates, neighbors, and kin, the same people who socialized together on other occasions, whereas today the "guest list" for such parties is more likely to contain the celebrant's elementary school classmates and accompanying parents or other adults. Such parties hence bring together a more ascribed group of men and women, people of different ethnolinguistic groups and walks of life, who may or may not know one another but gather gamely in groups to make small talk and socialize uneasily among themselves. I do not mean to pick on birthday parties in particular—they are, after all, for the children—but it is the nature of modernity in the lowland Philippines that much of the socializing that Cuyonon engage in today is on social occasions of these more ascribed, scripted, and mixed-attendance sorts. Of course, at these more "modern" gatherings one also finds "sociality," but (another value judgment here) how meaningful is it? For the most part I found such gatherings to be stilted and superficial affairs—and a far cry from the easygoing familiarity and other solidarity-enhancing cultural behavior that characterize more traditional Cuyonon social aggregations. I do not mean to reduce all of modern-day Cuyonon sociality to a caricature, and my uncharitable portrayal of contemporary social gatherings may be unfair to those Cuyonon who consider them to be pleasurable social occasions. I only want to suggest that there is a qualitative difference in the nature of Cuyonon sociality between traditional and contemporary social gatherings and that the direction of change in incidence is from the one to the other.

But second, and coming back to my simple evolutionary model, and because groups of Cuyonon men and women do still gather together much as they have all along, one can also argue that the more primordial modes of sociality do indeed continue as before, and in both form and function. At the least, however, one would have to say that these older modes have an attenuated role, providing cohesion and solidarity only in realms not yet penetrated by state-organized society or where they have not yet been replaced by gatherings of the sort just described. The basic notion is a familiar one—that there are "pockets" of "traditional society" here and there that have not yet been obliterated by the state or modernity—but I believe it has merit. And in support of my value judgments regarding the relative appeal of modern and traditional modes of Cuyonon sociality, I do know that many adult Cuyonon miss their older, more rustic forms of socializing. Having experienced some of them myself, I can say that it is with good reason.

Notes

I incurred many debts of gratitude during the course of my fieldwork on this topic, but I particular want to acknowledge the insights and generous assistance of Erlinda Daquer Abid, Regalado and Myrna Abid, Violeta Bacosa Jutare, Minnie Guardiano Sabando, Nanette Trampe, and Felix and Amelita Yara. I also thank Mirela Conner, Tom Gibson, Daniel Hruschka, Dorla Santa Cruz Lahwn, Charles Macdonald, and Kenneth Sillander for their helpful comments and suggestions.

1 Nicknaming practices were predominantly a male domain among Cuyonon, and as a male investigator I found this domain accessible and interesting. My focus here on the role of nicknaming practices in sociality and social solidarity should not be taken to imply that men are somehow more central to the business of social glue making than are women but only that the equally important activities of women in these regards are largely beyond the scope of this essay.

References

Cannell, Fenella. 1999. *Power and Intimacy in the Christian Philippines.* Cambridge: Cambridge University Press.

Carsten, Janet. 1995. "The Substance of kinship and the heat of the hearth: Feeding, personhood, and relatedness among Malays in Pulau Langkawi." *American Ethnologist* 22 (2):223–41.

———. 1997. *The Heat of the Hearth: The Process of Kinship in a Malay Fishing Community.* Oxford: Clarendon Press.

Eder, James F. 1982. *Who Shall Succeed? Agricultural Development and Social Inequality on a Philippine Frontier.* New York: Cambridge University Press.

———. 1999. *A Generation Later: Household Strategies and Economic Change in the Rural Philippines.* Honolulu: University of Hawai'i Press.

———. 2004. "Who are the Cuyonon? Ethnic identity in the modern Philippines." *Journal of Asian Studies* 63 (3):625–47.

Endicott, Kirk, and Karen Endicott. 2008. *The Headman Was a Woman: The Gender Egalitarian Batek of Malaysia.* Long Grove, IL: Waveland Press.

Fox, Robert B. 1982. *Religion and Society among the Tagbanua of Palawan Island, Philippines.* Monographs, no. 9. Manila: National Museum.

Gibson, Thomas. 1985. "The Sharing of substance versus the sharing of activity among the Buid." *Man,* new series, 20 (3):391–411.

Ingold, Tim. 1999. "On the social relations of the hunter-gatherer band." In R.B. Lee and R. Daly, eds., *The Cambridge Encyclopedia of Hunters and Gatherers*, 399–410. Cambridge: Cambridge University Press.

Macdonald, Charles. 2004. "Personal names as an index of national integration: Local naming practices and state-produced legal identities." *Pilipinas* 42:61–75.

Papataxiarchis, Evthmios. 1991. "Friends of the heart: Male commensal solidarity, gender, and kinship in Aegean Greece." In P. Loizos and E. Papataxiarchis, eds., *Contested Identities: Gender and Kinship in Modern Greece*, 156–79. Princeton: Princeton University Press.

Peterson, Nicolas. 1993. "Demand sharing: Reciprocity and the pressure for generosity among foragers." *American Anthropologist* 95:860–74.

Sillander, Kenneth. 2010. "Teknonymy, name-avoidance, solidarity, and individuation among the Bentian of Indonesian Borneo." In Zeng Yangwen and C. J-H. MacDonald, eds., *Personal Names in Asia: History, Culture, and Identity*, 101–27. Singapore: National University of Singapore Press.

Smith, M.G. 1982. *Stratification in Granada*. Berkeley: University of California Press.

Zorc, R.D.F. 1977. *The Bisayan Dialects of the Philippines: Subgrouping and Reconstruction*. Pacific Linguistic Series C, no. 44. Canberra: Department of Linguistics, Research School of Pacific Studies, Australian National University.

11

Egalitarian Islands in a Predatory Sea

THOMAS GIBSON

IN A SERIES OF ESSAYS written over the last twenty years, I have been slowly putting together an argument that the whole of island Southeast Asia should be regarded as a single, loosely integrated social system composed of social groups that have developed the ability to express their political disagreements with one another in a common symbolic code (Gibson 1990a). Many societies in the area have maintained pacifistic political cultures built on ascribed social equality, while others have maintained predatory political cultures built on ascribed social ranking. My analysis of the way the former type of society functioned was inspired by the work of James Woodburn on what he characterized as "immediate-return hunter-gatherers" (1982). My analysis of the relationship between the egalitarianism of the former and the ranking of the latter was inspired by Edmund Leach's account of similarly contrasting value systems among the Kachin of Highland Burma (1954). In this essay, I will develop this argument further by reference to Marilyn Strathern's claim that fundamentally different forms of human subjectivity and sociality are to be found in Melanesia, an area that has much in common culturally and linguistically with island Southeast Asia (1989).

Primary Ascribed Egalitarianism among Nomadic Hunter-Gatherers

According to the best archaeological and ethnographic descriptions available to us, it is plausible to assume that, prior to the "neolithic revolution," most foraging peoples lived in small, flexible bands and would have regarded the accumulation of material goods as pointless at best, and as burdensome at worst (Woodburn 1982, 1988). It was only the domestication of plants and animals that required the development of social mechanisms to assert and defend long-term rights in productive resources such as human labor, herds, and seed for future planting. Agricultural societies developed systems of kinship and marriage through which larger collectivities ("societies") were reproduced through the patterned exchange of goods and persons among smaller social units ("households").

By contrast, the members of foraging societies had no need to construct elaborate rituals designed to integrate individuals into corporate groups and to manage the transference of rights and obligations from one group to another at marriage. Woodburn summarizes ethnographic analyses of many foraging peoples that were made in the twentieth century by asserting that these were "societies of equals—equals in wealth, equals in power and equals in status. My argument is that they are societies of equals because in these societies equality is actively promoted and inequality is actively resisted through a set of coherent interlocked and mutually reinforcing institutional procedures" (2005:21–22). These procedures included direct access to material resources, personal autonomy in choice of residence and associates, and the obligatory sharing of key resources. I will call this form of egalitarianism "primary" as opposed to forms that develop as secondary reactions to systems of social ranking.

In fact, however, the situation is not quite as simple as the argument so far suggests. Many of the hunter-gatherers of Australia were organized into unilineal descent groups that were bound together through the systematic exchange of women under the authority of senior men (Lévi-Strauss [1949] 1969). It was the existence of hunting and gathering societies of this sort that led Woodburn to introduce his distinction between "immediate-" and "delayed-return" societies, a distinction that rests not on any techno-environmental differences between Australian and African hunter-gatherers but on whether social life is based on the immediate-return structures of personal autonomy in the choice of consociates and sharing within fluidly defined camps, or the delayed-return structures of reciprocal marriage exchange between corporate kinship groups. Woodburn went on to suggest that it was just this kind of delayed-return society of hunter-gatherers that would have been in the best position to undertake the domestication of plants and animals known as the "neolithic revolution." Delayed-return systems of kinship and marriage probably became more common following the neolithic revolution, developing alongside the domestication of plants and animals as the need to allocate rights to labor and productive property increased. In these kinds of kinship system, the resource-holding group has coercive power over the individual's labor, both directly through the arrangement of marriages and the allocation of children at birth to one group or another and by making access to essential productive resources conditional on obedience to elders.

Once under way, the higher demographic densities enabled by the neolithic revolution led agricultural societies to overwhelm and enclave foraging societies in most parts of the world. Foraging societies with delayed-return social systems would find it easiest to assimilate with expanding agriculturalists. Those with immediate-return systems would find it easiest to maintain their autonomy. Both the adaptability and the conservatism of the latter form of social organization are shown in island Southeast Asia by the persistence of egalitarian bands of foragers in the Philippines, Indonesia, and Malaysia, even where groups such as the Aeta and Batak of the Philippines abandoned their original languages in favor of an Austronesian lingua franca (Eder 1992) or groups such as the Batek and Chewong of Malaysia did so in favor of an Austroasiatic one (see the essays by Howell and Endicott in this volume).

While it is certainly possible that in a world without agriculturalists many hunting and gathering societies lived according to the principles of anarchic solidarity discussed in this volume, the fact remains that the hunter-gatherers of mainland and island Southeast Asia have been enclaved by agricultural societies for many centuries, and their forms of egalitarianism may have a secondary, reactive element as well.

Secondary Ascribed Egalitarianism in Agricultural Societies

Because of the vastly higher population densities that agriculture made possible as compared to foraging, a majority of humanity eventually came to live in groups organized in terms of kinship, some of which were far more stratified than others. When I conducted fieldwork among the Buid of Mindoro in the Philippines from 1979 to 1981, I encountered a radically egalitarian and pacifistic political culture. I also learned that Chinese historical sources indicated that the island of Mindoro had played a central role in long-distance trade between China and island Southeast Asia since at least the thirteenth century. The preservation of a writing system derived from Indic sources by the Buid, and by the Hanunoo Mangyan to their south, indicates historical connections to the cultures of the Java Sea beginning in at least the fourteenth century (Gibson 1986:11).

There was no question then of primary egalitarianism among the Buid. If the Buid and the other highland shifting cultivators of Mindoro and the neighboring island of Palawan were egalitarian and pacifistic in the late twentieth century, it was the product of a specific cultural response to the violent history of the region that began with the destabilizing effects of Portuguese, Spanish, and Dutch mercantilism in the sixteenth century and of their wars with local Islamic sultanates such as those of Sulu and South Sulawesi (Macdonald 1977, 2006, this volume). I argued that highland peoples like the Buid were best understood as adhering to a set of political values that had developed in systematic opposition to those of their lowland neighbors. Whereas lowland societies were built on the principles of ascribed rank, debt-bondage, and the valorization of long-distance trading and raiding, the highland societies affirmed the principles of ascribed equality, communal sharing, and the valorization of an inward-looking cultural conservatism. Compared to some of the other societies discussed in this volume, the Buid stand out in the extreme lengths they go to avoid any form of ascribed social ranking, asymmetrical social relations, or even the expectation of strong social ties within the family. Relations between men and women, adults and children, and even humans and animals are remarkably egalitarian.

Like many other shifting cultivators in Southeast Asia, when I conducted fieldwork among them in 1979–81 the Buid operated a complex system of intercropping, involving a succession of grain, root, and tree crops on the same swidden before it is returned to fallow. Rice, maize, sweet potatoes, cassava, taro, and bananas each made a roughly equal contribution to the diet. The key agricultural implements were the ax, bush knife, and dibble stick. The Buid always relied on trade to obtain the iron needed for the former two.

The Buid subscribed to a "labor theory of property" in that an individual may only be said to "own" the products of his or her labor. This means that land as such was traditionally a free good, which, if it belonged to anyone, belonged to the *afu daga*, "spirits of the earth." Only the crops planted in a swidden belonged to a person, and once the final tree crop ceased bearing fruit, all further claim to a previously cultivated plot was relinquished. Cultigens themselves were individually owned: both husbands and wives maintained separate swiddens, pooling the produce for domestic consumption but retaining clear title to their own swiddens should they divorce.

Husbands and wives were expected to help one another on their respective swiddens according to a "statistical" division of labor by gender. This division was not supported by social or mystical sanctions, and people could and did perform the tasks normally performed by members of the opposite sex. Buid agricultural techniques did not normally require the organization and control of large groups of workers. Most economic activities could be and were carried out by the members of individual households, even if they contained only a single member. Houses themselves were dispersed evenly across the landscape, being built at the edge of a swidden underneath the branches of trees so that they were difficult to spot until one was almost on them. There was usually one or two kilometers between houses. This meant that most social interaction between the members of different households was the result of a deliberate decision to interact. Social conflict was easily minimized through simple avoidance. At certain times of the year, however, cooperation between households was customary. The burning, planting, and harvesting of swiddens was usually carried out by large groups on a nonreciprocal basis: the sponsor of the collective labor team remained discreetly out of sight preparing a special midday meal for the helpers, and this meal and the sheer sociability generated by collective activity made participation in these occasions its own reward.

Whenever a pig or chicken was killed, its meat had to be shared out in exactly equal portions among all the members of the local community. In this distribution, no significance was attached to a recipient's age, sex, length of residence in the community, or genealogical tie to the sponsor of the ritual. The sharing of meat in this manner constituted the most frequent form of material transaction between households, occurring about once a week. As with labor teams, sponsors did not indebt recipients. One was entitled to a share of meat by virtue of one's membership in the community, not because of previous transactions one may or may not have had with a particular sponsor. There was thus a collective entitlement to a household's domesticated animals. In animal sacrifice, all social distinctions within the community were symbolically dissolved in a communal meal.

The sharing and cooperation that was expected between household members served as a model for proper social conduct in general and was extended to a wider range of individuals on certain seasonal and ritual occasions. But relations between members of a household were also capable of serving as a model for a breakdown in proper social conduct in general. If a husband and a wife began to quarrel, it was said that the spirits of the earth would withdraw their protection from the couple's children, making the latter vulnerable to the attacks of a whole range of predatory spirits. Continued quarreling thus put innocent bystanders at risk, and the community as a whole was under an obligation to intervene in marital disputes. This it did by convening a collective discussion, which any member of the community could attend. Pressure was put on the quarreling couple to come to some definitive resolution of their dispute. Whether this involved reconciliation or divorce was of no concern. Indeed, any attempt by one partner to prolong a marriage against the will of the other was condemned as selfish and possessive behavior.

While there was an inevitable factionalization of the community in the course of a divorce hearing, with some people taking the side of one spouse and some the side of the other, a deliberate attempt was made to define the dispute as being between the members of a single household. This was true even when the dispute had its origin in one spouse having an affair with a third party. Indeed, the chief cause of quarreling within a marriage was the jealousy of one spouse over the extramarital sexual affairs of the other. A collective discussion of a marital dispute was often the prelude to a divorce and the immediate remarriage of one of the spouses. If this was the case, the collective discussion served to determine the amount of compensation due the abandoned spouse and to regulate the formation of a new marriage. So frequent was divorce among the Buid, and so rare was it for an adult to remain unmarried for more than a few months, that a typical marriage might be said to have involved the transfer of an individual from one spouse to another. This transfer was regulated not by the individual's kin but by the community as a whole.

The satisfactory resolution of a marital dispute in a collective discussion was a necessary prelude to the restoration of the protection of the spirits of the earth. This was achieved by sacrificing a pig to them on the threshold of the house and sharing its meat both with the spirits and with all the members of the human community. Divisions within the elementary social unit, the household, were believed to bring about a state of mystical vulnerability in its weakest members. This danger provided a real incentive for the members of a household to resolve their differences quickly. Solidarity was reestablished with the most important spirit allies at the same time as it was reestablished within the household and community.

The collective nature of Buid ritual was not confined to sacrifices. The most common ritual activity was the séance. Virtually every adult man possessed a spirit familiar, which could be summoned at will by chanting at night. The mind of a medium was said to ride on the back of its familiar as it soared aloft and to be able to perceive the otherwise invisible predatory spirits that infested the forest and occasionally invaded human territory. Constant vigilance was required against these spirits, and an individual medium would chant by himself from time to time just to keep track of what was happening in the invisible world. When a predatory spirit actually "bit" a victim, however, more concerted activity became necessary. Groups of six to twelve mediums gathered to exert their combined force against the predatory spirit. Each chanted to his own familiar and strove to see and combat the enemy spirits for himself. From time to time the mediums would break off chanting and describe to their colleagues what they were seeing, where it was, and what it was doing. Other mediums would begin to perceive the same spirits and embroider the account of the first medium. Gradually an intersubjectively validated picture of the spirit world was built up in this way. These group séances were so common, taking place at times every night for weeks on end, that the invisible world came to seem comparable to the visible world. Spirit beliefs were thus legitimated through shared "empirical" experience, not by charismatic specialists who claimed privileged access to a higher reality as in shamanism nor through an appeal to a sacred tradition as in priestly religions. This "mystical empiricism" of the Buid, the emphasis on collective ritual activity and experience, gave their religion an extraordinary vitality and flexibility. Beliefs were continually being submitted to the test of the séance and being relegitimated in the present. Among the Buid, both ritual power and knowledge had an egalitarian basis (Gibson 1983, 1985, 1986, 1988, 1990b, 2005a).

The community where I lived in 1979–81, Ugun Liguma, was undergoing a deliberate process of radical transformation under the leadership of a man called Agaw. This transformation was inspired by the model of the leader of the community of Batangan, Yaum, who had persuaded the scattered households in his region to form a compact settlement a decade earlier, the better to defend their land from lowland peasant squatters. At the time of my arrival, Agaw had persuaded most of the households living in the valley of Ayufay to form a compact settlement. The traditional institutions of the collective discussion and group séance were being adapted to new ends, and the community of Ugun Liguma seemed to be well on the way to forming a kind of corporate group that asserted a collective right to its territory against all outsiders and individual rights to subdivisions of the territory among its members. A similar process was occurring in many other Buid communities, all based on the example set by Yaum in Batangan.

In May 2009, I was able to revisit the Buid for the first time in twenty-four years. I learned that they had achieved a remarkable degree of integration as a tribe of some twelve thousand members that included dozens of local communities. With the help of Frances Fisher, an American who began work as a Peace Corps volunteer in 1978 and continues to live among the Buid today, Yaum organized a nongovernmental organization called the Sadik Habanan Buhid (SHB) in 1985, which has come to represent most of the Buhid communities in Oriental Mindoro (Buid and Buhid are dialectal variants of one another). A sister organization, the Kalipunan Buhid, Inc. (KBI), represents the Buhid in Occidental Mindoro. In 1998 the Department of Environment and Natural Resources issued a Certificate of Ancestral Domain Claim (CADC) to the Buhid granting qualified exclusive use rights over an area of 94,000 hectares, the second largest CADC issued before the Indigenous Peoples Rights Act (IPRA) became operational in 1998 (Erni 2008:330). The act initiated a new process that could lead to the issuance of genuine land titles in the form of Certificates of Ancestral Domain Titles (CADT). This process is still under way for the Buhid (330–31).

Despite these transformations at the political and economic levels, in 2009 the Buid of Ugun Liguma exhibited remarkable continuities in the collective character of their religious beliefs and practices; in their consensual approach to solving disputes over spouses and land; in the equal status they granted old and young, male and female, parent and child; and in the positive value they attached to harmony and tranquility as opposed to competition and aggression. I will return in the conclusion to some of the reasons why this set of values may prove to have been preadapted to life in the postmodern world.

Optative Egalitarianism in Kachin Society

The argument that egalitarian and hierarchical values can coexist in a single social formation was originally inspired by that of Edmund Leach in *Political Systems of Highland Burma* (1954), where he observed an oscillation between egalitarian (*gumlao*) and hierarchical (*gumsa*) political systems among the Kachin and that neighboring peoples with quite different languages and cultures need to be seen as participating in a single social system. The Kachin lived largely by shifting cultivation in the hills surrounding the irrigated rice fields of the Shan, an ethnic group that adhered largely to Theravada Buddhism and lived under the rule of charismatic kings (Leach 1960).

One of the ways hierarchy was expressed among the *gumsa* Kachin was through the practice of asymmetric marriage exchange, such that Kachin chiefs bestowed female members of their patrilineage on men of either the same or lower rank, who paid as much bride wealth in return as they could afford, as a way of publicly demonstrating their wealth. Marriage was never supposed to be reciprocal: lineages stood in systematic relations of wife givers (*mayu*) and wife takers (*dama*) toward one another. Wife-giving chiefs attempted to model themselves on the Buddhist kings who ruled the Shan states situated in the valleys, but because of the ecological limitations imposed by shifting cultivation they could never sustain a sufficiently dense population of subjects for long. There was thus a natural tendency for *gumsa* domains to collapse back into a more egalitarian *gumlao* system.

The hierarchical implications of this system were avoided in egalitarian *gumlao* communities by arranging for three or more lineages to marry in a circle and by minimizing the size of bride wealth and compensation payments. But because of the asymmetric nature of marriage alliances and bride wealth payments, there was a built-in tendency for lineages in *gumlao* communities to again become ranked in relation to one another. It was this dynamic that led to the oscillation between egalitarian and hierarchical principles in Kachin social life (see Kirsch 1973; Friedman 1975; and Nugent 1982 for further developments of Leach's original argument). Recent ethnohistorical research has indicated that the transformation from ranked *gumsa* domains to egalitarian *gumlao* domains was not an oscillation generated by endogenous social factors but part of an irreversible historical trend generated by exogenous political factors such as the arrival of British colonialism and by exogenous economic factors such as the opium trade (Ho 2007). The important point for my argument is that very different moral and political systems can be built out of very similar cultural and social practices.

Bilateral Kinship as the Effect of Long-Distance Trade

Although similar systems of asymmetric marriage and social ranking existed in eastern Indonesia, the question I want to address in this essay is whether a similar opposition between egalitarian and ranked societies can be found in the Philippines and western Indonesia, where kinship systems tend to be organized around bilateral kindreds rather than unilineal descent groups, and where marriage tends to be seen as something that occurs within vaguely defined localized kinship groups and not between distinct kinship groups.

Elsewhere I have argued that the so-called bilateral kinship systems of Southeast Asia are better understood as symbolic systems that rely on the symbols of shared spaces such as wombs, houses, and territories and shared activities such as work, travel, and commensality to construct social groups. Lateral relationships among siblings, cousins, spouses, and siblings-in-law are more highly elaborated than lineal relations between parents and children (Gibson 1985, 1995). Based on reconstructed proto-Austronesian kinship terms, it seems likely that the development of bilateral kinship systems in Southeast Asia occurred only after the Austronesian migration into the region (Blust 1991; Benjamin, this volume). They are prevalent in the region's center, while unilineally based societies, many of which practice asymmetric marriage exchange, are found on the region's northern border in Highland Burma, on its western border in Highland Sumatra, and on its eastern border in eastern Indonesia.

Marshall Sahlins noted a generation ago that the Iban way of life, which is built around nuclear families occupying independent apartments in longhouses and having weak attachments to larger groupings, was only possible in the presence of a market economy in which rice surpluses accumulated in good years could be stored in the form of durable trade goods that could be converted to subsistence goods in bad years (1972). It is tempting to speculate that the development of bilateral systems of group affiliation in the central area that shifted the balance from ascribed to achieved status was correlated with the intensive nature of long-distance trade in staples in precisely this area over three thousand years ago.

Peter Bellwood has argued that the Austronesian-speaking inhabitants of the Philippines and Indonesia were drawn into networks of intensive long-distance trade with Austroasiatic-speaking agriculturalists in mainland Southeast Asia as early as the second millennium BCE (1995:105–7). Copper ores were mined first in the Philippines and mainland Southeast Asia, tin ores in the mountain chain running from China down through the Malay Peninsula, and iron in a number of more widely scattered locations.

> Java and Bali have few deposits of iron or other tool-making metals and no recorded early mining or ore-processing industries. Thus the inhabitants of the two most heavily populated islands of the archipelago, and large portions of Sumatra, were forced to import most, if not all, of the metals used for tools, weapons, vessels, armour and often for adornment and for ritual use.
> (Wisseman Christie 1995:246)

The unequal distribution of ores and fertile soil in Southeast Asia tended to generate relatively extensive long-distance routes for the trading of subsistence as well as prestige goods (251). The prevalence of bilateral kinship systems in the parts of mainland and island Southeast Asia with the best access to maritime trade routes may indicate a distinctive response to the development of a regional political economy that required a relative openness to trade with distant societies.

In some parts of this central zone, elite groups were able to gain control over long-distance trade and use the redistribution of prestige goods as the basis for a system of hereditary social ranks. All around the Java Sea, for example, local social structures were composed of hereditary nobles, free commoners, and "slaves" attached to noble houses. Marriage was hyper-gamous, and the ranks of individuals were determined by both of their parents. The highest-ranking noble families typically sought marriage alliances with their peers across the seas (Gibson 2005b:chap. 4).

These hierarchical societies were highly reminiscent of Lévi-Strauss's concept of *sociétés à maison* (1982, 1983, 1987). Lévi-Strauss introduced this concept to help analyze societies he saw as making a transition from kin-based to class-based social orders (Gibson 1995). It is significant, however, that where Lévi-Strauss does refer to Indonesia he devotes very little space to the "bilateral'" societies of the Philippines, Sulawesi, Borneo, Java, and Malaysia, turning as quickly as possible to the more familiar unilineal kinship systems of Sumatra and eastern Indonesia. This is what he does have to say about the bilateral systems.

> [In] Borneo as in Java the conjugal couple constitutes the true kernel of the family, and, more generally, of the kindred. Moreover, this central role of alliance manifests itself in two ways: as a principle of unity, underpinning a type of social structure which, since last year, we have agreed to call the "house," and as a principle of antagonism because, in the cases considered, each new alliance generates a tension between families on the subject of the residence—viri- or uxorilocal—of the new couple, and therefore of that of the two families which it is the couple's duty to perpetuate.
>
> (1987:155)

In the societies discussed in this volume, bilateral kinship was not used to build up noble houses at the expense of commoners but as the basis of social systems that ascribed equal status to all individuals at birth. In societies like that of the Buid any effort by an individual to achieve higher status or renown was frowned on. In societies like that of the Ilongot, adult males were expected to demonstrate their right to equal recognition by their bravery in raiding expeditions (Rosaldo 1980). In societies like that of the Iban, charismatic individuals could achieve high rank by recruiting large-scale groups through bilateral kinship networks to accomplish specific tasks such as headhunting raids or trading expeditions (Freeman 1967, 1970, 1979, 1981).

These variations in attitudes toward the ascription and achievement of social rank and equality are best explained by the different ways each kind of society experienced the predatory trading and raiding that was so prevalent in island Southeast Asia from about 1500 to 1900. Groups like the Buid that had been preyed on developed negative attitudes toward violence and domination, groups like the Iban that had been successful predators developed positive attitudes, while groups like the Ilongot that had been relatively isolated combined elements of both sets of attitudes (Gibson 1990a).

It is interesting to note that even in Highland Burma "the most stable *gumlao* communities appear to be those in which lineage is virtually neglected and loyalty to a particular place is emphasized instead" (Leach 1954:206). The idiom of shared space, which implies an achieved form of sociality, may be inherently more conducive to the expression of egalitarian relationships than the idiom of shared substance, which implies an ascribed form.

Instead of the oscillation between egalitarianism and hierarchy observed by Leach in Highland Burma, a more stable polarity between the egalitarian societies of the highlands and the ranked *sociétés à maison* of the lowlands developed in island Southeast Asia. Ethnohistorians have documented a pattern throughout the Philippines in which Christian lowlanders resisted efforts by Spanish missionaries to convert the highlanders because they found it useful to have an unadministered population with whom to trade, and presumably also to whom they could flee when they ended up on the wrong side of colonial law (Zuniga [1800] 1972; Worcester 1914; Keesing 1962; Jesus 1980).

Another difference between the regions of island Southeast Asia and Highland Burma relates to ethnolinguistic diversity. Highland Burma is populated by a wide variety of ethnic groups speaking languages belonging to completely different families such as Tibeto-Burman, Austroasiatic, and Tai-Kadai. Leach dismisses the striking differences in language and material culture between neighboring communities in Highland Burma as superficial cultural symbols used to express underlying social and political values that are shared across ethnic boundaries. Almost the opposite situation exists in island Southeast Asia, which is overwhelmingly populated by ethnic groups speaking languages belonging to the Western Malayo-Polynesian branch of the Austronesian language family. This means that the symbolic resources shared by adjoining societies in the latter area are likely to be richer and deeper than those that are shared in the former area. Thus social groups with remarkably similar languages and items of material culture may use them to express fundamentally different social and political values.

Achieved Ranking and "Dividualist" Subjectivity in the Papuan World

Leach's basic insight that the tribal peoples of mainland Southeast Asia have long had fundamentally different sets of political values available to them is thus borne out by the comparative analysis of societies in island Southeast Asia. On the other hand, Leach was quite wrong in his view that human subjects are everywhere driven by the same simple desire to maximize their power. As Raymond Firth noted in his foreword to *Political Systems of Highland Burma*, Leach posited a uniformly calculating and power-driven form of subjectivity that was most openly expressed during the Italian Renaissance (Firth 1954:vii). While the maximization of power is a factor for making some decisions in most societies, it is never the only one. In my analyses of Southeast Asian societies, people also want to reproduce and enhance the status of their kinship group, gain personal knowledge about the world in which they live, and achieve individual salvation in the afterlife (Gibson 2005b, 2007).

In *The Gender of the Gift* (1989), Marilyn Strathern argues for the existence of a form of subjectivity that differs radically from that of the "West" in Melanesia, the region that borders island Southeast Asia to the east. She argues that "Melanesians" possess fundamentally different concepts of subjectivity, agency, and social relationship than do "Westerners." She constructs her analysis of "Melanesia" on the basis of a crude contrast between Melanesian "dividuals," who engage in "sociality," and Western "individuals," who relate to one another through "society."

What Strathern means by *dividuals* and *sociality* is at one level quite general and refers to the subordination of individuals to the requirements of the social group in the societies based on delayed-return systems of agriculture and animal husbandry that I discussed above. In other ways, the system she describes is built on the structural integration and transformation of symbolic elements that are highly specific to Melanesia. While she called for an "injection" of "real history" to account for how Melanesia came to be such a unified symbolic whole, she made no attempt to carry out a historical analysis herself (1989:340–41).

In my view, much of what she has to say about Melanesia holds true for the wider category of "Austronesia" and so is directly relevant to my argument about the existence of multiple forms of subjectivity in island Southeast Asia. Peter Bellwood has attempted to supply a historical account of the origins of the common elements in Melanesian culture (1978, 1996). As he reconstructs it, when Austronesian agriculturalists expanded from Taiwan southward into the Philippines and Indonesia six thousand years ago, they entered a landscape inhabited only by a thin population of nomadic foragers who largely maintained their political autonomy while entering into mutually beneficial trade relationships with the newcomers. It was only when they reached Papua New Guinea in the east and the Southeast Asian mainland in the west that they encountered similarly dense populations of agriculturalists due to an independent agricultural and pastoral revolution that had occurred there several millennia previously. Peoples speaking languages belonging to several different Papuan families have lived alongside peoples speaking Austronesian languages in Melanesia for over three thousand years.

According to Bellwood, a system of ascribed social ranking was a distinctive feature of Austronesian political culture from the earliest phases of its expansion. It helped accelerate the maritime expansion of the Austronesians across the Pacific as younger siblings sought to escape subordination to their elders by founding new settlements on distant islands. He contrasts this dynamic with that typical of Papuan political cultures, which are dominated instead by the efforts of big men and great men to build individual reputations during their lifetimes, reputations that cannot be passed along to their children. In these Papuan systems equality (among men) is ascribed at birth but gives way to a vigorous competition for achieved rank. It is quite as opposed to the ascribed egalitarianism of foragers and agriculturalists like the Buid as is the ascribed ranking of the Javanese.

Bellwood suggests that many peoples of Papuan descent adopted the Austronesian lingua franca that developed during the expansion of the Lapita culture complex around 3500 BP (Before Present), along with many other symbolic elements. Some of them retained their long-standing Papuan rejection of ascribed rank, while others, especially in eastern Melanesia, embraced it (1996:22–23).

Such differences in basic political values do not enter into Strathern's analysis, as her primary goal is to characterize all the peoples of Melanesia as sharing a set of ideas about selfhood, agency, gender, and kinship that contrast with those of the modern West. What is important to Strathern about the West is the value it places on a dialectic between individuals and things conceived of as irreducible units with certain "natural" qualities, and society and culture as an artificial system of rules and constraints imposed on them from the outside (1989:135). What is most striking when reading Strathern's account of "Melanesians" alongside the societies based on anarchic solidarity discussed in this volume, however, is the coercive character of kinship and affinity among the former as opposed to the high degree of personal autonomy among the latter.

Tertiary Ascribed Egalitarianism
in the Civilizations of the Axial Age

Since it is precisely the contrast between egalitarian and hierarchical values that is central to the present analysis, in this connection we might expect to find more help from Louis Dumont, another theorist who identifies the core symbols of an entire region by contrasting them with those of the modern West. What was important to Dumont about the "West" is precisely the value it has placed on individualism and equality, as opposed to the holism and hierarchy he saw as essential to India. The contrast Dumont draws between the two civilizations is somewhat more subtle than that drawn by Strathern between the West and Melanesia, in that Dumont believes each contained the dominant symbolic elements of the other in a subordinated form. Thus those born into the ascriptive hierarchy of the Hindu caste system have always had available to them the option of an escape into the radical individualism of otherworldly asceticism. And while the modern West has progressively rejected one after another form of ascriptive ranking, it has a way of reasserting itself in the pathological form of racism (Dumont 1966).

Both Strathern and Dumont view the rise of capitalism in the seventeenth and eighteenth centuries as crucial to the formation of "Western" ideas of individualism and egalitarianism. Much of what they see as characteristic of the modern West, however, actually dates back to what Karl Jaspers called the "axial age," an age in which cosmopolitan ethical codes and cosmologies were developed in many parts of Eurasia to deal with the development of urban life, commodity markets, and chattel slavery (Jaspers 1953; Arnason 2004). These codes eventually gave rise to the world religions associated with specific exemplary and ethical prophets in Weber's sense, such as Siddhartha Gautama, the Hebrew prophets, Jesus, and Muhammad, and with the founders of philosophical schools such as Aristotle and Confucius (Weber 1963). There is thus nothing particularly modern or Western about these ideas.

Ethical doctrines such as karma, Judgment Day, and the "examined life" all tend to drive a wedge between individuals and their kinship groups or at least to create a psychic space between them. For the religious traditions, one's fate in the afterlife is meant to rest primarily on one's ethical choices as an individual, and one's soul bears only a contingent relationship to those of one's parents and siblings. Although all of these religions developed variants in which it is possible to lessen the suffering of family members in the afterlife, in principle one is held responsible for one's decisions in relation to the code for conduct outlined in the scriptures and as interpreted by learned professionals. For the philosophical traditions, universal ethical norms superseded particularistic loyalties to one's kin group.

These codes were embedded in cosmopolitan literary cultures: Sanskrit, Pali, Greek, Latin, and Arabic and their associated formal grammars and orthographies defined "civilizational" regions far wider than any political units and far more stable through time than spoken vernaculars (Pollock 2006). The production and reproduction of religious and literary texts took place in particular institutional settings such as royal courts, monasteries, and residential schools. Until the introduction of mass education and mass media in the nineteenth century, only a small minority of the members of each civilization was able to fully participate in these literary cultures. The literati who acquired the greatest degree of training in these institutions doubtless developed the most abstract sense of themselves as individuals standing against society, but their reflections on and interpretations of the scriptures and literary classics they reproduced slowly diffused into other social strata, both aristocratic and plebian.

In the major civilizations of Eurasia, the "dividuals" who continued to reproduce their kinship groups through ritual and gift exchange thus all had an awareness of another level of subjectivity in which they were individuals answerable to higher powers and/or principles in a way that transcended their obligations to immediate social groups. None of these codes abolished the experience of being born into a kinship group and being under an obligation to contribute to its reproduction over time. But they did introduce a critical perspective on them, limiting and subordinating these experiences to those relating to a transcendental order of reality.

Strathern and Dumont are thus quite wrong to associate the origin of all aspects of "Western" individualism and egalitarianism with the rise of modern capitalism in Europe. Something like it has been present since the dawn of urbanization throughout Eurasia. But it has always existed alongside a different kind of kinship-based subjectivity that has a lot more in common with Melanesian sociality than Strathern implies. Different forms of subjectivity are reproduced in every society by different kinds of institutions, and each of these forms has implications for the values that govern the political system. What needs to be explained about societies like that of the Buid is not so much the presence of egalitarian values as the complete rejection of any kind of social ranking, either achieved or ascribed.

In 1988 I began fieldwork among the Makassar of South Sulawesi in order to gain firsthand experience of an Austronesian society whose political culture was in many ways the opposite of that of the Buid. And, indeed, traditional Makassar society valorized ascribed rank and debt dependency, long-distance trade and warfare, and receptivity to foreign symbolic systems such as Sanskrit literature and Islamic scriptures (Gibson 1990b, 2005b, 2007). I concluded, however, that even in this kind of society ascribed ranking in the kinship system and the acquisition of mystical and scriptural knowledge by a religious elite were balanced by a basic sense of ascribed spiritual equality instilled through popular Islamic practices such as the performance of obligatory prayers in the mosque, visitation of the tombs of powerful *shaikhs*, and the ecstatic chanting of *dhikr* in collective Sufi rituals. We might term the effort to maintain this kind of "anarchic solidarity" in at least one sphere of life a sort of "tertiary egalitarianism." Other examples can be identified in the informal socializing described among Cuyonon Filipinos by Eder (this volume), among Bicolano Filipinos by Cannell (1999), among Muslim Malays by Carsten (1995a, 1997) and among Aegean Greeks by Papataxiarchis (1991).

The Dialectic of Ascription and Achievement, Equality and Rank

This brings us back to Leach's argument about the presence of multiple political systems in a single society but with the crucial caveat that Strathern was right to stress that forms of human subjectivity are just as variable across cultures as any other dimension of social life. Strathern, on the other hand, is wrong in her view that specific Melanesian societies can be characterized by a single set of political values and that "the apparently numerous social systems of Melanesia can be considered as versions of one another" (1989:340). Melanesia contains both the achieved ranking of the original Papuan cultures and the ascribed ranking of the later Austronesians. The two approaches may thus be seen as complementary when correctly understood.

If the societies of island Southeast Asia are understood as parts of a larger social system, it is one in which everyone is well aware of the

existence of competing sets of political values and everyone develops several
different kinds of subjectivity as they participate in the ritual and disciplinary
practices associated with different institutional settings such as houses,
mosques, and schools. A few people, like the Buid, live in societies that
entirely reject the hierarchical values of their lowland neighbors. Most live
in societies in which ascribed egalitarianism is appropriate in certain institutional arenas such as informal socializing, popular religion, or electoral
politics; achieved ranking in others such as war, long-distance trade, and
the acquisition of scriptural and mystical knowledge; and ascribed ranking
in yet others such as the reproduction of royal and noble households.

Still another form of ascribed egalitarianism is now taught throughout
the world in public schools and forms the subjective basis of nationalism
and electoral democracy, a model of the polity in which every citizen is
endowed with certain inalienable rights. This form of egalitarianism is
taught alongside another quite different form of subjectivity, one that
stresses the competitive achievement of differential ranks in graded exami-
nations. In postindustrial societies, the accumulation of "human capital"
through individual effort in the school system becomes the most important
route to securing economic resources in the form of salaried employment.
For the first time since the neolithic revolution, the reproduction of "society"
no longer depends on the reproduction of kinship groups. Children can
achieve autonomy from their parents at a relatively young age and certainly
do not have to wait for them to die to become completely autonomous. The
formation and breakup of households are increasingly determined by the
individual preferences of autonomous adults for companions who meet
their particular emotional, sexual, and social needs, and the rearing of
children is also seen more as a form of emotional fulfillment and self-
expression than an investment in a social relationship that can be drawn on
in the event of illness or old age. In short, "modern" individuals and
families look in many ways a lot more like the individuals and families
discussed in this volume than they look like the ones produced by most
agricultural societies since the neolithic revolution. It is perhaps this sort of
similarity that accounts for the affinity felt by so many of the authors in this
volume for the peoples about whom they have written. As Woodburn
notes, "[C]oexisting pressures for equality and for inequality ... are present
in the desires of every one of us as an individual and in the operation of the
political systems, and indeed of the kinship systems and the religious sys-

tems, of every human society" (2005:22). It is the peculiar merit of the peoples discussed in this book to live out the ideals of autonomy, equality, and fellowship more consistently and completely than most other peoples. We all have much to learn from them.

Note

The writing of this essay and the editing of this volume was made possible by an ACLS/SSRC/NEH International and Area Studies Senior Fellowship in 2008. Fieldwork among the Buid and comparative research on shifting cultivators in Southeast Asia were made possible by several grants from the Harry Frank Guggenheim Foundation. I owe all the participants in this volume a debt of many years' standing for their contributions to the study of the egalitarian peoples of Southeast Asia. My oldest debt in this regard is to James Woodburn, who alerted me as an undergraduate to the immense moral lessons we can all draw from such studies. My greatest debt is to Agaw, the visionary leader of Ugun Liguma, who passed away in the 1990s before I had a chance to revisit the Buid. He taught me a great deal about how to live according to a rigorous set of ethical ideals. I would like to dedicate this essay to him and his son Untoy, who was murdered by rightist militias in 2003 for asserting the rights of his people.

References

Arnason, Johann, ed. 2004. *Axial Civilizations and World History.* Leiden: Brill.

Bellwood, Peter. 1978. *Man's Conquest of the Pacific.* Auckland: Collins.

———. 1995. "Austronesian pre-history in Southeast Asia." In Peter Bellwood, James Fox, and Darrell Tryon, eds., *The Austronesians.* Canberra: Australian National University.

———. 1996. "Hierarchy, founder ideology, and Austronesian expansion." In J. Fox and C. Sather, eds., *Origins, Ancestry, and Alliance: Explorations in Austronesian Ethnography,* 18–40. Canberra: Australian National University.

Blust, Robert. 1991. "The greater Philippines hypothesis." *Oceanic Linguistics* 30 (2):73–129.

Cannell, Fenella. 1999. *Power and Intimacy in the Christian Philippines.* Cambridge: Cambridge University Press.

Carsten, Janet. 1995a. "The substance of kinship and the heat of the hearth: Feeding, personhood, and relatedness among Malays in Pulau Langkawi." *American Ethnologist* 22 (2):223–41.

———. 1995b. "The politics of forgetting: Migration, kinship, and memory on the periphery of the Southeast Asian state." *Journal of the Royal Anthropological Institute,* new series, 1:317–35.

———. 1997. *The Heat of the Hearth: The Process of Kinship in a Malay Fishing Community.* Oxford: Clarendon Press.

Dumont, Louis. [1966] 1972. *Homo Hierarchicus.* London: Paladin.

Eder, James. 1992. *On the Road to Tribal Extinction: Depopulation, Deculturation, and Adaptive Well-Being among the Batak of the Philippines.* Berkeley: University of California Press.

Endicott, Kirk. 1979. *Batek Negrito Religion.* Oxford: Clarendon Press.

Erni, Christian. 2008. "Non-violence in a frontier: The strategy of avoidance and the struggle for indigenous control over land and resources on Mindoro Island." In D. Geiger, ed., *Frontier Encounters: Indigenous Communities and Settlers in Asia and Latin America.* Copenhagen: International Work Group for Indigenous Affairs.

Firth, Raymond. 1954. "Foreword." In E. Leach, *Political Systems of Highland Burma.* v–viii. London: Athlone Press.

Freeman, Derek. 1967. "Shaman and incubus." *Psychoanalytic Study of Society* 4:315–44.

———. 1970. *Report on the Iban.* London: Athlone Press.

———. 1979. "Severed heads that germinate." In R. Hook, ed., *Fantasy and Symbol.* London: Academic Press.

———. 1981. *Some Reflections on the Nature of Iban Society.* An Occasional Paper of the Department of Anthropology. Canberra: Research School of Pacific Studies, Australian National University.

Friedman, Jonathan. 1975. "Tribes, states, and transformations." In M. Bloch, ed., *Marxist Analyses and Social Anthropology.* New York: Wiley.

Gibson, Thomas. 1983. "Primitive communism among the Buid?" Paper presented at the London School of Economics, Social Anthropology Departmental Seminar.

———. 1985. "The sharing of substance versus the sharing of activity among the Buid." *Man,* new series, 20 (3):391–411.

———. 1986. *Sacrifice and Sharing in the Philippine Highlands: Religion and Society among the Buid of Mindoro.* London School of Economics Monographs on Social Anthropology, no 58. London: Athlone Press.

———. 1988. "Meat sharing as political ritual: Forms of transaction vs. modes of subsistence." In T. Ingold, D. Riches, and J. Woodburn, eds., *Hunters and Gatherers.* Vol. 2: *Property, Power, and Ideology,* 165–79. Oxford: Berg.

———. 1990a. "Raiding, trading, and tribal autonomy in insular Southeast Asia." In J. Haas, ed., *The Anthropology of War.* New York: Cambridge University Press.

———. 1990b. *Predatory States in Island Southeast Asia.* Comparative Austronesian Project Working Papers, no. 2. Canberra: Research School of Pacific Studies, Australian National University.

———. 1995. "Having your house and eating it: Houses and siblings in Ara, South Sulawesi." In J. Carsten and S. Hugh-Jones, eds., *About the House: Buildings, Groups, and Categories in Holistic Perspective—Essays on an Idea by C. Lévi-Strauss,* 197–213. Cambridge: Cambridge University Press.

———. 2005a. "From humility to lordship in island Southeast Asia." In T. Widlok and W.G. Tadesse, eds., *Property and Equality.* Vol. 2: *Encapsulation, Commercialisation, Discrimination,* 231–51. New York: Berghahn Books.

———. 2005b. *And the Sun Pursued the Moon: Symbolic Knowledge and Traditional Authority among the Makassar.* Honolulu: University of Hawai'i Press.

———. 2007. *Islamic Narrative and Authority in Southeast Asia from the 16th to the 21st Century.* New York: Palgrave Macmillan Press.

Ho, Ts'ui-p'ing. 2007. "Rethinking Kachin wealth ownership." In F. Robinson and M. Sadan, eds., *Social Dynamics in the Highlands of Southeast Asia: Reconsidering Political Systems of Highland Burma by E.R. Leach.* Leiden: Brill.

Howell, Signe. 1984. *Society and Cosmos: Chewong of Peninsular Malaysia.* Singapore: Oxford University Press.

Jaspers, Karl. 1953. *The Origin and Goal of History.* Translated from the German by Michael Bullock. New Haven: Yale University Press.

Jesus, E.C. de. 1980. *The Tobacco Monopoly in the Philippines.* Quezon City: Ateneo de Manila University Press.

Keesing, Felix. 1962. *The Ethnohistory of Northern Luzon.* Stanford: Stanford University Press.

Kirsch, Thomas. 1973. "Feasting and social oscillation: A working paper on religion and society in upland Southeast Asia." Data Papers, no. 92. Southeast Asia Program, Cornell University.

Leach, Edmund. 1954. *Political Systems of Highland Burma.* London: Athlone Press.

———. 1960. "The frontiers of Burma." *Comparative Studies in Society and History* 3 (1):49–73.

Lévi-Strauss, Claude. [1949] 1969. *The Elementary Structures of Kinship*. Boston: Beacon Press.

———. 1982. *The Way of the Masks*. Seattle: University of Washington Press.

———. 1983. "Histoire et ethnologie." *Annales* 38 (2):1217–31.

———. 1987. *Anthropology and Myth*. Oxford: Basil Blackwell.

Macdonald, Charles. 1977. *Une Société Simple: Parenté et Residence chez les Palawan (Philippines)*. Paris: Institut d'Ethnologie, Musée de l'Homme.

———. 2006. *Uncultural Behavior: An Anthropological Investigation of Suicide in the Southern Philippines*. Honolulu: University of Hawai'i Press.

Nugent, David. 1982. "Closed systems and contradiction: The Kachin in and out of history." *Man* 17 (3):508–27.

Papataxiarchis, Evthmios. 1991. "Friends of the heart: Male commensal solidarity, gender, and kinship in Aegean Greece." In P. Loizos and E. Papataxiarchis, eds., *Contested Identities: Gender and Kinship in Modern Greece*, 156–79. Princeton: Princeton University Press.

Pollock, Sheldon. 2006. *The Language of the Gods in the World of Men: Sanskrit, Culture, and Power in Premodern India*. Berkeley: University of California Press.

Rosaldo, Michelle. 1980. *Knowledge and Passion*. Cambridge: Cambridge University Press.

Sahlins, Marshall. 1972. *Stone Age Economics*. Chicago: Aldine.

Strathern, Marilyn. 1989. *The Gender of the Gift: Problems with Women and Problems with Society in Melanesia*. Berkeley: University of California Press.

Weber, Max. 1963. *The Sociology of Religion*. Boston: Beacon Press.

Wisseman Christe, Jan. 1995. "State formation in early maritime Southeast Asia: A consideration of the theories and data." *Bijdragen van het Koninklijk Instituut voor Taal-, Land-, en Volkeukunde* 151 (2):255–88.

Woodburn, James. 1982. "Egalitarian societies." *Man*, new series, 17:431–51.

———. 1988. "African hunter-gatherer social organization: Is it best understood as a product of encapsulation?" In T. Ingold, D. Riches, and J. Woodburn, eds., *Hunters and Gatherers*. Vol. 1: *History, Evolution, and Social Change*, 43–64. Oxford: Berg.

———. 2005. "Egalitarian societies revisited." In T. Widlok and W.G. Tadesse, eds., *Property and Equality.* Vol. 1: *Ritualisation, Sharing, Egalitarianism,* 18–31. New York: Berghahn Books.

Worcester, Dean. 1914. *The Philippines, Past and Present.* New York: Macmillan.

Zuniga, Joaquin Martinez de. [1800] 1973. *Status of the Philippines in 1800.* Manila: Filipiniana Book Guild.

INDEX

Abai (Tebilun), 204, 208
accusatory dialogue, 232–33
achieved
  equality, 281
  kinship, 154–56, 158
  ranking, 282, 284, 287–88
adaptation to environment and egalitari-
    anism, 83
adat
  see customary law
adoption, 101, 119, 129, 158, 160, 185
Aeta, 10, 272,
affines, 28–29, 49, 66, 68–69, 71, 73, 80–
    81, 100–2, 121–27, 135, 137n. 9, 144,
    146, 150, 162–63, 164n. 1, 178–89,
    191–92, 278, 284
  respect for, 29, 69, 148–49
  transformation into consanguines, 149
  see also kinship
African
  hunter gatherers, 2, 7, 84, 271
  kinship systems, 20
age, 274, 288
  of parental generation, 189, 192
  relative categories, 5, 27–28, 30, 97–
    100, 135, 145, 183, 185, 187–92,
    196n. 17
agency, 26, 42, 129, 161, 283–84
agent as bounded individual, 43–44, 129
aggregates vs. groups, 26–27, 29, 34, 76,
    96, 119, 124, 126, 128–29, 133, 227,
    230, 249–50, 252–54, 256, 262
aggregation, 27, 29, 119, 144, 227, 229, 238,
    249–50, 253–57, 262, 267
  and dispersal, 227
  rules of, 17
  see also open aggregation
Ainu, 63
alcohol
  men's sharing of, 250, 254, 257, 264–65
Alcoholics Anonymous, 94, 106
alloparents, 27, 97
American colonialism, 265

Amish, 134
amity, 145, 227–28, 231–34, 237, 244
  and elders, 233
  and kinship, 145, 149, 153, 156, 163
  and mystical sanctions, 235, 237, 244–
    45, 275–76
  and shared activity, 161
  and social grace, 156
  and speechmaking, 231–33, 237
  as social value, 227
  see also consensus, harmony
anarchic, 8, 11–13, 19, 21, 89, 111, 135, 137,
    164, 244
  solidarity, 2, 4, 5, 7, 8, 12, 14, 17, 34–35,
    272, 284, 287
anarchism, 1–2, 8–11
  "actually existing," 10
  revival of after Cold War, 9
  in the Philippines, 10
ancestors, 27, 73–74, 102, 192, 195n. 8,
    195n. 11, 236
  as "source" (*puun*), 149
Andaman Islanders, 8
Andaya, Leonard, 195n. 5
Anderson, Benedict, 10–11, 13
animal relations to humans, 3, 29, 41, 45–
    46, 52, 58n. 12, 64, 67, 77–78, 94–
    95, 158, 217, 273–74
animism, 41, 45–46, 52, 58n. 12
Appadurai, Arjun, 241
Aristotle, 285
ascribed
  equality, 18, 270–72, 281, 284–85, 288
  group membership, 82, 90, 154, 157,
    267
  ranking or status, 6, 126, 266, 270, 273,
    281, 284–85, 287
Ashley-Montagu, M.F.
  on savage children, 23
assimilation of hunter gatherers, 10, 208,
    272
asymmetrical relations, 24, 28, 30

Note: page numbers within parentheses following the name of a contributor to this volume indicate the author's own chapter.

Design and typography
layout and production
by **H.G. Salome** of

Vermont USA
www.metaglyfix.com

Made in United States
Orlando, FL
06 April 2023